PERU

Highlights

Alexander Stewart

Edition 1

Bradt Travel Guides Ltd, UK
The Globe Pequot Press Inc, USA

radt

i

About this book

There are many heavyweight guidebooks to Peru bloated with long lists of budget hotels and overviews of public transport targeted at backpackers and independent travellers. This 'highlights' guidebook is more selective in the information it offers, and is written for the traveller on (or planning to go on) an organised tour. The book has two main aims: first, to help those considering a vacation to decide what they'd like to see and do, and therefore to construct their itinerary or liaise with tour operators in an informed way; and, second, to provide an entertaining, colourful and informative guide to carry on the trip itself. With that in mind, the book provides overviews of every town, national park and archaeological site that ranks as a possible highlight, a quick summary of practicalities and a short list of recommended accommodation. The selections are made by Alexander Stewart, who has been visiting Peru since 1997.

In addition we have called upon the expertise of local and international tour operators – those that know best what the country has to offer – to recommend their favourite itineraries and activities. Those tour operators were invited to contribute on the basis of their reputations for excellence; they also made a payment towards the production of this book.

These pages are unique in bringing together the selections of a top writer and experienced operators, ensuring that this is a useful guidebook available to those planning an organised tour to Peru.

Feedback request

If you have any comments about this guide (good or bad), we would welcome your feedback. Please email us on Ⓔ info@ bradtguides.com. Alternatively you can add a review of the book to Ⓦ www.bradtguides.com or Amazon.

Author

A fortunate childhood spent travelling to and from Africa and other destinations led to an incurable travel bug, which saw Alexander Stewart embark on a continued quest to see what else lay beyond his back door. He wrote his first guidebook more than a decade ago and has since produced numerous titles for a variety of publishers, on destinations all around the world. He has written about many of these places for national newspapers and specialist travel magazines including *Adventure Travel*, *Travel Africa*, *Traveller* and *Wanderlust*. When not managing or tinkering with travel websites as a displacement technique, he still travels extensively, with Peru something of a first love and a place to which he frequently returns.

Author's story

My own experience of Peru dates back to 1997 when I arrived there as a young backpacker, desperate to see the places I'd read about. A scruffy, budget hostel in Lima was a world away from the images of lost cities and Indiana Jones that I'd carried with me since I'd seen Harrison Ford in action. Soon though I was smitten. Highlights from that first, formative tour of the country stay with me to this day: uncovering ruins along the coastal desert, climbing in the Cordillera Blanca, trekking the Inca Trail independently, camping amongst the ruins and that first, unforgettable sighting of Machu Picchu. Sailing on Lake Titicaca and staying with a family without a word of English or Spanish. Developing a taste for Cusqueña and deep-fried pork. And of the wonderfully hospitable Peruvians who made me welcome. Since that initial visit, I have returned to Peru repeatedly. I've seen visitor numbers swell, independent trekking on the Inca Trail banned, Peru's food go global and new archaeological sites be uncovered – even as Machu Picchu celebrated the centenary of its own rediscovery. Peru's a country that continues to enthrall me, a place described by the 17th-century chronicler of Inca life, Guaman Poma, as, '*un espacio mágico*' – 'a magic space'.

Contents

(TDR/MP/FLPA)

Dramatic landscapes abound in Peru and provide superb opportunities for trekking. Pictured here, the breathtaking scenery near the Inca site of Choquequirao. (SS)

Introduction

Peru is an extraordinary country whose civilisations can be traced back 5,000 years. The story of these cultures is only now being told though, as archaeologists gain insights into the ruins that are all that remain of their empires and societies. Such a rich history has spawned temples, palaces and pyramids to rival any on Earth. Many are shown off around Cusco, which is synonymous with Machu Picchu, the myth- and mist-shrouded Inca citadel. However, Peru boasts more archaeological sites than any other South American country and there are countless examples of exceptional architecture throughout the entire country.

From the crumbling pre-Columbian citadels in the coastal desert, enormous forts in the cloud forest and enigmatic ruins that escaped the attentions of the conquistadors, to the grand colonial palaces and mansions built by the Spanish in Lima, Arequipa and Trujillo – history buffs will be spoiled for choice. And what ruins they are. Along the coast are the palaces of Chan Chan, the Pyramids of the Sun and of the Moon and the burial hordes of Sipán. Then there are the enigmatic Nazca Lines. In the highlands are the enormous fortress of Kuélap to the north and the surreal funerary towers of Sillustani in the south. And of course there's Machu Picchu, the most famous and celebrated set of ruins, so famous that we forget how little we actually know about a site only brought to the world's attention 100 years ago.

Peru remains deeply connected with its ancestral heritage and vigorously celebrates its past. However, the country is much more than the sum of its indigenous parts. Boasting breath-taking scenery and a variety of landscapes including coastal deserts, overlooked by vast Andean mountain ranges, in turn backed by dense jungle, Peru has natural wonders aplenty.

Beauty and solitude are available in abundance in the mountains. Parts of the Peruvian Andes are so unexplored they make the Himalaya look like a circus. Elsewhere adventure activities include trekking, cycling and world-class white-water rafting. Additionally, the country has some of the least-touched stretches of the Amazon within its borders, home to the greatest diversity of plants and wildlife on the planet. Jungle camps and luxury river ships are all available as means to explore this wilderness.

Socially and economically, Peru can be a mass of contradictions. Developed in parts yet still incredibly poor. Forward thinking but essentially conservative. Boasting a growing middle class and top-rate tourist facilities but also the setting for some genuine poverty. Despite its contemporary edges and tourist-class elements, it's still a traditional country, where it's quite possible to get off-the-beaten track, to see people in authentic clothing, pursuing age-old practices, fiestas and customs. This cultural dimension and the unforced blend of old and new lies at the heart of the country's appeal.

Traditional communities operating almost untouched on Lake Titicaca or in the highlands contrast powerfully with Spanish colonial cities full of character. Impressive centres such as Arequipa, Cusco and Lima are destinations in their own right with a sense of history that, like the Inca stonework, has resisted both Spanish invasion and earthquakes. It'd be a stretch to describe these cities as undiscovered, but despite the large influx of visitors, there's an authenticity and charm, with an emphasis on both the past that shaped them, be it pre-Columbian or colonial, and the future they're moving towards. Coupled with all of this, they boast a burgeoning food scene and cuisine that's gone global, luxury hotels, heritage properties and high-quality service to match.

With a diverse mix of cultures, both indigenous and immigrant, Peru is a multicultural melange. With its attitude and diversity, from snow-capped summits to sun-drenched beaches, peaceful ruins and riotous festivals, traditional villages and cutting-edge contemporary cities, it's one of the world's most multidimensional destinations, meaning that it will never cease to awe, inspire and fascinate the visitor. It's a place that you'll never forget; a place that will linger long in the memory after you've left.

List of maps

Introducing Peru

1 Background

Peru is a place of enormous antiquity and there is an extraordinary history to discover in the course of any visit here. Myths and legends abound, whilst the Incas, the best-known ancient civilisation, are in fact just one of many pre-Columbian groups to leave their mark on the country. Indeed, Peru is almost unequalled in terms of its archaeological wealth and ranks alongside the great archaeological centres of Mexico and Egypt. The arrival of the Spanish conquistadors in search of treasure heralded an extraordinary clash of cultures, the demise of the Inca Empire, and a period of colonial rule. More recently, the country has endured political turmoil and outbreaks of terrorism but has emerged from these troubled times to re-establish itself and rise to become one of the economic success stories of South America. What's more, Peruvians are justifiably proud of their heritage, maintain their traditions and hark back to their glorious past.

Peru at a glance

Location Western South America, just south of the Equator, bordered by Ecuador and Colombia to the north, Brazil and Bolivia to the east and southeast, Chile to the south, and the South Pacific Ocean to the west.

Area 1,285,216km² (20th-largest country in the world)

Status Republic

Population 29.5 million (2012 estimate)

Life expectancy 72 years (male), 77 years (female)

Capital Lima, population 8.5 million (2011 estimate)

Other large towns Lima, Arequipa, Trujillo, Chiclayo, Piura, Iquitos, Cusco, Chimbote, Huancayo, Pucallpa

Economy Important mineral resources including copper, zinc, gold and lead are found in the coastal and mountainous regions, whilst the coastal waters are rich fishing grounds. Coffee, sugar and cotton are also exported.

GDP US$301 billion (2011 estimate); per capita US$10,000 (2011 estimate)

Languages Spanish and Quechua are official languages; Aymara and Ashaninka, as well as a number of other native languages, are also spoken.

Religion 81% Roman Catholic, 12% Evangelical and the remainder follow various smaller or traditional beliefs.

Currency Nuevo sol (PEN)

Rate of exchange US$1= S/2.6, £1= S/4, €1= S/3.4 (Dec 2012)

Head of State Ollanta Humala

Prime Minister Oscar Valdés

National airline/airport LAN Peru/Aeropuerto Internacional Jorge Chávez

International dialling code +51

Time GMT −5

Electrical voltage 220V; 60Hz. Standard outlets accept round prongs but some have dual-voltage outlets and will accept flat prongs.

Weights and measures Metric, except for petrol (gas), which is measured in US gallons.

Flag Three equal, vertical bands of red, white and red, which symbolise the blood spilt in the pursuit of independence and peace. A coat of arms comprising a shield bearing a vicuña, cinchona tree and yellow cornucopia spilling out coins is set in the central, white column.

Public holidays 1 January, 1 May, 24 June, 29 June, 28-29 July, 30 August, 8 October, 1 November, 8 December, 25 December; also Holy Thursday, Good Friday, Easter Monday

History

Although the Incas are the best known of Peru's ancient civilisations, they are in fact just one of the groups to have helped shape the country and their time as the dominant society was relatively short. The first pan-Andean civilisation was the Chavín, who thrived around 2,500 years ago. Later, about 1,000 years ago, the Huari-Tiahuanaco united much of the continent before the Incas became the third culture to dominate South America. In between times a host of smaller cultures rose and fell, each contributing something to the colourful fabric of the continent and indelibly leaving their mark.

Pre-ceramic period

The earliest settlers, hunter-gatherers who exploited the rich natural resources as they travelled throughout the country in small groups, are thought to have arrived in South America some 10,000 years ago; from around this time there is evidence of fashioned stone tools in use in the valleys just to the north of Lima and also evidence of hunter groups in the mountains. Over the course of several thousand years differences began to develop between these groups, based on where they settled. Agriculture, including the cultivation of seeds and tubers such as potatoes, took root in the highlands around 8500BC and animals including llama and alpaca were domesticated around 4000BC. The coastal settlers took advantage of the rich fish supplies and so developed agriculture later, instead evolving their hunting style to include tools and weapons such as spears. Sophisticated early coastal settlers included the **Chinchorros**, who inhabited the area around Tacna and Arica in approximately 5000BC. As well as creating bone tools and fishhooks, this group began the practice of mummifying their dead, well in advance of the Egyptians. These **mummies**, the oldest in the world, were wrapped in the foetal position and shrouded in numerous layers of fabric.

Early cultures were also responsible for building large **ceremonial centres** such as Caral, which features six pyramids around a central plaza and is thought to have been home to 3,000 people. Dating from around 3000BC, it is considered the oldest complex site in the Americas, on a par with those found in India and Egypt. Highland sites such as Kotosh still show the decorations that adorned these temples and features such as **trapezoidal arches**, which were to become synonymous with the Incas, first appeared in architecture here. Sophisticated building techniques and a system of labour must have

5

The ceremonial centre of Caral dates from around 3000BC. (GS/C)

been in place to enable the construction of such sites, making these cultures surprisingly advanced.

Initial period

The years 1800BC to 1000BC are known as the Initial period, due to the initiation of the production of **ceramics** in Peru. The coastal people south of Trujillo and just north of Lima began with basic, undecorated pots that became increasingly sophisticated and colourful. At the same time these cultures developed metalwork and smelting and continued to push the boundaries of what was architecturally possible by building bigger and bigger complexes, which were used as tombs, ceremonial centres or oracles. Early highland pottery was more advanced and influenced by the proximity of the Amazon, right down to the design and incorporation of jungle animal motifs. At the same time, techniques for working gold were discovered. Highland groups also pioneered irrigation and the building of terraces, whilst horticultural techniques improved across the country. Elsewhere, the **Paracas culture** on the coast started

to produce **textiles** of extraordinary intricacy, using alpaca wool and incorporating rich colours and detailed patterns.

The Chavín horizon

The first major culture to unify all the disparate elements of Peru was the Chavín, who came to ascendancy in 1000BC and whose authority lasted for around 800 years. Rather than dominate through physical force, the Chavín were a cult whose influence, iconography and ideas emanated from an oracle called the **Chavín de Huántar**, east of Huaraz. The oracle was home to exceptional carvings including iconic figures such as the **Raimondi Stela**, a deity associated with agriculture and fertility that can be viewed as displayed or upside down with equally dramatic effect. The Chavín also made significant advances in weaving, pottery, agriculture and architecture, creating specially engineered buildings such as the central castle at Chavín de Huántar, which was honeycombed with watercourses. Ideas and iconography were spread across the coast and highlands, with the same imagery appearing in places many miles apart, suggesting that an exchange of ideas was taking place as cultures became more complex.

The peace and unification of groups couldn't last, however, and after 200BC violence flared up and settlements had to be fortified as groups fell out, sought to become locally important and factions began fighting. The period between 200BC and AD700 was nonetheless characterised by creative cultures that produced some of Peru's most impressive art; the **Paracas Necropolis**, named after a burial site, produced some of the finest pre-Columbian textiles in the Americas at this time, with a remarkable 398 threads per linear inch.

Early intermediate period

The **Moche** took over the region from the Piura River in the north to Huarmey in the south; they were at the peak of their influence from AD500 to AD600. Having a warlike culture, they established a stable state that endured for almost 1,000 years and their legacy of **impressive architecture** and carefully sculpted **portrait pots** endured far longer.

Quipu

None of the pre-Columbian cultures developed writing, meaning that there are no recorded histories for archaeologists to study. Instead all that we know of the ancient groups has come from the investigation of their artefacts. One of the most unusual are *quipu*. These are the knotted ropes developed by Andean societies and later used by the Incas as an alternative to writing and as a means of communication. The colour, position and number of knots on a particular piece of string related to an important piece of information – often to do with seasons, taxes or the local population – which could be deciphered by someone who understood what they were 'reading'. Each *quipu* was unique and could range from just a couple of strands to several thousand. Suppressed and destroyed by the Spanish, the knowledge relating to how to read them was lost and archaeologists are only now starting to understand how they worked.

(ML)

The pots are exceptionally detailed and the figures beautifully rendered, meaning that archaeologists can decipher daily details from the stories recounted on them. The Moche also specialised in making **erotic ceramics**. Their celebrated buildings included the Huaca del Sol y de la Luna, the Sun and Moon temples, close to Trujillo. These structures, decorated with elaborate friezes, are vast platform mounds commonly described as pyramids, and were the largest adobe structures in the Americas at the time of their construction. The Moche also built the adobe pyramid close to Chiclayo that hid the Lord of Sipán, a warrior priest buried with an enormous cache of treasure.

Typical Moche culture erotic pottery (ML)

At more or less the same time, the **Nazca** culture was leaving enduring marks on the landscape. The vast pampa around the Nazca River is covered in enormous patterns, polygons and designs including a hummingbird, monkey and killer whale, now collectively known as the Nazca Lines. The Nazca were also responsible for the construction of substantial **temple complexes** such as Cahuachi. Additionally, the Nazca created attractive **pots**, many of which were decorated with the same imagery as can be found in the desert, and further developed **mummification**.

Middle horizon

A terrible drought during the latter half of the 6th century contributed to the decline of the Moche. However, after AD700, Peru was again largely unified when the **Tiahuanaco** and **Huari** (Wari) cultures came together to dominate the Andes for three centuries. Originating on the central coast or inland close to Ayacucho, they expanded their territory aggressively, taking neighbouring lands and diffusing their ideas on art and religion widely. Tiahuanaco at its peak also controlled much of Chile and Bolivia. The group traded extensively, developed advanced farming techniques and built the largest stone city in the Andes. Inevitably, however, the farms failed and the trade in fine ceramics declined, leading to the demise of the Tiahuanaco. An increase in intertribal warfare followed, along with the construction of defensive forts and new ceremonial centres. Some 60 structures were erected in the region around Lima, including the adobe pyramid Huaca Pucllana, which now lies within the modern city.

Late intermediate period

The years from around 1000 to 1450 were dominated by the **Chimú** culture; they swelled and grew to control more than half of the Peruvian coast, from Tumbes to Lima. Initially they shared the land with other groups but following a devastating El Niño when their irrigation systems failed and their agricultural lands suffered, the Chimú began to take other tribes' land forcibly, including the territories controlled by the Sicán, descendants of the Moche. At the heart of the Chimú Empire stood Chan Chan, an enormous adobe complex close to Trujillo that covered 6km^2 and was made up of 12 palaces, which in time gave up some of the most substantial treasure troves in Peru.

The cloudforest-dwelling **Chachapoyas**, a powerful warrior culture, built Kuélap, an enigmatic and intriguing highland site. Close to Lima the **Chancay** people became locally significant, whilst further south the **Ica** and **Chincha** cultures established themselves and yet another group began to build funerary towers at Sillustani, close to Puno.

The Chimú continued to grow until they came into conflict with the **Inca**, who were also expanding their sphere of influence during the 13th and 14th centuries and making their presence felt in the region around Cusco. Over time the Chimú were defeated. Their empire was subsequently broken up, the Chimú were sent to other Inca lands and loyal Inca settlers were placed in charge of their old territories.

The origins of the Inca

The Inca believed that the first Inca, Manco Capac, emerged from the depths of Lake Titicaca and journeyed to Pacaritambo, close to Cusco. Eventually he thrust his staff into the soil and it promptly vanished, which he took as a sign from his father, the sun, that the valley was fertile and a fine place to stay. He named the place Qosqo ('navel of the earth') and built the first Coricancha, the Sun Temple.

In reality, the Incas probably evolved from smaller tribes in the Cusco area. Without any written documents, however, there is no recorded history and just a handful of oral narratives, allied to archaeological discoveries, determine what we know of them.

Inca in fact refers to the monarch, sometimes known as the Sapa Inca to help distinguish him from his subjects. The first eight Incas reigned from some time during the 11th century up until the early 15th century. Little is known of any of them apart from the last, Viracocha Inca, who exists in folklore and legend as the father of one of the great figures of Inca history.

Expansion of the Inca Empire

The expansion of the Inca Empire has largely been attributed to one man, **Pachacutec** who was the son of **Viracocha Inca**. He came to prominence in 1438, when the fledgling Inca state was under attack from a neighbouring highland tribe, the Canchas; Viracocha Inca and his appointed heir fled Cusco, whilst Pachacutec assumed control and fought off the Canchas. In the wake of the battle he usurped his father and exiled his brother. He went on to establish Cusco as a substantial stone city, commissioned the fortress Sacsayhuamen and began to grow the Inca Empire aggressively through military action. On the back of his initial victory, Pachacutec expanded the empire to include much of the Andes over the next three decades. In the course of this time, the empire conquered the cultures it came across and stretched from Colombia to central Chile, incorporating the Andean regions of Bolivia and northern Argentina, earning it the moniker **Tahuantinsuyo** – the 'Land of Four Quarters'. Four main roads led from Cusco to these far-flung corners. The Incas went on to impose their cultural identity, religion and way of life on those they subjugated, creating a country that was unified physically, ideologically and administratively, although many of the oppressed tribes were resentful of the new rulers. Pachacutec is also thought to have commissioned many of the Inca's most impressive sites, including Machu Picchu.

Independent Inca rulers

When Pachacutec died in 1463, his son **Tupac Yupanqui**, sometimes known as Topa Inca, succeeded him. He continued his father's work and further grew the empire so that it spread into Ecuador and further into Argentina. Interestingly, the Inca troops never fared all that well in the Amazon and the empire failed to progress far in this direction. During the course of this expansion, Tupac overcame the Chimú, who had previously boasted the largest empire. On his death in 1493, his son **Huayna Capac** withstood the challenge of his brother to ascend to the throne. He spent the majority of his life fighting first in the south and then in the north, securing territories and maintaining the Inca's dominance. He died in 1525, just before the arrival of the first Europeans and is considered to have been the last of the great independent Inca rulers.

The fall of the Incas

The arrival of the European army was preceded by European disease, which spread south from Mexico and struck down the Inca Huayna Capac and his heir. One of his sons, **Huáscar**, coveted the throne, as did his brother **Atahualpa**, who had been leading forces in Ecuador. The two brothers came to blows and civil war was inevitable; after a bitter struggle, Atahualpa triumphed.

Against this backdrop of disease and civil war, the Spanish conquistadors, comprising just 62 horsemen and 106 infantry soldiers, arrived in Peru on 24 September 1532, led by **Francisco Pizarro**. Landing at Tumbes, the small army quickly progressed inland.

Fatally, Atahualpa hesitated and failed to halt the Spaniard's advance. When the two met at Cajamarca, Pizarro laid a trap and tricked the Inca leader into coming down from his secure position, whereupon he was ambushed, his men butchered and the Inca himself taken prisoner. Atahualpa struck a deal to save his life, offering to fill a room with gold and two more rooms with silver. The Spanish agreed and Atahualpa asked his army to disband as a show of good faith; there has seldom been a more catastrophic misjudgement by one man. As the ransom was collected, the Spanish began to fear that a free Atahualpa would launch a counterattack. Scared of his potential retribution, they tried Atahualpa for plotting a rebellion and sentenced him to death by burning. Tradition dictated that the Inca had to be mummified and so, in a desperate bid to ensure his body was properly preserved after his death, Atahualpa converted to Christianity to escape the fire. Treacherously, the Spanish then murdered him on 26 July 1533 and burnt the body regardless.

Francisco Pizarro

The conquistadors were led by Spaniard Francisco Pizarro. An illiterate former pig farmer, Pizarro was a master tactician, a ruthless soldier and an excellent judge of human character. Initially he rose to a position of power in Panama, where he stumbled upon and named the Pacific Ocean. It was here that he first came across rumours of a wealthy kingdom to the south. With a compatriot, Diego de Almagro, he fitted out an expedition and went to see for himself. Although his initial exploration floundered, he secured support from the Spanish Crown along with the title Governor and Captain-General of Peru. With this backing he gathered a small army and returned for what was to become one of the most extraordinary accounts of colonial conquest. Having successfully led and masterminded the campaign, Pizarro established Lima as his capital. His partner Almagro became disillusioned and, disappointed by the spoils he received for his part in the conquest, set off to conquer Chile. Ultimately unsuccessful and increasingly bitter, he returned to Peru and fought Pizarro's army close to Cusco in 1538. Although Pizarro wasn't present, once his troops had triumphed he had his former partner put to death. In retaliation, Almagro's son assassinated Pizarro three years later, in the Plaza de Armas of the city he founded to secure his empire. The remains of the scourge of the Incas are thought to be interred in the cathedral in Lima.

(WC)

Pizarro established a puppet monarch, choosing Huáscar's brother, **Tupac Huallpa**, thereby ensuring he could exercise influence and power with minimum force. The Spaniards then marched on Cusco.

Cusco falls

As the Spanish progressed, they found support from the tribes that the Inca had subjugated. Buoyed by this backing, they continued, gathering supplies. Tupac Huallpa died during the march and was replaced by **Manco Inca**, a young prince descended from Huáscar. Although the remnants of the Inca army attempted to slow the assault, they had neither the weapons nor the tactics to truly oppose the Spanish cannons and cavalry and the conquistadors continued remorselessly. On 23 March 1534 they formally took control of Cusco and established Manco Inca as their puppet.

Manco proceeded to oversee a period of relative peace. Many conquistadors returned to Spain, whilst others stayed and were awarded land from which to derive an income. Battles continued, especially in the north, where Inca generals succumbed one by one to the Spanish, who now had a base, access to the sea and a means of resupply.

Rebellion

Pizarro left Cusco to establish Lima, as he needed a coastal capital from which to communicate with Spain. In his absence, his brothers squabbled and insulted Manco Inca, who subsequently rebelled. Having gathered an army, he laid siege to Cusco. In a desperate bid to preserve their power, the Spanish attacked his base at Sacsayhuaman and in a superhuman effort took the fortress, slaying countless Inca in the process.

Manco Inca escaped and retreated first to Pisac, then to Ollantaytambo and finally deep into the jungle, where he established the state of **Vilcabamba** in 1538. Hidden within impenetrable jungle, the state was small and a shadow of the former Inca Empire, but it was so far flung as to be safe from the Spanish. After two aborted attempts to catch and destroy Manco, the Spanish resorted to diplomacy. Aware of their tendency for duplicity, Manco refused their negotiations.

He was later brutally murdered by some renegade Spanish in 1541 in an attempt by them to curry favour with their lords. Manco's successor, **Sayri Tupac**, listened to the negotiations more favourably and, in 1557, he accepted an offer of property and money and quit his forest hideaway to live a life of comfort in Cusco.

Sayri Tupac's half-brother **Titu Cusi** took up the struggle and resistance in Vilcabamba continued, although the new leader's skills as a diplomat meant the Spanish had fewer pretexts to invade and a degree of peace prevailed. Although Titu Cusi's successor, **Tupac Amaru**, opted for confrontation again, he had few soldiers and no new weaponry at his disposal, meaning his rebellion was short-lived and easily extinguished. Tupac Amaru himself was eventually caught and beheaded in front of the cathedral in Cusco.

Depiction of the Battle of Ollantaytambo (FGPA)

The viceroyalty of Peru

Following the defeat of the Incas and once the group of rebellious conquistadors led by the disaffected Diego de Almagro had been put down, the Spanish established the viceroyalty of Peru in 1542. The new territory encompassed much of South America and was a source of enormous wealth and riches. Peru grew into the administrative centre of this empire, with Lima emerging as one of the most important cities in South America; the highest court was established here and all the goods leaving the continent had to pass through the city port of Callao, meaning that the Spanish Peruvians became wealthy and powerful. This newfound status was further enhanced by the discovery of what was literally a mountain of silver at Potosi.

The principles of rule were fiercely Roman Catholic and designed to reinforce Spain's control over their new colonies. No-one was entitled to hold land and in theory the Spanish Crown, which existed as a supreme ruling force, owned everything. Crown agents were appointed to oversee the rule and ensure that the Indians were treated not as slaves but as equals, albeit ones who hadn't yet converted to Catholicism. Yet in practice the good intentions failed, as greed and the logistical nightmare of running a distant colony ensured that laws weren't implemented. Individuals simply set out to line their own pockets and didn't blanch at exploiting the indigenous population to ensure they got what they wanted, whether it was by compelling them to work on the land or in the silver mines, where conditions were particularly unpleasant.

As their laws were flouted, so the Spanish began to lose control of their empire. The inefficiency of having Callao as the main port also meant that smuggling sprang up all over the continent and contraband left South America by various means. Coupled with this, pirates and privateers realised the potential riches on board ships leaving Peru and attacks became commonplace up and down the coast. The colonists also grew angry over the Crown's attitude to the Indians.

It wasn't until the **Hapsburgs** ascended to the Spanish throne that authority was established on the continent. As part of this new shift the viceroyalty was broken up into several parts, with Peru losing territory on all sides to new, rival viceroyalties. At the same time, taxes were increased and collected more assiduously.

Inca rebellion

The increase in the rate of taxation and the aggressive way in which they were collected inevitably caused problems and in 1780 a rebellion broke out, led by an Indian who adopted the name of the last Inca, Tupac Amaru. What started as a protest about taxation developed into an attempt to recreate the rule of the Incas. A crackdown followed but, although **Tupac Amaru II** was executed in 1781, the revolt sputtered on for a further two years, laying the foundation for Peruvian independence.

As revolution swept America and France, and Spain struggled against Napoleon in the early years of the 18th century, many South American colonies sensed an opportunity to change their circumstances. The exception was Peru, which had done well out of its relationship with Spain and still had close ties to the Crown. Consequently, as the liberating South American army started to work through the continent, it failed to attract much Peruvian support; indeed many Peruvians joined the Crown in trying to combat this movement.

Liberation and independence

The Argentine general **San Martín** had removed the Spanish from Argentina and Chile but needed to evict them from Peru to ensure they couldn't continue to take advantage of the wealth at Potosi and the port at Callao, and potentially pose a threat to him in the future. Having sailed from Chile to Pisco, he landed and began to battle his way towards Lima. As the Viceroy and the remnants of the royalist army fled, San Martín entered the city and declared independence in 1820. Giving pursuit to the royalist army, San Martín approached the other great South American liberator, the Venezuelan **Simon Bolívar**, for assistance. Bolívar refused to help, on the basis that he wanted the glory for himself. San Martín decided to remove himself from the equation and leave the field to Bolívar, who duly defeated the royalists at key battles in 1824 and became political supreme chief.

Fearing that they would be absorbed into Bolívar's rampant 'greater Colombia', the country that he had helped free turned on its liberator and following a military coup that would set the pattern for years to come, a group of military leaders came to power, led by a soldier called Gamarra, who became president. The Bolivian dictator Santa Cruz promptly attempted to invade Peru in a bid to unify the two countries, but the combined might of Chile and Argentina put paid to his plans and re-established Peru's independence in 1839. Gamarra returned to the presidency, retaliated against Santa Cruz's incursion by invading Bolivia in turn, and was subsequently killed in battle in 1841.

Prosperity and decline

A period of prosperity and development followed under the benign leadership of **Ramon Castilla**, who developed a rail network, invested in educating the Indian population and emancipated black slaves. Yet these good times couldn't last and his successor, Balta, spent more than he could afford on attempting to continue the development of the country and incurred enormous debts.

Throughout this period Spain had never formally acknowledged the loss of her colony and in 1864 sought to establish a toehold in South America by seizing the islands of Chincha, which had been a source of *guano* (see page 28), mined and exported to make vast profits. Peru sided with Ecuador, Chile and Argentina and formally went to war with Spain. The Spanish ships that had taken control of the islands shelled the ports of Callao and Valparaíso in 1866, but subsequently retreated to Spain. In 1871 an armistice was signed, although it wasn't until 1879 that Spain eventually acknowledged Peru's independence.

The War of the Pacific

Peace couldn't hold for long and when Chile went to war with Bolivia in 1879, Peru offered to mediate, only to be set upon by the Chileans as well. Although early Peruvian victories, in what became known as the War of the Pacific, included a significant battle at Iquique that signalled that things were going well, the Peruvian army was soon in disarray. By 1881 the Chileans had advanced as far as Lima. Two years later a treaty was signed that established peace but at the cost of Peru's southern provinces, including Arica.

In the aftermath of the war, Peru struggled to pay its foreign debt. A consortium of bondholders formed the **Peruvian Corporation** and undertook to pay off the debt in return for concessions and a lease of the national railways. Although humiliating, this at least ensured that the country remained afloat and improvements were subsequently made. Copper production ensured a new stream of revenue, whilst a series of reforms, including direct suffrage, along with public education programmes and municipal elections marked a period of development.

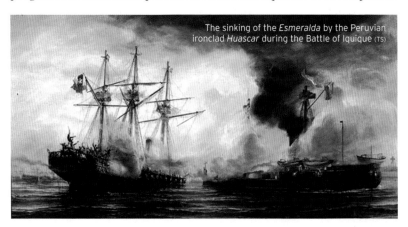

The sinking of the *Esmeralda* by the Peruvian ironclad *Huascar* during the Battle of Iquique (TS)

Political strife

The Depression affected Peru just as it did much of the world and premeditated the rise of the **Alianza Popular Revolucionaria Americana** (APRA), a Marxist outfit determined to resist economic imperialism, help the oppressed minorities of Peru and establish a united South America. Denied victory in the 1931 elections, APRA staged an uprising the following year in Trujillo where 50 army hostages were killed. The army bit back and murdered up to 5,000 people thought to be even slightly associated with the group. The tit-for-tat killing continued when APRA assassinated the president in 1933. APRA was subsequently outlawed but continued to operate covertly, to the extent that an APRA-endorsed candidate was on the verge of winning the 1936 elections when they were annulled and power was handed back to the military.

In 1941, Peru fell out with Ecuador and a border war saw some of Ecuador's southern territories ceded to Peru, a humiliation that rankled so much that border disputes continued throughout much of the rest of the 20th century. Further afield, Peru followed the USA in declaring war on Germany and Japan in 1945. In the same year, APRA was legalised again and promptly won sufficient seats for their candidate, Bustamente, to be elected president. He duly declared his independence from the party on whose ticket he had triumphed, so APRA staged an uprising in Callao. Promptly banned once more, the organisation was savagely suppressed, forcing its founder (Haya de la Torre) to seek sanctuary in the Colombian embassy for five years.

The 1950s were characterised by an increase in the dissatisfaction of the landless peasants, which culminated in a revolt in the Cusco area. Inconclusive elections in 1962 saw the military once again assume power, although an election was called the following year. New president **Belaúnde Terry** recognised the threat of the landless Indians and introduced agrarian reforms in 1963 that finally saw peasants assume ownership of the land they worked.

The army inevitably tired of this liberal stance and in 1968 forced Terry to resign, took control of the country and suspended many people's rights. The army seized control of Peru's industries, gave more land to the peasants and escalated national debt through further costly agrarian reforms. At the same time they reformed the education system, recognised the equality of women, built schools and encouraged the teaching of Quechua.

National problems and terrorism

Elections a decade later in 1978 finally saw the founder of APRA, Haya de la Torre, come to power. Within two years, however, he was defeated

An example of a revolutionary poster by the Movimiento Popular Peru (CPP)

at the polls by a resurgent Belaúnde Terry. The early 1980s were not progressive times; the fishing industry was badly hit by an El Niño (see page 26), Peru's currency collapsed, inflation escalated and the terrorist movements of the **Movimiento Revolucionario Tupac Amaru** (MRTA) or Tupac Amaru Revolutionary Movement and **Sendero Luminoso** (Shining Path), started to gather a following. In the 1985 elections, APRA returned to power but the policies of **President Alan García**, in particular his determination to pay no more than 10% of Peru's national debt, meant that international banks refused to loan the country any more capital. As things deteriorated, inflation soared and human rights abuses increased, peaking with the extreme violence inflicted in the name of the war on terrorism by a right-wing death squad assembled to combat the insurgents. People caught in the middle suffered horribly at the hands of both sides; it is calculated that some 50,000 people died or disappeared over ten years.

As things worsened, García nationalised the banks, leading to strikes, curfews and even higher inflation. The 1990 election was held with the country and economy on the ropes. At the end of his term, García went into exile, accused of embezzling millions of dollars. Whilst the novelist Mario Vargas Llosa battled APRA for authority, an unknown contender of Japanese ancestry, **Alberto Fujimori**, stole up and secured power. Having shut down Congress and dismissed the Supreme Court, Fujimori rewrote the constitution in 1993, allowing him to make brutal economic reforms and stand for a second term in office.

Fujimori

Successes in stabilising the economy – although at enormous cost to the average Peruvian – and the arrest of the leader of the Sendero Luminoso, Abimael Guzman, meant that Fujimori was re-elected in 1995. A further strengthening of the economy followed but it had a considerable impact on the country's human rights. Fujimori rewrote the constitution once more to enable him to stand for a third term and narrowly defeated Alejandro Toledo, a one-time shoe-shine boy and World Bank economist, in a contest characterised by dubious practices and threats.

Only once he was back in power did a mass of evidence emerge connecting Fujimori's right-hand man, **Vladimiro Montesinos**, to thousands of instances of corruption and intimidation to secure votes. Montesinos fled abroad, having stashed millions of US dollars in foreign bank accounts. Fujimori vowed to track down his one-time ally but in the course of a routine trip to Japan he faxed Congress to announce he wasn't returning to Peru and was resigning his presidency. To add insult to injury he declared that he was a Japanese national, meaning that he had held power illegally for ten years.

In 2005 Fujimori returned to South America, intent on contesting the next election. He was duly arrested in Chile on an extradition warrant and convicted of a number of charges, including ordering extrajudicial killings, embezzlement, corruption, bribery and wiretapping. He's currently serving three decades in prison but remains unrepentant. Montesinos is also languishing in prison for 20 years, convicted of bribery and of selling arms to Colombian rebels.

Peru in the 21st century

The new millennium has started brightly for Peru. In 2001 **Alejandro Toledo** became the first person of Quechua ancestry to be elected president. Unfortunately, such was the state of the economy and the depth of the recession he inherited that Toledo failed to deliver on his election promises and his popularity plunged to less than 10%. He did, however, establish a **Truth and Reconciliation Commission** to investigate the internal conflict, murders, rapes and disappearances that occurred between 1980 and 2000. The Commission reported that

Toledo on the campaign trail (IM/C)

70,000 people had been killed or had vanished; thousands of other lives were ruined, children orphaned, villages abandoned and communities devastated. Nonetheless, the process was seen as incredibly cathartic, with large numbers of people coming forward to testify to events they had witnessed.

At the end of Toledo's term, Alan García defeated Ollanta Humala in a run-off and was returned to power, despite his atrocious economic record during the late 1980s and self-imposed exile whilst charges of embezzlement expired. Under his second tenure, the economy strengthened due to mining and agricultural exports and Lima enjoyed an international resurgence after decades of decay. Controversy continued to plague García, however, with his entire cabinet forced to resign in 2008 over allegations of corruption and bribery. He also passed a law allowing foreign business to exploit natural resources in the Amazon, a move that led to violent reprisals from Amazonian tribes. Eventually Congress repealed the law.

Ollanta Humala subsequently won the 2011 election, defeating Keiko Fujimori, the daughter of jailed former president Alberto Fujimori. Having previously campaigned in a red polo shirt and called for a dramatic transformation in the style of Venezuelan President Hugo Chávez, Humala modified his radical stance, promised to respect democracy and spread the benefits of the decade-long economic boom to the poor. Early signs were promising but the president still faces untold challenges to reduce the gap between rich and poor and indigenous and white, whilst at the same time resolving how to develop or preserve the Amazon and ensure that Peru continues to make the most of the economic boom that has seen its economy become one of the fastest-growing in the world.

People

Peru has a diverse collection of inhabitants, with indigenous groups and immigrants making up the multi-ethnic mix. At the heart of the country is a substantial indigenous population, which accounts for approximately a third of the population. However, the division lies roughly along class lines, with the wealthier white and *mestizo* urban class in conflict with the indigenous *campesinos*, whose communities are often marginalised and under threat from mass migration to urban centres, development and projects such as road building. Sadly, discrimination and exploitation of these groups continues.

Aymara

The Aymara were one of South America's most successful cultures. Centred around Tiahuanaco on Lake Titicaca and spreading into the southern Andes, this highly organised and sophisticated group colonised the harsh altiplano. The lake remains central to the Aymara, with large numbers living on both the Bolivian and Peruvian sides. Due to the location and the harshness of the conditions, the Aymara remain poor. Nonetheless, they retain a strong cultural identity, with their own unwritten language, indigenous traditions and particular belief system. The mountains, water, wind and sun all feature in their religion, with mountains in particular prominent as places of worship where the Aymara can communicate with their god. Communities are strong and central to the Aymara – they come together to celebrate rituals throughout the year, whether it's for planting or harvest, to ask for rain or to celebrate Mother Earth (Pachamama).

Quechua

The Quechua are the other major indigenous group in Peru, although they are far more fragmented than the Aymara. Largely self-sufficient, they are inevitably poor agricultural communities. Their language, however, is more established due to its heavy association with the Incas. It has endured at least in part because communities are far flung and marginalised from modern Peru. Furthermore, the language is being more widely written, meaning that the connection to the Incas and the cultural identity of pre-Spanish Peru is strengthening.

Quechua musicians in traditional dress perform in a *passacaglia* in Lima's main square. (PA/C)

Amazonian tribes

There are also a host of indigenous communities in the Amazon Basin. Before the arrival of the Europeans, there were estimated to be in excess of 2,000 tribes living in this area. The introduction of colonial diseases such as influenza, to which they had no immunity, allied with forced labour and slavery, saw the number of indigenous Amazonians dwindle dramatically. It is now thought that there are around 400 tribes comprising some 250,000 individuals living in the Peruvian Amazon. All of the tribes continue to face threats from logging, mining and prospectors searching for oil or gas.

Mestizos

Most Peruvians can claim to have mixed blood, such is the blend of races and nations that have made the country home. In the wake of the conquistadors came the Spanish. The Peruvian children of Spanish couples became known as *criollos*, although this has since evolved to refer to anyone living along the coast. Intermarriage with the indigenous population followed and children of mixed race parentage were called *mestizos*. Almost half the population of Peru falls into these two categories.

Afro-Peruvian population

Over the years, a great many people of African descent arrived in Peru, often as slaves. It is thought that as many as 100,000 slaves were brought to Peru between 1532 and 1812 to replace the ravaged local workforce and to work on the cotton and sugar plantations; they helped to make Peru a rich and prosperous colony. Since independence, Afro-Peruvian communities have grown up in the coastal areas previously associated with the conquistadors and colonists, including cities such as Lima, Chincha, Ica and Piura. They now account for approximately 2% of the total population. In these areas, the vibrant culture has taken off and there are strong cultural identities associated with music, food, folklore, traditions and religion. Nonetheless, racism and marginalisation continue to be a problem and many communities are resolutely poor.

Asian and European population

Other groups to add to the melting pot include communities from China and Japan, who arrived in the mid 19th and early 20th century respectively, first as labourers and then as businessmen. A large number of Europeans also moved to Peru in search of opportunities and wealth. This small, successful elite quickly gained dominance in business and politics, ensuring that they became disproportionately powerful.

Culture

Although the Incas had no written text in the traditional sense, Peru has since developed a vibrant and well-established **literary tradition** that dates from the time of the conquistadors. Many of the Spanish left chronicles and accounts of their battles and to counterpoint these are the indigenous writings of Pedro Cieza de León, Inca Garcilaso de la Vega and Felipe Huamám Poma de Ayala.

Of Peru's contemporary writers, **Mario Vargas Llosa** is the most celebrated and he also won a Nobel Prize for Literature in 2010. Typically, he writes narratives intricately woven with Andean motifs and reflects the country's history and daily life. Good starting points are *Conversation in the Cathedral, Aunt Julia and the Scriptwriter* and *Death in the Andes*. The Peruvian poet **César Vallejo** is also feted for his use of language and imagination.

Historically, both **music and dance** have been an integral part of everyday life in Peru, especially in rural areas. **Traditional instruments** include the *queña*, a type of reed flute with a notched end, and the *charango*, a stringed mandolin originally made from an armadillo shell. Accompanying instruments include drums, harps, violins, guitars and of course panpipes. Depending on where you are in the country, keep an ear out for the waltz-like *huayno* in the highlands, with its soaring vocals and high-pitched instruments; the sultry *criolla* along the coast, which has African and Spanish flavours; and *chicha* in the urban areas, which is a fusion of Colombian dance and Andean music.

Visual arts

The most important school of **painting** to originate from Peru is the Cusco School, which reached its peak in the 17th and 18th centuries. The school consists of reinterpretations of traditional European themes by indigenous, often anonymous, artists and has a heavily religious theme; Catholic subjects are frequently fused with Andean imagery. Paintings are detailed, intricately decorated and often have gold applied to the canvas. They are also full of unusual and frequently bizarre details for the viewer to stumble across.

Although Peruvian cinema is in its infancy, **photography** is well established. The pioneering photographer Martín Chambi was responsible for the first iconic photographs of Machu Picchu in 1920, whilst Mario Testino is a more contemporary icon, famed for his work in the fashion world.

2 The Natural World

Peru's natural wonders are myriad and well known, for good reason. The country boasts an extraordinary natural variety from deserts to glacier-capped mountains, high plains to verdant rainforest, and Pacific Ocean beaches to vast inland lakes. Twenty eight of the world's 32 recognised climate zones are found across the country. As a result, Peru has an enormous biological diversity and supports a wide variety of life forms, from marine animals to river dolphins as well as favourites such as a llamas and alpacas, vizcachas and jaguars. In addition there are hundreds of bird species to see, with both migratory and resident species on the coast, condors and birds of prey in the mountains and glorious hummingbirds, parrots and macaws in the Amazon. These wild places and their inhabitants are protected by a network of more than 60 natural parks, which include some of the world's great wild spaces and rainforest reserves.

Geography and climate

Peru, the third-largest country in South America, is a country of great geographic and climactic extremes. At its most basic, the country can be divided into **coast**, **mountains** and **rainforest**. Much of the 2,250km coastline is desert although many of the major cities are also here, meaning that a little more than half the population lives in this region. Inland from this narrow strip, which makes up just 12% of the country, foothills quickly climb to a high plateau, dominated by the great summits of the Andes and gouged with deep gorges. The Highlands cover around 28% of the country's land surface and are home to just over a third of the population. Further east, the slopes of the plateau ease into the Amazon and this great jungle basin stretches inland, covering 60% of the country's land surface, but home to just 12% of the population. These regions segue seamlessly from one to the other, with dozens of distinct habitats gradually replacing one another as you progress east from the coast.

The **climate** varies across the country according to altitude, season and other factors. The coastal climate is affected by the cold Humboldt Current and chilly sea air coming into contact with the hot desert sands. Moisture is collected by the winds blowing onto the land, but it only condenses into rain during the winter months from May to November, forming a thick sea fog, known as *garúa*, which settles over the coast from the southern tip of the country to a point about 240km north of Lima. Apart from the occasional shower over Lima, however, it hardly rains. During the summer, from December to April, the coast is hot

El Niño

Peru is affected by a climatic effect known as El Niño. The effect was nicknamed 'Christ Child' when people noticed that the warming of the Eastern Pacific seawater associated with the phenomenon occurred around Christmas. The phenomenon isn't clearly understood, but every three to seven years the westerly trade winds from South America fail, meaning that the warm waters of the Pacific drift eastwards, causing the average water temperature to increase. The results of this are often devastating and widespread, and can include droughts, fires, crop failures and poor fishing. The most ruinous El Niño occurred during 1997, making headlines around the world and causing billions of dollars of damage.

and dry, especially in the north, with temperatures during this time reaching 25°C–35°C.

Inland, the dry season is from April to October. On the sierra temperatures are steady at around 20°C–25°C during the day but often plummet to below freezing at night. In the selva and jungle areas, temperatures at this time can climb to 35°C although a cold chill can still settle during the night. November to April is the wet season and at this time the sierra tends to be dry and clear in the morning but has showers during the afternoon. Temperatures are lower at around 18°C, but don't drop much further at night. The jungle is hot and humid during these months, with heavy rainfall possible at any time.

Habitats and vegetation

Coast

Peru's coastline stretches around 2,250km and is backed by a narrow strip of desert. In the north the jungles of Ecuador give way quickly to the sands of the Sechura Desert, which stretches south of Piura. Beyond this is the barren Chimbote region. Although both sections of coast are spectacularly dry, a number of rivers rise in the mountains to the east, almost making it to the sea, and support oasis towns such as Piura, Trujillo and Chimbote. These existed originally as agricultural centres since the river valleys can be very fertile and allow the growing of cotton, sugar cane and rice in the north and grapes, fruit and olives in the south.

South of Chimbote the mountains stretch right to the coast, apart from a short section of land just north of Lima. The land continues to be exceptionally dry, due to a dearth of rainfall, but is again watered by rivers rising at high altitude and flowing west. Oases exist here too, but tend to be further inland than in the north, to take maximum advantage of the water coming off the higher ground. The southern desert eventually joins the Atacama in Chile, which is one of the driest places on Earth.

Offshore the cold **Humboldt Current** drifts north following a sea trench that is as deep as the Andes are high. The strong tropical sun draws cool air into Peru from the Pacific, which then tends to condense into sea mist, known as *garúa*, which blankets sections of the coast at certain times of year (see *Geography and climate*, opposite). The mist provides precious little moisture, only enough to support some basic plants, and hardly ever condenses into rain. The cold current carries

27

Peru's dramatic coast is home to a wealth of seabirds and marine life. (J/D)

nutrients up from the deep Pacific Ocean and, along with the mist it generates, protects the coastal waters from the strong sunshine, making them perfect for fish; Peru has on occasion had the largest catch in the world. The fish in turn support lots of seabirds, whose droppings, *guano*, are harvested for export as fertiliser.

Mountains

Inland from the coast the **highlands**, also known as the **sierra**, stretch east some 240km in the north and some 400km in the south. They form a high plateau at an average altitude of 3,000m, although the highest peaks of the Andes tower over this and the deepest depths of the gorges and canyons that gouge the surface plunge far below this. Most major highland towns though, including Cajamarca and Cusco, can be found at this altitude. Much higher and the region known as the **puna** or steppe suffers from extreme temperature fluctuations from day to night, making it suitable only for llamas and alpacas.

The Andes stretch down the country, forming a spine. The highest summits are found in the cordilleras Blanca and Huayhuash, close to Huaraz. Mount Huascarán, just 97km from the coast, in the heart

of the Cordillera Blanca, is Peru's highest peak at 6,768m, making it one of the highest mountains in South America and a popular ascent for climbers and mountaineers. Above 5,000m the summits of the Andes are shrouded in tropical **glaciers** although there has been considerable shrinkage of these glaciers in recent years, attributed to global warming. The area is also prone to earthquakes and in the past enormous damage has been done by avalanches and rock falls triggered by tremors; in 1970 for instance, around 20,000 people were killed in Yungay when a mud and rock avalanche (debris that had slipped off Huascarán) drowned the town.

As the Andes soar skywards, deep **gorges and canyons** plunge below the sierra. The Colca Canyon, close to Arequipa, is thought to be twice as deep as the Grand Canyon. Deeper still is the precipitous Cotahuasi Canyon close by, where the river water is 3,354m below the canyon rim. Both canyons are great for white-water rafting and walking.

The sierra is also the location of Peru's only active **volcanoes**. Looming over Arequipa stands El Misti (5,822m), a picture-perfect cone that is considered one of the most potentially dangerous in Peru. The most active is Sabancaya (5,977m), which lies just south of the Colca Canyon. Beyond here is a region known as the **Valley of the Volcanoes**, where 80 volcanic cones stand over a sea of ash and cooled lava, testament to the seismic activity that helped shape this part of the country.

Pastoruri Glacier (see page 129) is situated in the Cordillera Blanca; even those without climbing skills will find it accessible. (EL/A)

Peru's flora has adapted to the diverse landscapes found throughout the country, such as this cold-resistent yareta (*Azorella compacta*) in the altiplano. (KS/MP/FLPA)

Flora

Owing to its diverse climate and wide range of landscapes, Peru has an exceptionally eclectic range of plants to discover; it's one of the most biodiverse places on the planet and the country is reputed to have 50,000 plant species within its borders. Many of these have long been used by the country's indigenous people as medicine – the best known of these is the coca plant (see *Chapter 4*, page 82), which is used to cure stomach complaints, ease hunger and altitude sickness. The leaves also play a role in certain religious ceremonies.

The **coast** is relatively barren, although some cacti do still grow here and oases are often palm-fringed. Inland, the hillier areas get enough rain and mist to sustain plants and shrubs. River valleys are also rich in flora. In the far north, around Tumbes, there's a small section of mangrove forest on the coast as well.

The **highlands**, above the tree line are home to drought-resistant plants such as clumps of spiky ichu grass, cushion plants and hardy herbaceous plants. Most plants are small and have developed ways of combatting the cold and lack of water, meaning that their leaves are usually little and fat. This area, especially around Huaraz, is also home to the spectacular *Puya raimondii*, one of the most remarkable plants you're likely to come across, which flowers just once in its lifetime (see *Chapter 6*, page 128). A member of the pineapple family, the *Puya raimondii*, also known as the 'Queen of the Andes', is the tallest flowering plant in the world, standing up to 10m tall and can have 8,000 small white blooms, which more than make up for the fact that it takes a century to flower.

On the **eastern side of the Andes**, cloud forest comprising rata rata, llaulli, tara trees and eucalyptus hides a wide variety of flowering plants, many of which are recognisable to visitors from Europe or North America. The bright yellow flowers of broom and the distinctive shaped lupins stand out amidst the scrub, whilst begonias, daisies, daturas, fuchsias and lilies are also all common. Bromeliads and several types of cacti are also prevalent, whilst Peru's national flower, the red and yellow kantu can be commonly seen in town squares. The most attractive and spectacular plants though are orchids. Peru is home to a huge number of orchids; the Machu Picchu Sanctuary alone boasts over 70 genera and more than 250 species, whilst there are thought to be around 3,000 in total. Look out for the large showy blooms of the Inca orchid or

The extraordinary *Puya raimondii* (JV/S)

Flor del Paraíso, the strikingly coloured purple and orange flowers of huakanki and the small, vibrant blooms of Huinay Huayna.

The **high Andes** up to 4,500m are also the last area in Peru where it is still possible to find *Polylepis* forest, made up of a group of tree species belonging to the rose family. The trees are often gnarled, with dark, dense bark and small leaves. Much of the forest is used by Andean peoples for medicines and it is also home to many bird species. The remaining stands are under threat and endangered though, with the trees being felled for wood.

Further east, the **Amazon** is home to great trees as well as canopy plants and epiphytes that survive perched high above the ground on trees or in the crook of a branch. The most sizeable trees include the ceiba or kapok, the trunk of which can be 3m wide and which can grow up to 50m tall. Butress roots support the tree, which is often festooned with vines and lianas. Useful trees include rubber trees, Brazil nut trees and wild mango, whilst walking palms, thatch palms and aguaje palms are used to make either the floors or roofs of houses. There are though plenty of species still not documented or known to science within the forest and new discoveries are made every year.

Amazon

The Amazon stretches away to the east of the Andes. It covers about half of Peru but supports just a tiny fraction of the population. The **rainforest**, or selva, is watered by the rivers that rise in the mountains and drain east, and by heavy rainfall generated by the prevailing south–east trade winds that cross the continent from the Atlantic and condense into rain as they hit the highlands.

Cloudforest at altitude gives way to dense rainforest lower down; trees extend down from about 3,000m with the jungle considered to start at about 1,500m. The rainforest is vast and stretches towards Colombia and Brazil long after the last Peruvian town has been passed. On this eastern side of the mountains, drops and descents are gentler in general, although there are still plenty of deep valleys created by rivers. The most distant source of the Amazon is a glacial stream that issues from Nevado Mismi, in the Arequipa district and flows into the Quebrada Apacheta. This in turn joins the Apurímac, then the Ucayali, which later merges with the Marañón to form the Amazon proper.

Wildlife

Peru has a wealth of wildlife, which acts as a major draw for many people visiting the country. Bear in mind though that even a trip to the Amazon is unlike an African safari or an expedition to the Galápagos; most mammals are extremely difficult to see in the thick jungle and you are unlikely to spot many animals, especially some of the larger elusive mammals, unless you're on a wildlife watching trip. You are, however, likely to see a wealth of birds and other, smaller mammals. The variety of habitats, from the Amazon jungle to high sierra and Andean mountain slopes mean that there are many places to see lots of different types of animal and bird. National parks and reserves are detailed in the main body of this book but the following section provides an overview of what is out there. It also provides an introduction to the country's extraordinary range of avifauna, as well as its reptiles and amphibians, though not the invertebrates which are too numerous to mention. For tips on spotting wildlife, see page 40.

Cats

South America's only big cat is the fabled and elusive **jaguar**, which hides in the Amazon lowlands. It is up to 2m long, strongly built and has black rosettes on a light tawny fur.

Puma, powerful cats with tawny fur and some distinctive dark face markings, are occasionally spotted in the hills. Opportunistic hunters, they prey on deer but will take almost anything, including domestic livestock. This has meant that they have been hunted and persecuted by farmers and the numbers of this impressive cat, which was once revered by the Incas, are much reduced.

Smaller cats include the **pampas cat** and the **Andean mountain cat**. Shy and rare, neither is well known and little is understood about their habits and preferred habitats, although they hunt small rodents, vizcachas and ground-dwelling birds. In the rainforest you may also encounter the slinky jaguarundi, slender **margay** and smaller **ocelet**. The latter is the cat most commonly seen by visitors.

Capybara live in large groups alongside rivers in the Amazon. (SS)

Amazon Big Five

Traditionally people go on safari in Africa to search for the Big Five, the most impressive mammals seen on the savanna. Peru, and in particular the Amazon, doesn't have creatures on this scale, but if you rein in your expectations you can still see some truly extraordinary animals. Although many are elusive, nocturnal or sufficiently rare to be difficult to see, if you take your time, enjoy the rainforest for what it is rather than a chance to simply tick boxes off, then you'll have an exceptional wildlife experience. There are more details in the main text but here are our Big Five:

• Jaguar: the biggest and best-known feline and South America's only big cat
• Tapir: South America's largest land mammal
• Capybara: the world's biggest rodent
• Pink river dolphin: one of a handful of freshwater dolphin species
• Manatee: the Amazon's biggest aquatic animal

Bears

Hard to see but high on most people's wishlist are Andean or **spectacled bears,** which are the only member of the bear family found in South America. Small and dark with shaggy fur, these bears have white markings around their eyes, hence their popular name. Although not especially rare, these bears are very shy and shun contact with people due to a history of persecution; there are some in the vicinity of Machu Picchu though and it's also possible to encounter them on the approach to Manu. Spectacled bears are resourceful and will eat

Spectacled bears are the only surviving species of bear native to South America. (SS)

Ukuku

The bear plays a large role in Andean folklore and is a central figure in some festivals, where it is known as ukuku. The festival of the Snow Star, Qoyllur Rit'i, takes place in early June and sees up to 30,000 people gather in the mountains of the southern Andes accompanied by dancers, often young men, dressed as ukuku and representing the bear. The Incas saw the bear as a threshold animal, half human and half savage, which could connect the spiritual and physical worlds. A bear could be clownish but also authoritarian; during Qoyllur Rit'I the ukuku carry whips to enforce order. The bear's wider role though is to protect the pilgrims from the spirits of the damned that wander the glaciers of the Andes. It is also responsible for transporting blocks of ice back down from the glacier as a symbol of the healing powers of the apus or gods who reside on the summits.

carrion, invertebrates and eggs, as well as berries and roots. They are also known to raid farm crops on the edge of cloudforests. The bears are excellent tree climbers and will forage amongst the branches for shoots and new leaves, and will even construct 'nests' to sleep off the ground.

Primates

Peru has a number of primates that are concentrated in the Amazon, where more than 20 species are found. The need for trees and a primary diet of leaves and fruit means that cloudforest is the highest habitat suitable for them. Unlike African primates, most New World monkeys have evolved a prehensile tail – in effect a fifth limb used for grasping tree branches. The exceptions are the marmosets and tamarins. Look out for the common **woolly monkey**, which can readily be seen in Manú. Other species, such as the **yellow-tailed woolly monkey** and **night monkey**, the world's only truly nocturnal monkey, are much rarer and restricted to small territories. Large black **spider monkeys** can be spotted swinging through the primary forest in large groups, using their long thin limbs and prehensile tails to help them travel at speed. Other forest monkeys to look out for include **capuchins**, **pygmy marmosets** and **saddle-back tamarins**.

Primates such as the yellow-tailed woolly monkey are worth searching out. (KS/MP/FLPA)

Camelids and deer

The most visible animals in the Andes are the camelids, including llamas and their relatives. Related to Old World camels, they are smaller, stockier and perfectly adapted to life in the Andes. **Llama** are the most common and have been domesticated and used as beasts of burden for

Llamas are widespread and commonly seen in the Andes. (JML & FR/B/FLPA)

a long time. Prior to the introduction of cattle and horses, they were the largest domestic animals in the Andes. Their surefootedness and tolerance for the narrow trails of the mountains marked them out as perfect creatures to carry things for the Incas, especially as the wheel was never adopted due to its impractical nature on this terrain. By European standards though llamas are too slight to carry much weight and can't be ridden. The Incas also used them for milk, meat, bone and leather; their droppings were even used as fuel.

Alpaca are smaller and more sheep-like, with shorter neck and legs, a blunt muzzle and a bushier coat. The easiest way to tell a llama from an alpaca is that llamas have a characteristically high tail and longer ears, which curve inwards. Alpacas have also been of use to people in the Andes for centuries, their fine wool is used for clothing and their meat is also eaten. Alpaca steaks are increasingly popular in Nuevo Andino cuisine.

There are also two wild camelids. **Vicuña** stand just 1m high and are much more graceful and elusive than their larger counterparts. Their tawny brown wool is reputed to be the finest of any living creature, meaning that for extended periods they have been hunted and poached, almost to the point of extinction. Today their numbers are on the rise again, especially within protected areas such as the Pampas Galeras Reserve close to Nazca, but they are still considered to be vulnerable. Traditionally, vicuña are rounded up annually during a *chaccu* and sheared of their wool as part of a three-day festival. The second wild camelid is the **guanaco**. A little taller than the vicuña, they are still much smaller than both llamas and alpacas. They have a grey face, shorter ears and often appear wide-eyed and startled. Their fur can be brown or cinnamon-coloured. Found throughout the tip of South America, the northern limit of their range is in central Peru; you're most likely to see them in Tacna and Arequipa.

As well as camelids, you may also encounter high altitude deer. **Huemal** are endangered but can be seen in areas where there is plenty of *Polylepis* woodland and cover, particularly in the Cordillera Blanca, Vilcanota and Huascarán Biosphere Reserve. They are barrel-chested and short-legged, with y-shaped antlers, each with two prongs. More common are **white-tailed deer**, which can be found throughout the Americas. Much more numerous, they are more tolerant of people and can often be seen by trekkers in the Andes.

Other mammals

The largest forest land mammal is the **tapir**, a bulky, pig-like animal with a long snout and sooty brown fur. It is known as *sachavaca*, 'forest cow', in Quechua. Those found in the Andes of Peru, particularly in the far north of the country, are related to the lowland, Amazonian animals more commonly seen

An endangered huemal deer (TDR/MP/FLPA)

Vicuña in the Pampas Galeras Reserve (SS)

Peru wildlife experiences

Peru has a range of habitats and each showcases a different type of terrain and consequently supports a different type of animal or bird. Travel to the following five wildlife hotspots for the widest range of wildlife experiences.

Pampas Galeras Reserve

Close to Nazca, this reserve is home to large herds of vicuña; try to arrive during the shearing festival of *chaccu* to see a traditional ceremony in action. See page 169.

Ballestas Islands

Lying off the Paracas National Reserve are these rocky islands where thousands of marine animals and seabirds feed on the plankton-rich waters. Humboldt penguins, sea lions and birds such as Peruvian boobies, Inca terns and red-legged cormorants can all be seen. See page 157.

Humboldt penguin (CR/MP/FLPA)

Colca Canyon

Close to Arequipa, this is the best opportunity for spotting Andean condor; the vast birds can often be seen rising on thermals before soaring off to search for carrion. See page 182.

Pacaya Samiria

Close to Iquitos in Peru's northern Amazon rainforest lies the country's largest protected area, home to countless birds, amphibians, and butterflies as well as pink river dolphins, manatees, giant otters and tapirs. See page 248.

Manú National Park

Close to Puerto Maldonado in Peru's southern Amazon rainforest, jaguar, ocelot and tapir compete for your attention with scores of bird species. See page 253.

in countries such as Brazil. They are largely nocturnal and browse swampy ground for fruit and grass.

Peccaries or wild boar are stocky beasts with biggish heads and surprisingly spindly legs. The most common are the **white-lipped peccary** and **collared peccary**.

Peru has several sloths, the most common of which is the **three-toed sloth**. Up to 1m long, they have small, round heads and substantial claws that help them to hang upside-down on branches as they move slowly through the canopy.

Three types of **anteater** make Peru their home and all three are found in the eastern reaches of the Amazon; they are the silky anteater, the southern tamandua and – the most spectacular of the three – the **giant anteater** which is very rarely seen. It is the largest, reaching 2m in length from the tip of its long tube-like snout to the end of its feathery tail. The giant anteaters have powerful front legs and long curved claws for digging, although they use their long tongues to catch insects.

Giant anteater foraging for insects. (IA/MP/FLPA)

The **South American fox** is known locally as *culpeo* or *zorro*. It looks not dissimilar to a European red fox, with a reddish grey body and white chin. It feeds on rodents and rabbits and is relatively common.

The **coati** is from the raccoon family. Predominantly a lowland species it can also be seen in the Andes, where it resides in the humid cloudforest. It has a long ringed tail, pointy snout and is omnivorous, feeding on invertebrates, eggs, fruit and the rubbish left behind by tourists. You may also see **weasels** and **skunks**.

Peru is a mecca for wildlife enthusiasts. (ss)

Spotting wildlife

A lot of the animals that you might see in Peru, especially in the rainforest, are rare and elusive. Wary of people, they can be hard to spot. If you want to catch a glimpse, try and adhere to the following rules:

Look out too for **river otters**, which live in clear water streams, feeding on fish, molluscs and crustaceans. They can be seen in the Amazon but are also found in the Urubamba Valley close to Machu Picchu. Playful, sociable **giant otters** can also be found in the Amazon although they are under threat from hunting.

In the Amazon River and its tributaries keep an eye out for **pink river dolphins**, with their distinctive colouring, prominent ridge along their back instead of a dorsal fin and long beaks; they are incautious and easy to spot.

The frankly rather bizarre looking **manatee** is the region's largest mammal; manatees can grow up to 3m long and weigh 440kg. They are gentle herbivores, however, and feed on water hyacinths and

Be quiet

Animals will often be aware of you long before you are of them, so tread lightly and talk in hushed voices.

Be attentive

Lots of forest animals are excellently camouflaged and the dappled light, dense vegetation and deep shadows can make it hard to see them. Keep your eyes and ears open.

Look and listen carefully

You don't have to focus on the Big Five. Keep an eye out for smaller mammals, insects and birds, and you'll be amazed at the variety of creatures you can see.

Stay together

Work as a group and you'll probably see more. Stay close and walk with a guide, who is more experienced at spotting wildlife, but remember that many eyes are better than two.

Be out early or late

Wildlife is naturally more active around dawn or dusk, so you should be too.

Wear appropriate clothes

Subdued colours will draw less attention to your shape; khaki, green and brown may not be great on the high street but they excel in the forest or highlands.

Bring binoculars

Animals and birds will tend to be some distance away and can be hard to see with the naked eye. Use compact binoculars to bring the world closer to you.

aquatic vegetation. Relatively common close to Iquitos they are nonetheless considered an endangered species due to hunting.

Rodents

There are plenty of rodents in Peru and in addition to rats and mice, there are several types of cavy, robust rodents that include *cuy* or **guinea pig**

Montane guinea pig (HP)

in their family. As well as the **domestic guinea pig**, which Peruvians keep in houses and use for food, you may also see **montane guinea pigs** and **yellow-toothed cavies**. Closely related to the cavies is the **mountain paca**, a larger and fatter rodent that is found in cloudforest and close to Machu Picchu. The largest rodent though is the **capybara**, which can be more than 1m long and is found in the Amazon, where it hunts for fish and lizards and grazes on grasses.

Peru is also home to short-tailed **chinchillas** – distinguishable by their exceptionally fine and dense fur – but these cute rodents have been considered endangered in the country for some years. More common and equally cuddly are **viscachas**. Although their dense grey fur blends in with the rock and scrub they are often seen when they sun themselves in the early morning or late afternoon.

Marine wildlife and fish

On the coast or offshore on islands such as the Ballestas, you'll see large numbers of **fur seals** and **sea lions**. **Dolphins** can frequently be spotted as well, but Peru is rarely visited by whales. **Fish** frequently found in the coastal waters include tuna, marlin, swordfish and sea bass, along with manta rays.

Sea lions congregate around the Ballestas Islands. (GL/FLPA)

Responsible wildlife watching

Avoid any activity that disturbs or upsets an animal; no photograph is worth disrupting a creature's routine. Make sure you don't have a negative impact on the landscape or environment either. Don't litter, don't throw matches into the outdoors, discourage your guide or driver from leaving authorised paths and. dissuade them from attempting to attract an animal's attention. Nor should you feed wildlife, as animals quickly learn to associate people with food.

Reptiles and amphibians

A great many reptiles can be found in the Amazon, including **river turtles, lizards, leaf-iguanas** and **geckos.** More substantial reptiles include caimans, Peru's **crocodile;** there are four types of caiman in Peru with the **spectacled caiman**, which grows up to 2m, the most usually seen. The **yellow-footed tortoise** is the only tortoise in the Amazon and it grows up to 1m long.

The yellow-footed tortoise is the largest on the mainland of South America. (PO/MP/FLPA)

There are also numerous **snakes** such as the attractive but venomous coral snake, fer-de-lance, bushmaster and Peruvian pit viper, as well as anacondas which kill by constricting their prey. Non-venomous species include whipsnakes, tree snakes, racers and frog-eating snakes.

Peruvian **frogs** can be very large and vocal, especially along the Amazon, where species include gaudy poison dart frogs and tree frogs. **Toads**, such as the substantial cane toad are also common. You may even encounter salamanders, although these are much rarer.

Insects and other invertebrates

The Amazon is alive with insects, spiders and other invertebrates. These include ants, beetles, katydids, stick insects, praying mantis and dragonflies. Peru is also justifiably famous for its **moths and butterflies**, which appear in every size and hue; there are some 3,500 recorded already with more being added to this number all the time. The bird-eating spider is one of the world's largest arachnids – but, unless specifically searched for, it – and other tarantulas – are seldom seen.

Birds

South America is home to around a third of all bird species on earth; Peru boasts 1,850 recorded species alone, which is the second-highest single country number after Colombia. On this basis, Peru really shines as a wildlife destination for birdwatchers and even the casual twitcher will be able to observe a range of spectacular species. In the course of a day in the Amazon you might see up to 20 species, whilst in a week you can expect to spot around 100 – just don't forget your binoculars. A number of lodges now boast towers or canopy walkways that you can ascend to look out over the forest. Do this at dawn for your best chance of seeing a range of birds. Alternatively, keep an eye out for clay licks, which provide nutrients for macaws and parrots, flowering trees that attract a wide range of species, and fruiting trees, which attract both birds and mammals.

There are numerous **birds of prey** in Peru, especially in the Andes where they can hunt rodents. The **Andean condor** *Vultur gryphus*, the only vulture to be found in the mountains, is symbolic of the region. A scavenger with a bald head and a short bill for eating carrion, it nests in inaccessible cliffs but can often be seen soaring on thermals. The birds are impressive in size and their wingspan can be more than 3m, but they have small, chicken-like feet that are too weak to grasp or kill and they only feed on carrion, despite the sensationalist stories in newspapers reporting that condor occasionally snatch unguarded infants from mothers tending flocks of llama. Other vultures of note include the impressive **king vulture** *Sarcoramphus papa*, **turkey vulture** *Cathartes aura* and **black vulture** *Coragyps atratus*.

King vulture
(TDR/MP/FLPA)

Other birds of prey that hunt in the Andes include the common **Aplomado falcon** *Falco femoralis*; they hunt in pairs and often take prey whilst in flight. A relative, the **mountain caracara** *Phalcoboenus megalopterus*, is an omnivorous scavenger, who has adopted a roll akin to that of crows and ravens elsewhere. Look out too for large hawks such as the **puna hawk** *Buteo poecilochrous*, **black-chested buzzard eagle** *Geranoaetus melanoleucus*, **red-backed hawk** *Buteo polyosoma* and cinerous harrier *Circus cinerus*. In the cloudforest you might see smaller hawks, although they're harder to spot and scarcer. Species include the **white-throated hawk** *Buteo albigula* and **white-rumped hawk** *Buteo*

Condor - bird of the Incas

The Andean condor, known as *kuntur* in Quechua, was revered by the Incas and featured heavily in their mythology. The bird was believed to be immortal, and represented intelligence and strength; it was thought to tow the sun over the mountains every day. The Inca also believed that the bird could forecast things, both good and bad; the death of a condor during the Inca festival of Inti Raymi a year before the Spanish conquistadors arrived was thought to foretell the end of the empire.

(DT/FLPA)

leuchorrous. The powerful **black-and-chestnut eagle** *Oroaetus isidori* and **solitary eagle** *Harpyhaliaetus solitaries* can be found in Manú, where they sometimes prey on primates.

At dusk you might spot several species of owl: the **Magellanic horned owl** *Bubo magellanicus* can be seen in the Sacred Valley, whilst **pygmy owls** and **screech owls** are found in the cloudforest. **Nightjars** also hunt insects after dark, using their speed and agility to catch them on the wing.

Woodpeckers are widespread in the cloudforest, where they mainly live in trees, using their bills to find food, hollow out nest sites and communicate. One species though, the **Andean flicker** *Colaptes rupicola* lives on the high grasslands and plains, choosing instead to make holes in earth banks or adobe walls for its nest.

The plains are also home to the largest bird in the Andes, the **puna rhea** *Rhea tarapacencis*. This giant, flightless bird is the South American equivalent of the ostrich. It lives on the high altiplano and can sometimes be seen running across the plains. It is quite rare, however, having been hunted for its meat and eggs. **Tinamous** also live on the highland plains, and looking like partridges they were once domesticated for their meat and eggs before the introduction of the

Andean flicker are carefully camouflaged. (AK)

ubiquitous chicken. Furtive, ground-dwelling birds, they crouch to hide and will only take off when almost stepped upon, erupting from the long grass at the last moment.

The high saline lakes of the Andes are home to three separate species of **flamingo**, with especially large concentrations found on the highland lakes northeast of Arequipa. Other **water birds** to watch out for include herons, egrets and ibis, whilst lakes are often home to waders and other migrant species from April to May and August to October. Sandpipers, plovers, lapwings, snipes and avocets are all common.

Toucans and parrots are prominently associated with the tropical forests of South America and are found throughout the Amazon region. The **white-throated toucan** *Ramphastos tucanus* is unmistakable with its black plumage, bursts of red and orange and a white throat. You can also spot the **grey-breasted mountain toucan** *Andigena hypoglauca* in the high altitude cloudforest, along with **Andean** and **mountain parakeets** *Bolborhynchus orbygnesius* and *auriforms*. Small and noisy with predominantly green plumage, parakeets move in flocks and communicate constantly. Equally vociferous are **macaws**, which fly in large flocks. Common macaws include the descriptively named **blue and yellow macaw** *Ara ararauna*, **scarlet macaw** *Ara macao* and **red and green macaw** *Ara cloroptera*.

Hummingbirds are similarly beautiful. They evolved in the Andes and now include a wide range of species, including some of the smallest in the world. They are uniquely adapted to extract nectar from flowers and usually hover when feeding; some larger species have to perch though. Hovering requires birds to beat their wings at almost 80 beats per second and it is this frantic activity that generates the familiar humming sound that has given rise to their name. Most hummingbirds have iridescent plumage and extravagant tail feathers. More than 130 species can be found in Peru, including metaltails, sunangels, rackettails, trainbearers, sheartails and sylphs as well as the world's largest hummingbird, the **giant hummingbird** *Patagonia gigas*, which measures a whopping 23cm.

Brightly coloured **cotingas** are only found in the American tropics, many of them in the high Andes. They are known for their bright feathers, which are used to impress females. Amongst their number is the spectacular **Andean cock-of-the-rock** *Rupicola peruviana*, which can be

The Andean cock-of-the-rock is widely regarded as the national bird of Peru. (H/D)

seen in the cloudforest and at Manú. Males sport bright orange-red plumage and a very distinctive crest and can often be seen performing courtship dances in front of other would-be suitors. There are also pigeons, doves, ovenbirds and antbirds, swallows, thrushes, wrens and dippers, blackbirds and tanagers.

Conservation

A major challenge for conservation is to preserve biodiversity in areas close to dense rural populations. Deforestation, erosion, industrial pollution and urban sprawl are all serious issues. What's more, inroads are constantly made into the rainforest and every new discovery of oil or gas threatens to increase the amount of traffic to this fragile area.

Habitats such as Andean cloudforest are not suitable for agriculture as the shallow topsoil washes away too easily once exposed and fields have to be left fallow for long periods. Yet, new roads have opened up areas and tracts of countryside have been severely degraded; sections of the highlands are routinely burnt to prevent forest encroachment and provide pasture. Furthermore, the clear-cutting of forest for firewood, valuable hardwoods and the clearing of land for farming, drilling or mining has led to considerable erosion.

Without the correct logistics, support and ability to enforce environmental rules, the Peruvian government is hampered in its conservation efforts; it wasn't until 2008 that the first Ministry of the Environment was established. What's more, conservation needs are often in direct conflict with poverty-driven pressures; striking a balance between the needs of wildlife, poor rural communities and large-scale multinational companies is a difficult juggling act, especially when socio-economic issues inevitably take precedence.

Positive strategies include the creation of a network of reserves and national parks, improving the use of land, introducing sustainable projects in the Amazon and educating the local population as to the benefits of and need for conservation. Peru has managed to do more to preserve its rainforest than most South American countries; **Manú**, **Tambopata** and **Pacaya Samiria** are some of the biggest protected rainforest areas in the world, with tourist numbers carefully regulated. Forests are re-seeded, logging restrictions are enforced to a degree, and reforestation projects have been initiated. The single biggest factor, however, may be the continued growth of ecotourism in the rainforest region, with sustainable tourism an offshoot of this.

3 Planning a Trip

Planning a trip to deepest darkest Peru needn't be daunting although there is so much choice it can be difficult to know where to start, especially if the time you have for travelling is tight. Initially, ask yourself what you want to do. Deciding whether you're interested in walking, history and culture, or whether you want to watch wildlife or see extraordinary landscapes, will help you to tailor your trip to your personal interests and might inform where, when and how you travel. It covers important considerations such as timing your trip, what to look for in a tour operator, the types of opportunities available, and basic preparations and practicalities including gear to take, vaccinations and finances. Essentially though, remember that it is far better to focus on one area rather than try to cover everything Peru has to offer in a single trip.

When to visit

It is possible to visit Peru at pretty much any time of the year, depending on what you want to do and where you want to go. However, the country's topography and varied geography mean that choosing when exactly to travel for the best conditions is complicated.

The climate is essentially wet or dry; temperature is affected by altitude. In general though, the busiest periods for foreign visitors are **June to September**, although you will find that there are variations according to region, and high season does change depending on where you are in the country.

The high season for **coastal Peru** is September and again from late December to March – the early summer months, when conditions on the coast are hot and sunny, especially in the north. Summer lasts until April. After this the region is affected by the sea mist *garúa*, which cloaks the coast from May to October and makes the beaches and sea much cooler; the southern beaches in particular are deserted at this time, with people heading to the far north and Máncora or Tumbes instead. That said, if you're considering swimming or surfing, the Humboldt Current makes the water off Peru chilly at the best of times. Rain is very infrequent and aside from the odd shower over Lima, the coast remains dry year-round.

In **the highlands** the seasons change more noticeably. The high season lasts from May to September, when the weather is generally warm and sunny, making it ideal for walking. The start of this period is particularly pleasant but bear in mind that if the rains last longer then May can be wet. The mountains are coldest and wettest from December to March, and although they can be explored at this time, the highest passes will be inaccessible and the lower foothills will be muddy. Bear in mind that the **Inca Trail** is closed in February if you are thinking of trekking to Machu Picchu.

The **Amazon** is best visited during the dry season, which lasts from April to October, when temperatures are bearable, humidity is lower and rainfall is reduced. The ideal months to explore are July and August. In the rainforest it rains a lot, of course, so you should expect some rain at all times of the year.

During the wet season, from December to May, the temperature can hit 40°C and heavy rain will wash out access roads. Coupled with this, wildlife watching becomes harder and you're likely to see far fewer species.

For more information on Peru's climate, see *Chapter 2*, page 26.

Public holidays

A particular reason to visit Peru might be to witness some of the extraordinary **festivals** that take place annually. Many of these occur during the wetter months but, for example, the **fiesta of La Virgen de la Candelaria** in February, **Carnaval** on the weekend before Ash Wednesday, and **Semana Santa** (the Holy Week that ends on Easter Sunday) continue despite the inclement weather. Other festivals to be aware of include **Q'ollyor Riti** in late May or June, **Inti Raymi** on 24 June, the **Feast of Santa Rosa de Lima** on 30 August and **El**

Feast of the Virgin of Candelaria, Puno
(RG/PP)

Señor de los Milagros, a celebration of the Lord of the Miracles, on 18 October. During these times and over national holidays local tourism is at its highest. The main national holidays are as follows:

1 January	New Year
1 May	Labour Day
28–29 July	Independence (Fiestas Patrias)
7 October	Battle of Angamos
1 November	All Saints' Day (Todos Santos)
2 November	All Souls' Day (Dia de los Muertos)
24–25 December	Christmas (Navidad)

Itinerary planning

Types of tour

If you simply look online or browse tour operator brochures, the choice of tour may appear overwhelming. To start the process of building an itinerary, ask yourself why you want to go to Peru and what it is that you hope to see whilst there. If time is tight and you don't have weeks and weeks to explore, focus on a particular region. Essentially Peru can be broken into **four areas** that are each much more manageable in a single trip; the north, central highlands, the south and the Amazon. It is possible to combine some of these areas, and flying between places will enable you to cover more ground and enjoy greater flexibility, but

you're unlikely to be able to see and do everything. Although trips can be tailored to suit your specific interests, most offer a series of standard inclusions. Many of the adventure activities listed below depend on decent weather so they're better during the dry-/high-season months. This applies particularly to walking, but try to aim for the shoulder seasons when there are fewer crowds.

Adventure and activity trips

If you're looking for activity then Peru is the place for you. The country has world-class **mountain biking** throughout, **white-water rafting** from Arequipa or Cusco, **kayaking** on Lake Titicaca or the Urubamba River, **hang-gliding** off the cliffs in Lima or in the Sacred Valley, horseriding in the hills, **surfing** at Trujillo, Huanchaco or Máncora, and much more to get your adrenaline flowing. **Diving** is also available off the Paracas Peninsula or from Tumbes. For walking, see below, page 54.

Archaeology

Peru is synonymous with archaeological sites. Machu Picchu is the established draw, but there are dozens more Inca and pre-Incan sites to discover. From the Sacred Valley of the Incas to the more remote ruins on the coast and the vast pre-Columbian fortress of Kuélap, Peru boasts the greatest array of archaeological treasures in the Americas. Highlights include Choquequirao; the Huacas del Sol and de la Luna near Trujillo; Chavín de Huantar on the eastern slopes of the Cordillera Blanca; Sicán, Sipán and Tucumé close to Chiclayo; and the Nazca Lines near Nazca.

Birding

Birding trips may be lodge-based or involve a river cruise. Peru has a wealth of birdlife, with the majority of it concentrated in the cloud- and rainforest. Visit between September and December for the best chance to see birds and be sure to visit a selection of habitats for the chance to spot the widest range of species. Highlight regions include Chiclayo, Huascáran Biosphere Reserve, Paracas National Reserve, Manú Biosphere Reserve and Tambopata National Reserve.

Boat cruises

One of the most intimate ways to explore the Amazon is on board a river cruise. Sail from Iquitos on a luxurious vessel and drift through the channels and waterways of the rainforest with the chance to see bird and animal life that otherwise wouldn't be accessible to you. Most boats include naturalist guides who bring the ecosystems to life, and trips include stops at traditional villages for a glimpse of daily life.

Colonial history

In addition to ancient sites, Peru has a wealth of colonial treasures to uncover. Fine examples of colonial **architecture** can be seen throughout the country, with well-documented and beautifully maintained examples to be found in centres such as Arequipa, Cusco and Lima.

Cultural tourism

Discover the culture of Peru if you really want to get to know the destination. Join a community project to scratch below the surface and spend time in local communities or enjoying traditional markets such as the daily Mercado Modelo in Chiclayo, the Sunday markets in Chinchero, Huancayo or Pisac, and the waterfront market in Iquitos to get a feel for the minutiae of daily life here.

Tourist information

The official government tourist agency in Peru is called **PromPeru**. They don't have any international offices so you can't visit them in advance. However, their informative website (Ⓦ www.peru.info), which is available in English and Spanish, is a good way to gather information before you start. Once in Peru, look out for tourist information offices called **íPeru**. Run by PromPeru, they can be found in most major cities, including Arequipa, Cusco, Huaraz, Iquitos, Lima, Puno and Trujillo.

Natural history

Peru has some exceptional natural history locations and landscapes. The best trips feature a variety of these and include **nature reserves and protected areas.** Some operators focus on particular regions, be they the Andes or the Amazon, or draw attention to certain types of animal or plant. Whichever you choose, make sure your tour includes the services of a naturalist guide who speaks your language.

Walking

Walking and trekking are the most obvious activities in Peru, with the peak season being May to September when conditions are dry. Beyond the classic Inca Trail to Machu Picchu, there are dozens of other treks, many on ancient Inca paths, that visit extraordinary archaeological or natural sites. Whether you want a one-day walk through Andean villages or an epic expedition along less-trodden trails, there's something for you. In the north, close to Huaraz, the Cordillera Blanca and Huayhuash are home to beautiful mountain routes. Southern Peru close to Arequipa and Cusco has a network of trails which visit sites such as Choquequirao. Alternatively, tackle the Ausangate Circuit for a genuine wilderness experience. Whilst most trekking involves camping, your equipment is frequently carried by porters or mules. There are also some lodge-to-lodge options for people looking for a little more comfort.

Booking your trip

Tour operators have the responsibility of delivering the trip of a lifetime. Most will strive to meet their obligations and ensure that you get what you thought you'd paid for – the tour operators featured in this guide are good examples of this attitude, but others may cut corners. To help you decide who to travel with, make a list of questions and compare responses. Take your time, do your research and chances are you'll have a wonderful trip.

There is, of course, the decision of whether to book with an operator in your own country or commit to travel with an operator in Peru. By using a company at home, you can plan an itinerary more easily, you may get a cheaper flight to Peru, payment is more straightforward and, as long as the agent is bonded, you'll have a greater degree of financial protection. Booking an itinerary through a Peruvian operator will usually be cheaper, but you will find communication slower and you will have less protection if something goes wrong.

See pages 56–7 for details of our recommended tour operators.

Choosing a tour operator

It's important that you choose a reputable, reliable tour operator for your trip so consider the following when making your decision:

Online reviews

Check independent reviews of the operator online; search forums and blogs for first-hand reports. No agency is infallible but how they respond to issues is a good indicator of the type of service you'll receive.

Testimonials

Ask the operator to supply credible testimonials from satisfied customers and if possible speak to someone who has used the outfit before.

Time established

Poor operators don't last long in this highly competitive market, especially when it comes to trekking and the Inca Trail.

Availability

Ensure that you can speak to the operator by phone or email easily. If they don't respond be wary, and equally if they don't answer questions posed to them then consider your options.

Cost

Cheapest may not be best. With regard to trekking this is almost always the case and it's generally an instance of you get what you pay for. Cheap operators are more likely to be cutting corners and exploiting staff or porters as well, so think carefully about snapping up a great deal because if it sounds too good to be true, it probably is.

Special interest

There are a number of niche operators dedicated to particular interests. If you'd like to focus on a special interest, these operators are more likely to be able to give you your trip of a lifetime.

Guides

Guides are an essential part of the holiday experience and someone who is good, speaks your language, knows their stuff and is passionate about sharing their knowledge is invaluable. Make sure to ask about the quality of guides, their experience, training and language abilities before committing.

Recommended tour operators

ALPA-K
① +31 (0)644 50 2854/+51 (0) 43 421629
Ⓔ info@alpa-k.net Ⓦ www.alpa-k.net

ALPA-K is a travel agency based in Huaraz, Peru, in the proximity of the majestic Cordillera Blanca and Huayhuash. They love to share their passion for Peru, so you can discover all the richness this magnificent country has to offer. ALPA-K is at your disposal to help you customise your dream vacation.

Amazonas Explorer

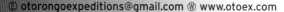

① +51 (0)84 25 2846
Ⓔ enquiries@amazonas-explorer.com Ⓦ www.amazonas-explorer.com

Based in Cusco, Inca capital and gateway to Machu Picchu, Amazonas Explorer has 30 years' experience organising the best quality trekking, biking, canoeing, rafting, cultural, family and environmentally friendly adventures throughout Peru. They have the best gear, guides, food, transport and logistics available and offer both fixed departures and customised itineraries.

Otorongo Expeditions
① +51 (0)65 224 192/+51 (0)965 307 868
Ⓔ otorongoexpeditions@gmail.com Ⓦ www.otoex.com

Owned and operated by American/Peruvian naturalists, Otorongo specialises in personalised itineraries for all types of adventure in the Peruvian Amazon. Tailor-make your trip: choose from camping in the rainforest to jungle lodging or cruising on the Amazon. They work extensively with local communities to promote environmental sustainability in tourism.

Rainbow Tours
① +44 (0)20 7666 1272
Ⓔ info@rainbowtours.co.uk Ⓦwww.rainbowtours.co.uk

Rainbow Tours Latin America specialists have been providing expert advice and tailor-made tours to the region for over a decade. Rainbow's trips in Peru offer plenty of opportunities to visit the iconic sites or combine them with lesser-known destinations in order to soak up the rich culture and history of the region.

Reserv Cusco

Ⓣ +51 (0)84 26 1548 Ⓔ arturo_c34@hotmail.com
Ⓦ www.reserv-cusco-peru.com Ⓦ www.incajungletrail.pe

Reserv Cusco are specialists in trekking and outdoor trips including the Inca Jungle Trail to Machu Picchu. They offer the most beautiful trek itinerary to Machu Picchu over four days and three nights, with excellent guides, their own lodge, good food and reliable organisation. You may visit them on the second floor of Plateros 326 in Cusco.

SouthAmerica.travel

Ⓣ +44 (0)20 3026 0287 (UK); +1 800 747 4540 (US)
Ⓔ bradt@SouthAmerica.travel Ⓦ www.SouthAmerica.travel

SouthAmerica.travel is the 4* & 5* South America specialist to Peru, Chile, Brazil, Ecuador, Argentina, Bolivia, Paraguay, Uruguay and Colombia. They've been sharing their passion for South America since 1999 through offices in Seattle, Buenos Aires, Lima, Rio de Janeiro, and Stuttgart. Call from anywhere in the world! See their website for local phone numbers in 44 countries.

Destinos Turísticos

Ⓣ +51 (0)84 228 168 Ⓔ destinos@travelagencyperu.com
Ⓦ www.travelagencyperu.com and www.reisburoperu.com

Since 1996, Destinos Turísticos has been welcoming foreign visitors to Peru. They can help with all your travel needs: hotel reservations, transfers, excursions and travel arrangements. They are a licensed operator for the Inca Trail. Their friendly international staff speak Spanish, English, Dutch, Portuguese and German offering a professional, personalised service.

Walking Perú

Ⓣ +51 (0)973 58 2815
Ⓔ info@walkingperu.com Ⓦ www.walkingperu.com

This tour operator based in Cusco, specialises in personalised tour packages designed to meet each group's preferences. You'll find traditional tours like the world wonder of Machu Picchu, plus a variety of the best trekking tours, including the Inca Trail, the snow-capped Salkantay, and Choquequirao. Well-trained staff ensure that you have the best experience possible.

Your itinerary: 20 top attractions

The first step in planning an itinerary is deciding which places you absolutely must visit; use the brief synopsis of my top 20 recommendations to help you start narrowing down your choices. Once you have identified what you want to see or do, you'll have a basic route to discuss with your tour operator, who can help refine your trip, add their own recommendations and sort out the logistics.

Peru is blessed with a great many highlights. Allowing for the inevitable element of subjectivity, the following are suggestions for places that would rate as essential for first-time and repeat visitors, depending, of course, on individual interests, budgets and time available.

Cities

1

Lima
A resurgent city that's pioneering Peru's gastronomic renaissance and which boasts some of the country's finest museums, as well as impressive archaeological sites hidden amidst residential districts.

(R/D)

2 Cusco

The former capital of the Incas is an extraordinary open-air museum packed with Inca and colonial treasures that celebrates its past but has all the amenities and attractions of the present, too.

(SS)

3 Arequipa

Beautiful and enigmatic, with colonial era treasures and architecture, the 'White City' has a stunning setting below the picture-perfect volcanic cone of El Misti and is within easy reach of great climbs and deep gorges.

(SS)

4 Trujillo

Colonial architecture and a surprising cosmopolitan atmosphere make Peru's third-largest city a charming, colourful place to visit, with easy access to good beaches a bonus.

(SS)

Archaeological sites

5 Machu Picchu

Synonymous with Peru, this superlative Inca site with hundreds of terraces and extraordinary features is awe-inspiring.

(PZ/S)

6

Choquequirao

As spectacularly sited as Machu Picchu at the end of a breath-taking trek, Choquequirao welcomes far fewer visitors to its plazas and decorated terraces. There are a number of unusual features here, and many sights are still hidden in the jungle.

(SS)

7 Kuélap

An enormous ruined citadel in the Andes, Kuélap is considered to be the greatest pre-Columbian fortress in the Americas, with massive stone walls protecting hundreds of houses. (LG/PP)

8 Sicán

The site of a number of adobe pyramids that stand on a coastal plain amidst an ancient carob forest full of birdlife. They have given up some exceptional treasures.

(A)

9 Chavín de Huantar

This large ceremonial temple, dating back 2,500 years and hidden amidst the Andean mountains, boasts exceptional stone carved heads, obelisks and subterranean chambers.

(SS)

Natural wonders

10 Sacred Valley
Close to Cusco and carved by the Río Urubamba, the valley is home to traditional Andean towns, awesome Inca architecture, unusual sites and some splendid places to stay.

(SS)

(GJ/S)

11 Lake Titicaca
An enormous inland ocean that is home to ancient floating islands made of tortora reeds, as well as traditional communities living on rather more stable islands.

12

Colca Canyon

Twice the depth of the Grand Canyon and one of the deepest canyons in the world, visit this gorge for adventure sports, idyllic Andean villages and the chance to see condor up close.

(J/D)

13

Cordillera Blanca

Snow-capped summits, glacier-gouged scenery, improbably coloured lakes and some world-class walks make these mountains an essential stop.

(MF/C)

14 Valley of the Volcanoes

A surreal landscape of volcanic cones sprouting from a sea of ash and cooled lava below Coropuna, which shows the after-effects of the area's enormous seismic activity. (E)

Off-the-beaten path

15 Máncora

Laidback northern town that's popular with surfers for its superb beaches, big breaks and vibrant nightlife.

(K/D)

(WAA/G)

16 Ayacucho
Highland town full of folklore and fascinating archaeology that is at its best during Semana Santa, when parades and processions mark Holy Week.

(C/D)

17 Cordillera Huayhuash
The Cordillera Blanca's cousin, with more remote routes, wilder treks and some seriously spectacular scenery that's ideal for the more experienced walker.

18 Manú Biosphere

One of the largest conservation areas on earth, with exceptional wildlife and bird-spotting opportunities contained within the cloud- and rainforest here.

(SS)

(LC/MP/FLPA)

19 Pacaya Samiria

Peru's largest protected area with 130 species of mammal, including pink dolphins, giant otters and manatees. This is the place to head for a prime Amazonian experience.

20 Islas Ballestas

Found off the coast of the Paracas National Reserve, these rocky islands, the Peruvian Galápagos, teem with bird and marine life including sea lions and penguins.

(TDR/MP/FLPA)

Red tape

All visitors to Peru require a **passport** valid for at least six months after the end of their stay. Most nationalities, including those in the European Union, North and South America, South Africa, Australia and New Zealand, do not require a **visa** to enter the country though; visitors are allowed a 30- to 90-day stay. This is stamped into your passport and onto a tourist card – an Andean Immigration Card or Tarjeta Andina de Migración, which must be returned when you leave the country. Ask for the maximum allocation upon arrival. If you lose this card you will be forced to queue up at the immigration office for a replacement.

If you do require a visa, you will need a valid passport, a departure ticket from Peru, two colour passport photos, an application form and proof that you have sufficient funds to support yourself during your stay.

Thirty-day extensions can be obtained at immigration offices in major cities such as Arequipa, Cusco, Lima, Puerto Maldonado, Puno and Trujillo. Technically you can extend your stay three times, up to a maximum of 180 days in total. After this you must leave the country but can cross back over the border immediately, at which point you will receive a new 90-day stay and the process begins again.

Getting there

Lima is the focus point for arrivals. The main airport, **Aeropuerto Internacional Jorge Chávez**, is a major transport hub and has a mass of modern facilities. Direct flights from Europe originate in Amsterdam and Madrid. From other European cities, including London, connections must be made in one of these, or in gateways including Atlanta, Dallas, Houston, Miami, Los Angeles and New York in the US.

Airlines with routes to and from Peru include **KLM** (⊛ www.klm.com), **Iberia** (⊛ www.iberia.com.pe) and **LAN** (⊛ www.lan.com). From the US, **American** (⊛ www.aa.com), **Continental** (⊛ www.continental.com) and **Delta** (⊛ www.delta.com) also fly routes to Lima. **Air Canada** (⊛ www.aircanada.com) flies to Lima from Toronto. Once in Lima there is an extensive network of **domestic flights** to a number of cities within Peru operated by airlines including LAN, StarPeru and Toca. Most popular is the flight from Lima to Cusco; if Cusco is your intended destination when flying to Peru, you are likely to land in Lima, where you'll have to overnight, before continuing your journey the following day.

Health and safety
With Dr Felicity Nicholson

In general, you should stay safe and healthy on a trip to Peru. You won't need an extensive medical kit full of drugs and bandages as a typical tour is very safe. Your tour operator ought to provide guidelines and information on what you will need though, to balance sensible caution with realistic risk.

Inoculations
There are no requirements for vaccination regardless of where you are coming from. It is wise, however, to be up-to-date with **tetanus, polio, diphtheria, typhoid** and **hepatitis A**. **Yellow fever** vaccination is likely to be recommended if you are travelling to areas east of the Andes, and occasionally for longer-term travellers to the west coast. This vaccine is not suitable for everyone and needs to be discussed with a travel health expert. You may also choose to consider immunisation against hepatitis B, rabies, cholera and tuberculosis.

Personal first-aid kit

To make life comfortable consider taking a small kit for routine scrapes and bruises. Basic items might include:

- Painkillers such as aspirin or paracetamol
- Sticky plasters (Band-Aids) or small dressings for minor cuts and abrasions
- Alcohol-based hand rub or a bar of soap in a plastic box
- Insect repellent to deter irritating biting beasties
- Anti-diarrhoeal medicine such as Ciprofloxacin or Norfloxacin
- Antihistamine cream or tablets for allergic reactions and hayfever
- Antimalarial tablets
- Good drying antiseptic to treat wounds and minimise the risk of infection
- Antiseptic such as dilute iodine, potassium permanganate or gentian violet
- Antifungal cream such as Canesten to prevent fungal infections
- Suncream SPF 30 or higher to protect you from the strong sun
- Motion sickness medicine if needed
- Antibiotic eye drops
- Thermometer
- Scissors, safety pins, tweezers

Travel clinics and health information

A full list of current travel clinic websites worldwide is available from the International Society of Travel Medicine Ⓦ www.istm.org. For other journey preparation information, consult Ⓦ www.nathnac.org/ds/map_world.aspx. Information about various medications may be found on Ⓦ www.netdoctor. co.uk/travel or Ⓦ www.emedicine.com. Other useful sites include Ⓦ www. fitfortravel.scot.nhs.uk (a useful source of general travel health information) and Ⓦ www.nc.cdc.gov/travel (includes updates on specific destinations and information for those with limited mobility or those travelling with children). Both the US State Department (Ⓦ http://travel.state.gov/) and the British Department of Health (Ⓦ www.nhs.uk/nhsengland/healthcareabroad) also provide dedicated travel information.

Deep-vein thrombosis (DVT)

Prolonged immobility on long-haul flights can result in deep-vein thrombosis (DVT), which can be dangerous if the clot travels to the lungs to cause pulmonary embolus. The risk increases with age, and is higher in obese or pregnant travellers, heavy smokers, those taller than 6ft/1.8m or shorter than 5ft/1.5m, and anybody with a history of clots, recent major operation or varicose veins surgery, cancer, a stroke or heart disease. If any of these criteria apply, consult a doctor before you travel. Ensuring that you are well hydrated and trying to move around during long periods of travel can also help to reduce the risk.

Malaria

Malaria is a mosquito-borne disease that can be found in parts of Peru. Consider taking **antimalarial tablets** unless your trip is restricted to Lima, the coastal region south of the capital or the highlands including Arequipa, Cusco and surrounds, and Lake Titicaca. In general, it is better to be safe than sorry as the disease is particularly unpleasant and can even be fatal. There is no vaccine, but several types of oral prophylactics are available. Malarone (proguanil and atovaquone) is recommended for short trips as, although it's expensive, it is effective and has fewer side effects. Chloroquine may be recommended for trips to the jungle around Puerto Maldonado and this is a weekly tablet, which is easy to take and very cheap. Jungle areas around Iquitos require different medication, including Malarone, doxycycline or Mefloquine (lariam). None of the drugs is 100% effective. Visit a travel clinic for up-to-date advice about the most suitable option.

For on-the-ground advice on preventing malaria, plus other health issues to consider whilst in Peru, see *Chapter 4*, page 78.

Women travellers

Women travelling alone in Peru ought to have fewer gender-related issues compared with visiting some parts of the world. On an organised tour, guides and facilities staff should be highly professional. That said, machismo is alive and well in Latin America and you may encounter staring, flirtation and wolf-whistles in public places. If you are fair-skinned or have blond hair, then be prepared for this to escalate. In general this behaviour is not meant to be insulting and shouldn't be that bothersome; either ignoring the provocation or issuing a firm 'no' should diffuse the situation.

At the risk of stating the obvious, single women travellers might want to be especially circumspect when choosing what to wear; in the highlands and traditional communities clothing is quite conservative. Skimpy clothing might not only offend but, however unfair this seems, be perceived as provocative or an advertisement of availability. Generally speaking, if you use common sense, don't walk alone at night in unfamiliar places, don't take unlicensed taxis, and always remain aware of your surroundings, you ought to avoid any unpleasant encounters.

The range of toiletries available in Peru is not nearly as wide as in Western supermarkets, nor is there much of a range when it comes to items such as sanitary towels or tampons. The choice becomes even more limited when you leave the main centres and arrive in the Andes or Amazon. It is therefore a good idea to arrive in Peru fully equipped in terms of hygiene-related products and toiletries. Bear in mind that travelling in the tropics can induce heavier than usual periods.

Disabled travellers

Peru isn't especially accommodating of travellers with disabilities. There are virtually no signs in Braille or telephones for the hard of hearing, for instance. Public places and streets rarely accommodate mobility- or sight-impaired people and you will need the assistance of a companion more than you might in a Western city. There are, however, upmarket hotels in most major centres that will have disability-adapted features.

What's more, increasingly large numbers of tour operators are conscious of meeting the needs of less-mobile or otherwise less-able travellers. When planning your trip make sure to enquire of your tour operator which facilities accommodate disabled travellers.

What to take

When travelling in Peru, you don't want to have to lug around a suitcase that you can barely lift. Consider the kinds of activities that you'll be doing and where you'll be staying and pack accordingly. Most hotels offer a laundry service but it isn't standard in jungle lodges or on river cruises. To make sure you don't leave anything behind make a checklist in advance.

Clothing

What you take to wear will probably make up most of your luggage, depending on the type of trip and sort of accommodation that you opt for – you'll need a lot more spare clothing for instance on a multi-day trekking expedition than if you stay in small boutique hotels where there's the option for fresh laundry to be returned to you within 24 hours. In general, bank on a change of clothing per day. When touring the country, look to travel in lightweight, comfortable clothes made of natural fibres. The highlands are at altitude and nights are cooler than you might expect, so bring a range of warm clothes and possibly a windbreaker. A waterproof is a good idea even if you aren't travelling during the rainy season and is invaluable if you intend to venture into the rainforest.

Footwear

On a standard tour you won't need any special footwear but decent, well broken-in walking shoes or boots are essential if you are contemplating treks, mountain ascents or forest walks. Sandals are useful when exploring towns, navigating boats or pottering about after a day wearing heavier footwear but watch out for ants and other bugs in the rainforest.

Photographic gear

Few people would consider going to a country as photogenic as Peru without a camera. However, you need to recognise that wildlife photography is a specialised field and balance your expectations accordingly. For the best results a digital SLR is preferable to a point and shoot camera. A high magnification lens is essential for capturing wildlife or birds; 200mm is essential for long distance, whilst 300mm or more is required for good wildlife photography. Zoom lenses (eg: 70mm–300mm) are generally more affordable and allow for greater compositional flexibility than a fixed or prime lens. It also means you

A tripod is vital for supporting long lenses. (SS)

won't have to swap lenses and risk moisture or dust getting onto the camera sensor. Magnification can be boosted with a converter but the compromise is clarity and an increased risk of camera shake. Ultimately, if you're serious about photography you should buy the best lens that you can afford. Use an ultraviolet (UV) or daylight filter to protect the lens and add a polarising filter for dramatic effect when taking scenic shots, reducing the glare from lakes and rivers or preventing over exposure. To get the best results consider a proper means of supporting your camera, whether it be a tripod, which can be heavy, or a beanbag, which can be used as a prop on a car, rock or other surface. Save weight by travelling with it unzipped and empty and filling the bag with corn, rice or beans upon arrival.

When using a digital camera, make sure that you have a supply of batteries and memory cards with lots of spare capacity. Check that you have all the requisite cables, connectors, plugs and adaptors as well. If you are planning on taking a lot of pictures, invest in a portable storage device. Use a well-insulated camera bag to keep all your kit together and prevent dust from working its way into your things. Keep a sachet of silicon crystals in with the camera to absorb excess moisture caused by humidity.

Electricity

On an organised tour you won't have to worry unduly about electric power, aside from the requirement to charge batteries for electronic equipment or for a hair dryer or electric shaver. Electric power in Peru is 220V 60Hz. Plugs are either American flat-pin or twin flat and round pin combined; take a universal adaptor plug to accommodate your various equipment plugs.

At some lodges or on some cruise boats the voltage may vary as it is provided by generator or solar panel. If you are charging sensitive equipment, consider using a surge protector to prevent your kit from frying. Check with your guide or tour manager to make sure that the electricity supply is reliable enough to use with your equipment before plugging it in.

Luggage

A hard case protects things better, but on a high-activity trip a duffel bag is more suited to standing up to the rigours of being on the move. A small backpack to hold your passport, ticket and other essentials is also a good idea.

Other essentials

Don't forget to bring sunscreen, a hat and sunglasses to protect against the strong rays. You'll need a comfortable, well-fitted day pack to carry binoculars, field guides and other kit during the day. A toilet bag should be packed with razors, deodorant, tampons, lip salve and anything else you consider essential. A basic medical kit is a good idea (see page 69 for suggestions on what this should include). A penknife and torch might also prove invaluable. Be sure to take out travel insurance that covers health and medical protection (including cover of any medical expenses incurred abroad) and all activities you might want to undertake, such as trekking or white-water rafting.

Your tour operator ought to provide a more comprehensive list of what you might need to take.

Organising your finances

When visiting Peru on an organised tour most people don't need to take a great deal of money with them as major costs such as airport transfers, transport, guide services, internal flights, park fees and accommodation will have been covered in advance. With regards to food, most city hotels are booked on a bed-and-breakfast basis. Coastal lodges tend to be half-board and jungle lodges are full-board. Some tours are booked on a full-board basis throughout though, so make sure you check what you are paying for. Drinks tend not to be covered.

If everything is paid upfront then you'll only have to carry sufficient cash to cover **day-to-day expenses** such as drinks, tips and souvenirs. This shouldn't add up to more than US$500 and hard currency is the easiest way to carry this sort of sum. US dollars can be readily converted to local currency, but pounds and euros are not widely accepted.

To protect against theft, take larger sums of money as **travellers' cheques**. Alternatively, use a **credit or debit card** to withdraw money, either dollars or soles, from banks or ATMs. Bear in mind though that small towns won't have an ATM and there's always the risk elsewhere of machines being out of order. Credit cards can be used to pay extras at most upmarket accommodation but they are less widely accepted by shops or even restaurants. Visa is by far the most widely accepted followed by MasterCard. Brands such as Maestro and American Express are less recognised.

4 On the Ground

If you're visiting Peru with a tour operator or travelling on an organised trip, you'll usually find that the ground operator and/or their appointed guide will handle most of the day-to-day practicalities such as checking into hotels, liaising with staff, organising fees or choosing an appropriate place to eat or to change or withdraw money. Nonetheless, it's useful to have some idea of the basic dos and don'ts and some knowledge as to how things work on the ground. This chapter will take you through the most important elements, from health and safety to foreign exchange, telecommunications and cultural etiquette, with the aim to ensure that you feel more confident. It might appear daunting at first but you needn't worry and, in the main, local guides are very good at helping out or intervening when some on-the-ground knowledge is required.

Health and safety in Peru
With Dr Felicity Nicholson

Peru is not an especially hazardous country to visit and by and large travel here is relatively low risk. The overwhelming majority of trips pass off without incident but it is still worth being aware of the more common health risks, whether sunburn or malaria, and other aspects of health and safety; follow the commonsense guidelines below and your trip should be trouble free. For details on pre-departure inoculations and other health advice, see *Chapter 3*, page 69.

Malaria

Malaria is a virulent and unpleasant disease. Be aware of whether there's a risk in the area you're travelling to and guard against contracting it by taking a course of antimalarials. See *Chapter 3*, page 70 for more information. Unfortunately, no prophylactic is 100% effective so you must take all reasonable care to avoid being bitten by *mosquitoes* in the first place, as they are responsible for transmitting the disease. Mosquitoes are most active around dusk and in the evening, so make sure you wear a long-sleeved shirt, long trousers and socks. Apply a DEET-based insect repellent to exposed flesh and sleep under an impregnated mosquito net. If there is no net and you think there's a risk, burn a mosquito coil but do make sure the room is air-conditioned or has a fan. Malaria normally manifests itself within two weeks of being bitten, but it can be as short as seven days and as long as a year. If you do suspect you have any malaria symptoms, which include alternating fever and chills, feeling tired, lethargy, and headaches, go to a doctor, tell them your travel history and ask to be tested.

Sunburn, heatstroke and dehydration

The tropical sun can be very strong and overexposure to it can lead to short-term sunburn or sunstroke and in the long term increases the risk of skin cancer and premature skin aging. Wear a T-shirt and use waterproof sunscreen to prevent it being washed off if you go swimming. If you're walking in direct sunshine, wear loose clothes and a hat and use a high factor sunscreen (at least SPF 30) that also guards against UVB. Protect your eyes with UV-protecting sunglasses, which also combat the harsh glare. A side effect of strong sunshine is dehydration, so make sure that you drink lots of water to compensate, even if you don't feel especially thirsty.

Travellers' diarrhoea

It's not unusual to suffer a dose of travellers' diarrhoea when visiting an unfamiliar destination, and Peru is no exception. Abide by the maxim 'Peel it, Boil it, Cook it or Forget it' and you'll protect yourself

Local dishes can be delicious but make sure they're properly cooked. (EC-M/PP)

from both diarrhoea and other, rarer but more unpleasant diseases such as cholera, dysentery, hepatitis and typhoid. Remember to wash or peel fruit and heat food properly and thoroughly. Cold food, raw food, salads, food bought in markets or at food stalls and things like ice or ice cream all carry greater risks. With regards to water, generally drink bottled water and if you're in the mountains or trekking, make sure to filter or boil any water sourced close to camp before you consume it. If you do suffer a bout of diarrhoea then make sure to drink lots of extra water to rehydrate. Dissolve sugar and salt in small quantities in the water to replace those you're losing or use rehydration sachets, and eat bland foods so as not to tax your digestion. If you have a fever or blood in your diarrhoea it may be dysentery so seek medical help.

Bilharzia

Freshwater snails in lakes and rivers transmit this unpleasant parasitic disease. It cannot be caught in hotel swimming pools or the sea. Should you contract bilharzia whilst swimming in a lake or river, it is easy to treat. It is not pleasant, however, and is best avoided.

HIV/AIDS

HIV is present in Peru, as are other sexually transmitted diseases, so if you do indulge, use condoms or femidoms to reduce the risk of transmission.

Car accidents

One of the biggest risks to travellers is dangerous driving. Usually on a tour you will be driven by people familiar with the roads and the idiosyncrasies of Peruvian road use. If you feel uncomfortable at any point, don't hesitate to ask your driver to slow down. Alternatively, if you are driving yourself, take extra precautions, avoid driving at night and pull over if conditions get too bad.

Skin infections

Each mosquito bite or small abrasion is an opportunity for a skin infection in warm, humid climates. Reduce the risk by cleaning and covering the slightest wound. Use a good quality antiseptic such as dilute iodine, potassium permanganate or gentian violet. **Prickly heat** or heat rash is a pimply rash that is most likely to be brought on by humidity. Reduce the irritation and itchiness by taking cold showers, using talc and sleeping naked under a fan or in a well air-conditioned room. Hot, moist climates are also ideal for **fungal infections**, so wash frequently around the armpits, crotch and between your toes, dry thoroughly and wear 100% cotton socks and underwear.

Altitude sickness

Acute Mountain Sickness (AMS) can affect people from 3,000m upwards and manifests itself initially as a persistent headache, coupled with dizziness, loss of appetite, nausea and vomiting. It most obviously affects those who ascend to altitude too quickly, usually by flying from low levels straight to a high-altitude destination, or by climbing or walking up a mountain too quickly. If the symptoms are mild they can easily be managed by resting. If they persist or are stronger then the patient ought to descend to a lower altitude immediately, where the symptoms should subside. The golden rule for avoiding altitude sickness, which can affect anyone regardless of fitness, age or other factor, is to ascend to altitude slowly, ideally descending to a lower altitude to sleep. Alcohol, cigarettes and heavy food exacerbate the risks.

Wild animals

The animals that you encounter in Peru are rarely dangerous but neither are they domesticated. In the wrong circumstances they could quite easily cause you an injury, so stay clear of wild animals. Attacks are rare but to further reduce the risk never approach a wild animal on foot, never swim in rivers or lakes without checking for the presence of caimans, never leave food out close to where you sleep, and don't run away from a predator as this can trigger the instinct to chase.

Rabies

Be aware that all warm-blooded mammals can carry rabies, although in Peru you're most likely to run the risk of contracting it from feral dogs. If you are bitten, scratched or saliva gets into an open wound then scrub the area with soap and running water, treat it with alcohol or an iodine-based disinfectant and ask for medical advice or help as soon as possible.

The specific **treatment** for a potential rabies exposure if you have not had rabies vaccine before travel includes a blood product called rabies immunoglobulin (RIG) along with a series of rabies vaccines (four to five doses given over a month). Ideally the RIG should be human but in Peru when it is available it is likely to be horse (equine or ERIG). Sometimes if the RIG is not available it is not mentioned, but you should always have this if you have not had a full course of pre-exposure vaccine, so contact your travel insurance providers to ensure that you obtain the correct treatment.

Snake and other bites

Snakes are very secretive and bites are generally rare. The same goes for **spiders** and **scorpions**. In all cases, minimise the threat by wearing closed shoes and trousers when walking in the bush or jungle, and by watching where you put your hands and feet, especially in rocky areas. In the evening check bedding and in the morning shake clothes thoroughly before dressing. If you are bitten, try to identify the creature that bit you without putting yourself at further risk. Bites can be painful and frightening but they rarely deliver enough venom to be life threatening. It is important to keep the victim calm and inactive, and to seek urgent medical attention.

Otherwise, and aside from mosquitoes, the most irritating insect bites are likely to be from **horseflies** and **sandflies**, which are not harmful.

Watch out for **ticks** and check yourself carefully after walking in grassy places. Ticks are usually straightforward to remove but attach themselves more firmly over time; leaving them in increases the chance of infection. Remove them gently but firmly, using tweezers. Do not jerk or twist the body but pull the tick away steadily at right angles to your skin, in order to avoid leaving the head parts behind – this can cause infection or an allergic reaction. Typhus, carried by ticks, can also sometimes occur, causing a fever and a reaction around the bite area. Seek advice if there is spreading redness around the bite and/ or you have a fever and/or aching joints.

Other diseases

There are a host of other diseases that can occur, such as Chagas disease (which may have done for Charles Darwin), Dengue fever, Leishmaniasis and Leptospirosis. However, travellers are rarely at risk from these and in the main they are treatable if the worst case scenario occurs. As a rule though, if you suffer a fever or can't identify what's making you ill, seek urgent medical help.

Coca

Coca leaf has been grown and chewed in the Andes for centuries; it's as central to the Andean culture as coffee is to the Arabs and tea is to people on the Indian subcontinent. Originally reserved for the Inca himself, it was popularised during the Spanish colonial period and chewed almost incessantly by overworked labourers as a relief from the cold and hardship. A quid of coca leaves is chewed with a mixture of lime and potash called *llipta*, to release a natural anaesthetic that combats hunger and relieves the effects of altitude, although people are at a loss as to how it works. It also provides a healthy dose of vitamins and iron, meaning that it is easy to understand why Andean people swear by it. Today though, it is more closely associated with its derivative, cocaine. Once considered a powerful painkiller, abuse and restriction have helped turn cocaine into the monster it is today. In reality, coca leaf is far removed from the heavily refined final product that crops up in cities the world over; it's just the raw material from which the drug is eventually made. However, the enormous profits that come from cocaine production mean that *campesinos* and farmers living in poverty can be persuaded to grow large coca crops for drug cartels. The war on drugs, which sees fields torched, swathes of jungle spayed with poison and attempts to eradicate all growing of coca leaves in the Andes, overlook the historical, cultural and beneficial nature of the leaf and also ignore the poverty that drives farmers to make money from growing it. The fact that the war is fought in the Andes, rather than on the streets of the urban West, is another contentious issue that polarises Peruvians who point out the traditional nature of the leaf in Andean society.

(L/D)

Crime

Most people affected by crime are victims of **opportunistic theft**. In general though, Peru is very safe. If you are in a tour group the chances of serious crime are small. Watch out for **bag snatchers** and **pickpockets** in large crowds, close to money changing facilities, tourist hotspots or at markets and train stations. If you are accustomed to the security of a larger group, be extra vigilant when out walking on your own or in smaller numbers. To make yourself less of a target, leave expensive items at home, leave valuables in a hotel safe, use a money belt or keep your wallet in an inside pocket, don't get large amounts of cash out in public places, carry cameras and other equipment in a day pack or by their straps, and appear vigilant. Watch out for unusual activity designed to distract you and alert others if you see something suspicious. Keep copies of important documents such as your passport, and note down serial numbers for cameras and the like; you may want to email them to yourself. If you are the victim of theft or a scam, report it to the police or local authorities immediately. The police will provide you with a report and incident number, which is vital for an insurance claim.

Drugs

Peru abides by all the usual drug laws so don't dabble. If someone does offer you drugs, be aware that they may be an undercover policeman and you may be being set up in order to extract a bribe. Sentences for possession and trafficking are high and prison conditions are not pleasant. However, coca leaf (see box, opposite) is grown and used legally for medicinal and cultural purposes; you may find that you can't bring it back to your home country though.

Banking and foreign exchange

The Peruvian nuevo sol (S/) comes in notes of S/10, S/50, S/100 and S/200. It's also divided into 100 *céntimos*, with copper- and silver-coloured coins worth S/0.05, S/0.10, S/0.20, S/0.50, S/1, S/2 and S/5. The nuevo sol currently trades at around US$1 = S/2.6, £1 = S/4 and €1 = S/3.4. Most upmarket hotels, particularly those in major tourist towns such as Arequipa, Cusco and Lima, will accept payment in US dollars but other currencies are much less recognised. Restaurants, shops and markets work in the **local currency**. Make sure you have small denomination notes as places, especially in more rural areas, may not have change or be able to break a big note for you. Foreign currency can be converted into nuevo sol at banks or bureaux de change, known locally as *casas de cambio*; bank rates will be less favourable. You may encounter long queues and have to fill in a variety of forms. No-one will accept damaged or torn bills, so make sure you travel with crisp, clean

Tipping

Knowing how much and when to tip is often a tricky business in a foreign country, particularly when the gap between wealthy visitor and poorer local is so wide. In Peru, the staff at hotels and those in airports often rely on tips to make up their income. In most situations a tip of around 10% is acceptable, depending on the level of service. High-end restaurants often add a service charge to the bill but you can leave a little extra for the waiting staff; a further 5% is often enough. Taxi drivers don't expect tips but make sure you agree a rate before setting off and then leave a little extra after. If you are on an organised tour it's customary to tip for good service; tips are usually given at the end of a stay or at the end of your trip. Discuss the amount with your tour operator before you travel. If you go on a trek and have a team of porters working with you, then tip generously; these people receive very low basic wages and work incredibly hard on your behalf. Make sure to tip the whole team, from guide, to cook to porter, with a larger amount for the guide and senior crew and an even split for the porters. Try to give the money to individuals directly, to ensure it ends up in the right hands.

notes. **Banks** tend to be open 09.00–18.00 on weekdays, although they may close for lunch. In the cities they also open on Saturday from 09.00 to 12.30. **Street traders** tend to congregate together. They will probably offer better rates for small transactions but beware of scams, check the calculations carefully, count the notes you receive before handing over your cash and look out for forgeries. You should avoid changing large amounts of money on the street and if you do use the service, think about taking a taxi afterwards to avoid being followed by someone who knows you've got cash in your pocket. Soles can be changed back into dollars at banks or a *casa de cambio* at Lima airport. Visa is the most widely accepted credit card by far, followed by MasterCard, but Maestro, American Express and Diners are also valid although they are less recognised. There's often a charge for using credit cards, meaning that, assuming your card provider doesn't hit you with a fee, it is frequently cheaper to withdraw money from an ATM on the card than actually using it to pay for something. **ATMs** are increasingly widespread and within main cities and towns you shouldn't have a problem finding one. Smaller towns, rural areas and the jungle still require you to carry cash. If you are using **travellers' cheques**, then be aware that you'll need to change them in banks in the main centres, as you may struggle in the smaller towns.

Food and drink

Eating out

Peru is enjoying some extensive exposure on the back of a culinary revolution in the country that has seen its blend of fusion cooking exported across the world; the country's cured-fish *ceviches*, spicy mashed potato *causas* and tender alpaca steaks – though possibly not its roasted guinea pig – are going global. Charismatic celebrity chefs such as Gastón Acurio and Virgilio Martinez have brought regional

Peru's best food towns

You'll find great food all around Peru but look out for these gastronomic centres in particular:

Lima

The city pioneering the Peruvian gastronomic renaissance, with award-winning restaurants, celebrity chefs and a signature fusion food that blends Spanish, indigenous and Asian influences to mouth-watering effect. See page 97.

Chiclayo

This northern coastal town has a wealth of seafood on offer, and also specialises in a heady stew where the meat is simmered in beer and cilantro for hours before the dish is cooked. See page 140.

Trujillo

Located on the coast, this town serves up delicious seafood but is a particularly good place to try *ceviche*, fish 'cooked' in citrus juice, and *chupe de camarones* – shrimp chowder. See page 132.

Cusco

Look out for local specialities, including rich soups and a variety of pork dishes as well as plenty of roast guinea pig, amongst the high-end and celebrated restaurants here. See page 201.

Arequipa

In keeping with the locals' fiery temperament, the food here is spicy, with specialities including *rocoto relleno*, spicy bell peppers stuffed with beef and vegetables. See page 173.

Essential Peruvian flavours

Pisco sour

Peru's national drink, this potent cocktail of grape brandy, lime juice and sugar is fresh and sharp but packs a kick. Contemporary versions include fruit or infusions of purple corn or coca leaves but make sure to try the uncomplicated classic.

Ceviche

Raw white fish marinated in lemon juice, onion and spicy peppers, usually served with corn on the cob or sweet potato.

Cuy

The legendary guinea pig, usually roasted and served whole but nowadays also available in a variety of contemporary forms, including guinea wellington or served with an Asian sauce.

Causas

An architecturally impressive yellow potato-based terrine that's often layered with avocado, tomato, seafood, chicken or vegetables.

Pisco sour – sweet, tart and delicious (IP/S)

specialities to the attention of a far wider audience and international diners have responded incredibly favourably, with gastronomes around the globe singing the praises of Peruvian food and Peruvian restaurants springing up across the Americas, Spain and in London. Lima stands at the centre of this gastronomic renaissance, but there are fine food outposts all over the country and a number of food festivals, such as La Mistura, that are gaining a similar following.

As you move around the country you'll discover a wide variety of ingredients and foodstuffs being used in the different regions and notice that each has its own speciality. On the **coast**, the enormous amount of fish found offshore means that you'll enjoy a wealth of seafood. *Ceviche*, white fish marinated in citrus juice, is the standout dish, although *chupe de camarones*, a shrimp chowder, is also delicious. Fish include sea bass (*corvina*), salmon and snapper. They tend to be served cooked in garlic (*al ajo*), fried (*frito*) or baked in white wine, tomatoes and onion

Chicharrones
Artery-hardening chunks of crispy, deep-fried pork.

Chupe de camarones
A delicious, buttery shrimp bisque that has a host of other ingredients as well.

Aji de gallina
Shredded chicken served in a rich walnut sauce with a hefty dose of spice.

Anticuchos
Beef heart shish kebabs cooked with cumin, garlic and peppers.

Inca Kola
Vibrantly coloured and bubble-gum sweet, this soft drink, the popular alternative to Coca Cola, is widely available and easily identifiable by its yellow colour.

Maté de coca
A highland staple, coca tea is widely drunk and is often served to help stave off the effects of altitude.

Inca Kola – improbably coloured and impossibly sweet (C)

(*a la chorrillana*). You'll also come across lots of shellfish, including mussels and scallops. Octopus (*polpo*) is another favourite. Along with fresh seafood, the northern coast also specialises in a heady goat stew cooked with cilantro (*seco de cabrito*) and served with beans or rice. In the **highlands**, food is heartier and often based around corn or potato; there are hundreds of types of tuber grown here. Soups and broths are widespread, with a lightly spiced beef broth containing noodles (*sopa a la criolla*) and chicken soup (*caldo de gallina*) especially widespread. Stir fry beef with onions, chilli, tomatoes and potato (*lomo saltado*) is ubiquitous, while roasted guinea pig (*cuy*) is considered a delicacy – it tastes a little gamey. You'll also come across trout (*trucha*) fished from Lake Titicaca. In the **jungle**, fresh fruit is readily available; meals are often accompanied by fried banana and palm hearts. You'll also be served river fish or shrimp, along with *tamales* made of mashed yucca and stuffed with seasoned chicken (*juanes*). By eating in lodges you should ensure you're not served endangered turtle soup or monkey meat. **Desserts** everywhere are sweet concoctions, including flan and caramel topped with meringue (*suspiro a la limeña*). Look out too for a purple corn pudding served with pineapple and dried fruits (*mazamorra morada*). Local fruits include custard apple (*cherimoya*), guava, mango, passion-fruit and soursop (*guanábana*); try them as juices, smoothies or ice cream.

Drinks

Most hotels and lodges provide bottled water – don't be tempted to drink unpurified or unfiltered water. Drinks range from the lurid Inca Kola to soothing herbal teas such as camomile (*manzanilla*) or coca (*maté de coca*). The latter won't make you high but will ease altitude sickness and soothe stomach complaints. The quality of **coffee** is improving; usually you will be served a small jug of coffee essence which you add to a mug of hot water. Milk is also served separately. The national drink is *pisco*, a type of grape brandy used to make heady cocktails, that is best bought in Ica. The Ica Valley is also where some of Peru's best **wines** are produced, although they're not really a patch on neighbouring Chile's. **Beers** though are good and include the delicious and drinkable Cusqueña and Arequipeña. Whilst in Lima you'll come across Cristal and Pilsner, and Trujillo produces a type of ale, Trujillo Malta. In the Andes you may also be offered strong homemade corn beer (*chicha*). On the coast a non-alcoholic corn drink, the purple-coloured **chicha morada** is also readily available.

Shopping

Lima and a number of the other main cities boast an excellent selection of shops, at least by Latin American standards. Items likely to be required by tourists are readily available in **shopping centres** or at **mall complexes** such as LarcoMar in Miraflores. However, once in more rural areas or the rainforest, the only shops are likely to be gift shops associated with the big hotels or lodges. There are also a host of regular **markets** in both big centres such as Cusco and much smaller towns where items are usually cheaper if you want to pick up a souvenir. One of the largest and liveliest markets is **Mercado Modelo** in Chiclayo. Operating every day, it's a good place to come for handicrafts and herbal medicines. Some of the best **handicrafts** though are found

(AB/PP)

Buying local crafts

When buying crafts, there is often room for bargaining and sellers are usually open to negotiation and may quote a price based on the premise that you'll bargain them down. This doesn't mean the initial price was inflated or that you're being ripped off, it's just part of the game. Don't respond aggressively or by offering a ridiculously low amount in return; remember that the goods you're haggling over are often handmade and have taken a lot of skill, time and effort to create. Simply suggest a lower price and see where the two of you settle. If you want to gauge the price of something, ask at other shops or stalls selling similar items before you actually contemplate buying anything. There are no fixed rules for bargaining but remember that essentially you want to secure a fair price, not necessarily the lowest one.

in the Mantaro Valley, close to Huancayo. Travel to small villages such as Cochas Grande and Cochas Chico, or attend the main Sunday market in Huancayo itself to pick up woven goods, carvings and jewellery. Other Sunday markets of note include the well-established weekly event in Pisac and the marginally less-touristy market in Chinchero, both in the Sacred Valley close to Cusco. In each there are two separate locations, one for craft and artisanal goods and another for food and produce. Should you find you arrive back in Lima without a souvenir, head to the vast Petit Thouars market in Miraflores to search out that perfect present.

What to buy

You'll be spoiled for choice when selecting a souvenir, as Peru has a long tradition of producing high-quality arts and crafts. Silver and gold handicrafts are good value, whilst jewellery is often unusual; silver filigree earrings and jewellery boxes can be found around Huancayo. Saint Mark boxes, known as *retablos*, are beautifully intricate. Originally introduced by the Spanish, these simple, portable altars containing detailed figures of saints evolved to include all manner of folk influences, Quechua rituals and native customs. In Cusco in particular, look out for reproductions of paintings in the Cusco-School style, which fuse Spanish religious imagery with indigenous elements and icons. Traditional carved gourds, *mate burilado*, are popular, whilst woodcarvings, elaborate Baroque-style frames and musical instruments are also readily available.

Textiles

The Andean people have long used alpaca or llama wool to create intricate textiles, usually decorated with anthropomorphic or geometric designs. Indeed, at one time woven cloth was the most valuable commodity in the Andes. The earliest high-quality examples are

from the Paracas culture, who incorporated animal motifs and specific symbols to tell a story. The Incas inherited this tradition and continued it, although their textiles tended not to be embroidered. These days Alpaca clothing, including scarves and jumpers are much sought after. Arequipa and Cusco are weaving centres, whilst Ayacucho is the heart of the textile industry. Look out too for hand-woven blankets and ponchos. The knitted earflap hats, *chullos*, are available everywhere but some of the finest can be found on the islands in Lake Titicaca. Lima also has several high-class shops specialising in Andean textiles.

Traditional, colourful textiles make high-quality souvenirs. (LG/PP)

Pottery

Peruvian pottery dates back to the pre-Columbian cultures. The Nazca culture specialised in painted vessels decorated with animal and bird motifs, the Moche recorded the minutiae of daily life on their pots, and the Incas decorated their ceramics with geometric, symmetrical shapes. The arrival of the Spanish saw an evolution in techniques as they introduced the potter's wheel, the enclosed kiln and lead glazes. Contemporary examples of these original ceramics can be picked up in most major centres and at craft markets.

Peru has a fine tradition of beautiful pottery. (gy/S)

Media and communications

Internet

The internet is widely available in Peru, though it tends to be more readily available in towns and cities and speeds may be slow by North American or European standards. **Internet cafés** are common and **Wi-Fi** is increasingly plentiful too, particularly in upmarket hotels. Internet access is limited in rural areas and in the jungle, where it may be restricted to the larger lodges.

Telephone

In Peru, public **pay phones** are operated by Telefónica Peru and are prolific. You'll need a prepaid phone card, *tarjeta telefónica*, which can be bought at supermarkets, newsstands and from pharmacies. Telefónica Peru's 147 card is the most common and best for long-distance calls;

you dial 147 then enter the unique code on the back of the card, listen to a message about how much time you have left and then dial the number you want. The **international telephone code** is +51. Some internet cafés also have private phone booths. There are three main **mobile** (cell) phone providers in Peru: Telefónica, Claro and Telmex, and their use is increasing. You can buy or rent mobile phones in major cities. They're generally cheap and offer pay-as-you go plans.

Media

The main **newspapers** in Peru are *El Comercio* and *La República*, which lean towards the government and the left respectively. Numerous tabloids also compete for your attention at newsstands with lurid, sensationalist stories and eye-catching headlines. For a rational round-up of weekly news and current affairs pick up a copy of *Caretas*, and to find out what's on where browse an edition of *Rumbos*.

Along with the ubiquitous international **television** channels there are a number of domestic stations, although their output is packed with soaps and Hollywood blockbusters.

The airwaves are full of **radio stations**. Along with the state-run Radio Nacional there are three national stations operating from Lima: Radio Programas de Peru, a talk station; Radio Panamericana, a music station; and Radio Americana, which has a mix of news and music. You'll also be able to pick up international broadcasts such as the BBC World Service.

Language

The official language is **Spanish.** There is some variation in terms of pronunciation and spelling between Latin American Spanish and European Spanish but you shouldn't have any problems making yourself understood. **Quechua,** an ancient indigenous language, has some official status and is widely spoken in parts of the country, often where Spanish isn't. It's a guttural language that's difficult to pronounce, but locals will appreciate you trying a handful of words or phrases, for politeness sake if nothing else. Another indigenous language, **Aymara** is used by the communities around Lake Titicaca. English is not widely spoken except in the largest cities or in areas where tourism is important. That said, visitors on organised tours shouldn't find themselves in a situation where they need another language.

Parts of Peru are ideal for learning Spanish and there are some very good language schools in Cusco in particular.

Business and time

Opening hours
In general, urban businesses operate during the week from 09.00 to 18.00 Monday to Friday. Some open on Saturday too, usually along similar hours. For bank opening hours, see *Banking and foreign exchange*, page 83. Forget going shopping or trying to change money on a Sunday. In smaller towns be aware that businesses often close for lunch, usually from 13.00 to 15.00. Some restaurants only open for meal times, although others are open all day. Bars and clubs open around 18.00 but don't get going until much, much later and can go on through the night.

Time
Peru is five hours behind GMT and on the same time as US Eastern Standard Time. There is no Daylight Saving Time in Peru. Bear in mind that locals have a relaxed attitude to time keeping and being late is a regular occurrence.

Cultural etiquette

On the whole, Peru is a very relaxed and friendly country. Nonetheless, it's important to remember to travel sensitively and be aware of local traditions, customs and ways of thinking. Allowances may be made for minor *faux pas* but you should endeavour not to make too many mistakes. **Politeness** is a trait of Peruvian society and in some circles greetings can be very formal. Always remove hats or headgear when meeting someone or entering a building. Men greet each other with a handshake; women or men meeting women usually share a kiss on the cheek. A polite good morning (*Buenos días*) or good afternoon (*Buenos tardes*) is usually offered, as are business cards. When dealing with officials make sure to remain courteous at all times, it won't help your cause getting angry or being rude. Politeness should extend to bargaining, when a pleasant negotiation will more than likely get you the desired result. A friendly but firm no thank you (*no gracias*) is better appreciated than a rude brush off as well. Sooner or later in Peru you'll encounter **begging**. Whether you give is up to you but try to determine if the person begging is doing so out of necessity or as a means of preying on tourists. Regardless though, don't give money to

Respect the traditions and heritage on display throughout Peru. (S/D)

children, it encourages parents to exploit their kids. Most Peruvians take great care over their appearance and even the poorest will often be **smartly turned out**. You should mirror this as you will be judged on how you dress in certain situations. Whilst urban and younger folk can be very fashionable, people in highland or rural communities tend to be more **conservative**. Bear this in mind as you travel around the country. Women should err on the side of conservatism and carry at least one long skirt as, rightly or wrongly, skimpy clothing can be considered an advertisement of availability. Men should make sure they don't wander about bare-chested in public places. As a rule though you can wear what you like in touristy areas or at the beach.

Gay travellers will find that Peru doesn't have an especially active scene and the country is essentially fairly reserved when it comes to the subject. Lima and Cusco are the most open cities and have a number of gay-friendly venues. Most of the country, however, doesn't have separate venues or set ups. In general though, travel for gay and lesbian visitors is safe and easy and you shouldn't encounter hostility.

Peru Highlights

5 Lima

For much of the year sea smog, known as *garúa*, shrouds Lima and the city looks washed out and monochrome. Combine this with years of negative reports and a reputation for being shabby, unsafe or simply boring, and it's no wonder the alluring former capital of Spanish South America, degenerated into little more than a stepping stone on the way to Machu Picchu. Lima, however, has another side; it is, in fact, one of South America's most underrated capitals and the ideal introduction to what you'll discover elsewhere in Peru. The oldest city in the Americas, it has world-class cuisine, architecture dating back over five centuries, well laid out museums, an eclectic and multi-cultural vibe, and an irresistible energy. All of this puts it on a par with cities on the continent commonly considered far hipper and more happening. Combining South American and Spanish influences, grime and glitz, Lima is as fresh and sharp as the *ceviche* and *pisco* sours for which it's famous.

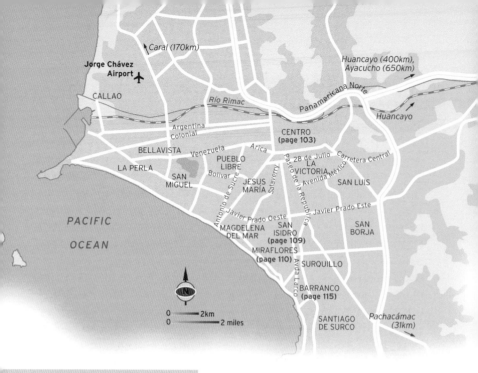

History

Lima has a protracted and colourful history and was once one of the most alluring cities in the Americas. People have lived at the mouth of the Rimac River for more than 7,000 years and as you fly in to the airport it's possible to see some of the large adobe pyramids these early residents built, now surrounded by the city's urban sprawl. The pyramids date from around 3000BC, long before the arrival of the Spanish and even before the rise of the Incas. By the time of the Incas, in the 15th century, the local shrine and oracle called Pachacámac was already ancient, having been established around 1,000 years earlier. The Incas simply incorporated these structures into their religion and built a convent at the site. When the Spanish subsequently arrived, there were about 400 temples along the river, backed up by a network of peaceful communities.

In 1535 Francisco Pizarro, who had previously captured Cusco, founded Lima. This settlement was established as the capital so that the conquistadors had a coastal city and connections with Spain via a well-protected harbour, as well as relatively easy access to the Andes. The city was christened Ciudad de los Reyes ('the City of Kings'), after the Magi and the kings of Spain. The name failed to stick, however, and by the late 16th century the city was known as Lima, a corruption of the Quechua name for the Rimac River.

Lima rapidly grew into a place of power and prestige. The Viceroy of Spanish South America made his home here, as did the Spanish Inquisition. The University of San Marcos, the first university in South America, was also founded here. Prosperity followed as Lima evolved into an important commercial centre and a hub for the import and export of goods to and from South America. The city walls were built later, in response to raids by privateers and pirates, amongst them Sir Francis Drake in 1579, who had heard of Lima's fabled wealth. The walls, however, couldn't protect the city from the catastrophic earthquake which rocked Lima in 1746. The quake razed the majority of the colonial buildings, flattened the adobe structures and instantly reduced the city to a shadow of its former self. Thousands of people are thought to have died during the earthquake and as a result of the illnesses and diseases that followed in its wake. Despite extensive efforts to rebuild and resuscitate the city, Lima struggled to recover. Under the guidance of the flamboyant Viceroy Amat though, the city shook off its cloistered atmosphere and took the opportunity to rebuild along a more open plan, with wide avenues, pretty gardens and mansions influenced by the Bourbons.

Whilst the rest of Peru was liberated earlier, Lima had to wait until 1821 to be set free from Spanish control by San Martín. Subsequently,

A faded but colourful colonial façade in Lima (SS)

Practicalities

All **flights**, including domestic flights from elsewhere in Peru, arrive at Jorge Chávez Airport, some 16km outside the city centre. At the airport a hotel shuttle or a tour representative will usually meet people on an organised tour. If that doesn't happen, transport into town is easy and frequent, although expensive. **Taxis** run from outside the Arrivals Hall and a **shuttle bus** also operates from the airport to the centre of town. In the Arrivals Hall there are **car-hire** desks for all the usual international companies, who tend to have more reliable and better-maintained vehicles than local operators. Here you will also find **exchange bureaux** and **ATMs** that accept Visa, MasterCard, American Express, Maestro and Cirrus; the rates of exchange will be better in town though. In the main hall there's an **iPerú information desk** open 24 hours a day, public telephones, internet access and a postal service.

If you arrive by **bus**, you should hail a taxi from the bus terminal as the area around the depot is generally not safe either during the day or at night.

Lima, laid out across a broad alluvial plain, is large and sprawling, making exploring on foot difficult. The **original centre** straddles the banks of the Rimac, several kilometres inland from the sea. This area is the old colonial heart and is still the city's architectural and cultural centre. To the west of the centre is the sea and a finger of land on which stands **Callao**, Lima's rather run-down port. Down the coast from Callao lie the districts of **San Miguel, Magdalena del Mar, San Isidro, Miraflores** and **Barranco**. Although the downtown area

Accommodation

There are almost no hotels close to the airport, so you will have to head into the centre, even if you are simply moving on from Lima the following day. Make sure that you have somewhere booked before you set off and, if it has not been arranged by your tour operator, see if the hotel in question will arrange to pick you up, either as part of the room rate or for an additional fee.

Exclusive
Gran Hotel Bolívar Ⓦ www.grandhotelbolivarperu.com
JW Marriott Hotel Ⓦ www.marriott.com
Miraflores Park Hotel Ⓦ www.mirafloorespark.com
Swissôtel Lima Ⓦ www.swissotel.com

(MC/PP)

can be walked easily enough during the day, you are better taking a **taxi** to the main sites. This is especially true if you want to travel from the centre to San Isidro, Miraflores or Barranco, where the majority of sites of interest, hotels and places to eat or drink outside the centre lie.

The Lima **public transport system** appears chaotic and impenetrable but is actually quite efficient and offers visitors an authentic experience of Lima life. **Buses** and shared minivans called *combis* or *collectivos*, which are distinguished by size, can all be flagged down. The routes or destinations they are travelling to are listed on the front or written on the side.

Upmarket
Casa Andina Miraflores Centro Ⓦ www.casa-andina.com
Country Club Lima Ⓦ www.hotelcountry.com
Second Home Peru Ⓦ www.secondhomeperu.com
Sonesta Posadas del Inca Miraflores Ⓦ www.sonesta.com

Moderate
Casa Bella Ⓦ www.casabellaperu.net
Hotel Antigua Miraflores Ⓦ www.peru-hotels-inns.com
Libertador San Isidro Ⓦ www.libertador.com.pe

Budget
Hostal El Patio Ⓦ www.hostalelpatio.net
Inka Lodge Ⓦ www.inkalodge.com
The Point Ⓦ www.thepointhostels.com

the city again fell into disrepair. The city walls were torn down in 1870 as expansion continued east and south beyond the protective ring. Without these defences, the Chileans easily overran the capital during the War of the Pacific in 1881; it took two years for the city to be liberated again, during which time it endured extensive damage whilst occupied.

During the early 20th century there was a substantial influx of poor and unskilled people to the city, which saw the population swell. Despite attempts to create sewage systems and open spaces to offset the boom, the city has struggled to keep pace with the number of new residents and overcrowding has been a problem ever since. More than eight million people now call Lima home, even if they live in large shantytowns (or *pueblos jóvenes*) on the outskirts.

In stark contrast there's another side to the contemporary city, a side decorated with wealth and opulence and centred on the suburbs of San Isidro, Miraflores and more recently Barranco. These areas are home to the emerging middle-class *Limeños* who are re-engaging with their city, helping to energise it and re-establish some pride in the capital as it seeks to recapture some of its glorious past.

Neglect and poverty are still evident all over the city, but new money

Mural in Barranco (see page 114) (JG/A)

is ensuring an improvement in infrastructure and the regeneration of run-down areas, along with the conservation of the UNESCO-listed historic centre. While issues of race and class pervade the place the cocktail of cultures, attitudes and peoples remains endlessly fascinating. Although its grandeur has faded, the city clings on to its elegant past with grand colonial and municipal buildings, wide plazas, smart suburbs and artistic quarters. Positive press and the continued export of Peruvian cuisine and chefs from the city ensure that Lima's international stock continues to rise and there's something of a renaissance in the city, evidence that the capital's time is set to come again.

Lima highlights

City centre

There are a host of sights, fine-art museums and excellent restaurants to take in amidst Lima's chaotic centre.

Museo del Oro

Alonso de Molina 1100 Ⓦ www.museoooroperu.com.pe ⊘ 10.30–18.00 daily

Once a must-see site, the **Gold Museum** was massively discredited when the majority of its exhibits, some 7,000 pieces, were declared to be fakes. The museum maintains that the pre-Hispanic gold pieces that are on display now are authentic but it is wise to take what you see here with a pinch of salt. There are also textile and ceramic exhibits.

Museo Andrés del Castillo

Jr de la Unión 1030 Ⓦ www.madc.com.pe ⊘ 09.00–18.00 Wed–Mon

Contained within an attractive 19th-century mansion, the **Andrés del Castillo Museum** is home to a breathtaking private collection of Nazca textiles and Chancay pottery.

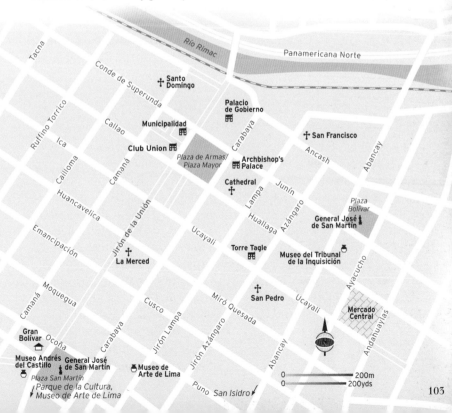

Eating out

Whilst in Lima, take advantage of the burgeoning food scene here; a lot of local life revolves around meals and it's worth taking the time to savour some of the dishes on offer. One of the great food cities of the world, Lima is full of eateries, both grand and small, that can rustle up delicious versions of Peru's unique fusion food, a complex blend of indigenous, African, Asian and Spanish flavours. Look out for *ceviche*, nutty stews, *anticuchos*, potato terrines and much more.

Astrid y Gastón (International) Cantuarias 175, Miraflores ⊕ 01 242 4422

Canta Rana (Peruvian) Barranco ⊕ 01 247 7274

Central (Peruvian) Santa Isabel 376, Miraflores ⊕ 01 242 8515

Chez Wong (*Ceviche*) Enrique León García 114, La Victoria ⊕ 01 470 6217

El Rincon Que No Conoces (Peruvian) Bernardo Alcedo 363, Lince ⊕ 01 471 2171

La Mar (Peruvian) Av La Mar 770, Miraflores ⊕ 01 421 3365

La Rosa Nautica (Peruvian) Espigon 4 Costa Verde, Miraflores ⊕ 01 447 0057

Malabar (Peruvian) Av Camino Real, San Isidro ⊕ 01 440 5200

Matseui (sushi) Manuel Bañon 260, San Isidro ⊕ 01 422 4323

Panchita (Peruvian) Av Dos de Mayo 298, Miraflores ⊕ 01 242 5957

Restaurant Huaca Pucllana (South American) Av Arequipa 4698, Miraflores ⊕ 01 445 4042

Xocolatl (chocolates) Manuel Bonilla 111, Miraflores ⊕ 01 242 0143

Entertainment

Lima has a more **contemporary nightlife** scene than most other cities in Peru, with the suburb of **Barranco** the hippest and liveliest place to hang out. For mood-lifting drinks to start a night out, go to Ayahuasca in Barranco (San Martín 130) or Malabar (Camino Real 1101) in **San Isidro**. The former is set in a three-storey mansion with an Andean postmodern feel, while colourful, contemporary Malabar is coolly chic.

For something more **folksy**, try the *tabernas* in Barranco, such as La Noche (Bolognesi 307), where you'll find authentic, live Andean music, criolla, Latin jazz and affordable drinks. To **dance**, head to any of the *peñas*, or music clubs, in Barranco; Del Carajo (San Ambrosio 328) and La Candelaria (Bolognesi 292) are considered two of the classic hangouts for traditional music fans.

Museo de Arte de Lima (MALI)

Paseo Colón 125 ⓦ www.mali.pe ⊘ 10.00-19.00 Tue-Sun

The **Lima Art Museum** contains the country's most spectacular permanent collection of art, with pieces from all the major periods of Peru's history. Textiles, paintings, furniture, modern art and video installations compete for your attention in this *beaux-arts* structure designed by Alexandre Gustave Eiffel, and give a good introduction to the country's present art scene as well as the foundations from which it grew.

Museo del Tribunal de la Santa Inquisición

Jr Junin 548 ⊘ 09.00-13.00 & 14.30-17.30 Mon-Fri

This substantial colonial mansion, which has been restored impeccably, used to be the headquarters of the South American Spanish Inquisition and is now the **Museum of the Inquisition**. The first court was held in 1584 and it remained active until 1820. The tribunal room remains beautifully decorated with a carved wooden ceiling, whilst the dungeon still effectively conjures up sobering images of the atrocious torture that was carried out here.

Iglesia de Santo Domingo

Jr Camaná ⊘ 05.00-08.00 & 09.00-12.30 Mon-Sat, 09.00-13.00 Sun

The pink-painted **Dominican church**, dating from 1549, is one of the most attractive in Lima, with intricate chapels and courtyards to admire. It also houses some of the city's most venerated artefacts, with the skulls of celebrated saints such as Santa Rosa and San Martín de Porres, the first saint of the Americas and the first South American black saint respectively, on display here. An adjacent convent contains the saints' tombs.

Monasterio de San Francisco

Jr Lampa, on the corner with Ancash ⓦ www.museocatacumbas.com ⊘ 09.30-17.30 daily

This Baroque Franciscan church, the **Church and Convent of San Francisco**, dates from 1674 and is one of the most spectacular buildings in the city. The cathedral was one of the few large buildings to survive the devastating earthquakes of 1687 and 1746. It has subsequently been strikingly restored to its original yellow and white colouring.

An attractive building in its own right, with a dramatic stone façade and twin towers, it's celebrated for its collection of artwork, fine tile work and extraordinary 17th-century **library** containing 25,000 books, many of which pre-date the Spanish Conquest. The sprawling subterranean

The extensive library in the Monasterio de San Francisco (SS)

catacombs are a rather grisly additional attraction, and are where as many as 75,000 bodies were interred before Lima's main cemetery was built. You can file past the bone-filled crypts and admire a well lined with skulls and femurs for a glimpse of the city's past.

La Merced

Plazuela de La Merced, Jr de la Unión y Miró Quesada ⊘ 08.00–12.45 & 16.00–20.00 Mon–Sat, 07.00–13.00 & 16.00–20.00 Sun

A church has stood on this site since Lima's first mass was celebrated here in 1534. The current church, **Our Lady of Mercy**, is probably the most important religious building in Lima and is still actively used as a place of worship and pilgrimage by Peruvians. Much of the current building dates from the 18th century and is resplendent with an impressive Baroque frontage worthy of its status, made from white granite. Inside are more than 20 impressively carved **altars**, some of which are made of mahogany. Also look out for some attractive tile work and a number of eye-catching religious paintings.

San Isidro and around

San Isidro is one of Lima's most affluent areas. A smart residential district south of the centre, it has a selection of good hotels and fine restaurants as well as an attractive park, centred on an old olive grove planted by San Martín de Porres in the 17th century. There is also a large golf course here and it is in close proximity to a handful of good museums.

Shopping

The capital has the widest variety of shopping in Peru. The main shopping street is **Jirón de la Unión**, a pedestrian precinct running from the Plaza Mayor, where you can find boutique shops, big brand names and other outlets.

The **LarcoMar mall** on the clifftops at the end of Avenida Larco in Miraflores has great views of the Pacific Ocean, a decent food court and is home to global brands such as North Face, L'Occitane and Giuliana Testino (a local designer and the sister of photographer Mario Testino). Watch out for paragliders who jump off the nearby cliffs and cruise past the shoppers and diners in the mall.

For contemporary and good quality crafts, head to Barranco and **Dédalo** (Paseo Sánz Peña 295), an early 20th-century mansion close to the oceanfront that's full of handicrafts, clothes, bags and jewellery made by local artisans and designers. **Agua y Tierra** (Diez Canseco 298 y Alcanfaes) in Miraflores is a good bet for crafts from the Amazon. Alpaca jumpers and other items can be bought from **Alpaca 111** (Av Larco 671) and **Alpaca 859** (Av Larco 859), whilst silver jewellery, antiques and religious art are available from Avenida La Paz in Miraflores.

For a different shopping experience, head to one of the many markets, making sure to take your wits and haggling skills with you. **Gamarra market** in La Victoria has more than 20,000 shops and small factories, making this clothes emporium the biggest in South America. Last-minute crafts, textiles, alpaca clothing and reproduction canvases can also be found at the vast **Mercado Indio** in Pueblo Libre, which shouldn't be confused with the smaller, more up-market collection of stalls by the same name in Miraflores. In Miraflores look out too for the strip of craft markets on Avenida Petit Thouars, which sell a wide range of good quality arts, crafts and souvenirs. For a food-shopping experience, follow the local chefs to **Mercado de Surquillo** in Miraflores to see where the freshest seafood, meats and fruits are sourced.

Lima boasts a wide range of contemporary shopping arcades and more traditional markets. (SS)

Huaca Huallamarca

C Nicolás de Rivera 201 & Av Rosario ⊘ 09.00-17.00 Tue-Sun

This *huaca*, or temple, hidden in a residential, suburban area, consists of a restored **adobe pyramid**, built by the Lima culture in around AD200. A small museum describes the site in detail and also houses a mummy from within the structure. The pyramid is often illuminated for special occasions and presentations.

Museo Larco

Av Bolívar 1515 Ⓦ www.museolarco.org ⊘ 09.00-22.00 Mon-Sun

Founded in 1926, the privately owned **Larco Museum** is housed in an 18th-century colonial mansion that was itself built on top of a 7th-century pre-Columbian pyramid. The scholarly museum features three sections; the main part houses gold and silver exhibits as well as a magnificent textile collection and hundreds of examples of pottery. Look out for sacrifice vessels, the gold ceremonial suit of the Lord of Chan Chan and a detailed textile from Paracas that would have

Ancient sites often sit within modern residential districts, such as Huaca Huallamarca. (DT/PP)

shrouded the body of a deceased ruler and dates from around 200BC. A warehouse contains additional material, whilst an erotic art museum is

full of frivolous, erotic-themed antiquities. The museum serves to illustrate that not all of Peru's past is Incaic, with much of its vast 44,000-piece collection dating from the Moche and Chimú cultures. The latter were especially good at phallic art. The museum is in the Pueblo Libre district and can be easily visited on the way to or from the airport as it is just 20 minutes away.

Museo Nacional de Anthropolgía, Arqueología y Historia

Plaza Bolívar, Pueblo Libre

Ⓦ http://museonacional.perucultural.org.pe

⊘ 09.00-17.00 Tue-Sat, 09.00-16.00 Sun

This stately mansion – in which the leaders of the struggle for independence, San Martín and Bolívar, once both lived – now houses one of the largest collections of artefacts from pre-Hispanic cultures in Peru. Exhibits of the **National Archaeology and Anthropology Museum** include ceramics, carved stone figures and tools, metalwork, jewellery and textiles. Objects of particular interest include the impressive granite **Tello Obelisk**, and **Estrela de Raymondi**, a 2m tall sculpted stele from the site of Chavín de Huantar. Other rooms are dedicated to the Nazca, Paracas, Moche and Chimú cultures, while a scale model of Machu Picchu will clarify the layout of the original for when you get there.

Museo de la Nación
Javier Prado Este 2465, San Borja ⊘ 09.00-18.00 Tue-Fri

What looks like a large, ugly concrete monstrosity adjacent to a main road is in fact Lima's **National Museum**. It's laid out clearly and is full of interesting information and permanent exhibits that cover aspects of Peruvian archaeology and art. Follow the exhibits through the highlights of the pre-Conquest cultures; a visit here before you see the actual sites will help put them in context and ensure you get more from the various ruins when you reach them.

Miraflores

San Isidro gives way to Miraflores, set above some precipitous cliffs, which is effectively the core residential and commercial district of Lima. Fashionable and well tended, it has some smart properties and a wide range of shops, good hotels and recommended restaurants. There are also a number of pretty parks in the district and along the seafront.

Huaca Pucllana
Av General Borgoña y Tarapacá ⊘ 09.00-16.30 Wed-Mon

This pre-Columbian **archaeological site** of painstakingly precise brickwork now stands amidst the tower blocks and buildings of Miraflores. Sitting right alongside the modern city, you bump into it

Lima's Gaudi-inspired Parque del Amor (SS)

Lima landmarks

To see the best **colonial architecture**, head to either Plaza de Armas (Plaza Mayor) or **Plaza San Martín** as both have attractive buildings surrounding them; San Martín is dominated by a statue of the Liberator (General José de San Martín). Alternatively, stroll down **Calles Ucayali, Conde de Superunda, Huancavelica** or **Jirón de la Unión. The Torre Tagle Palace** on Jirón Ucayali is the best surviving example of **colonial architecture** in Lima. Dating from 1735, it has a beautiful Baroque stone doorway standing amidst two exquisitely carved dark-wood balconies; now occupied by the Foreign Ministry, it's not possible to access the inner courtyard, although you can poke your head round to see the patio and take in the intricate carvings.

The central **Plaza Mayor**, just south of the Rimac River, is a UNESCO World Heritage Site. Once a market and meeting place, the plaza – also known as the Plaza de Armas – marks the spot where Pizarro founded the city in 1535. It also hosted bullfights before important buildings such as the gated Palacio de Gobierno (Government Palace), the cathedral, the Archbishop's Palace, the Municipalidad (Municipal Palace) and the Club Union were built around the edges, usually on top of existing Inca or other structures. In the centre stands a bronze fountain dating from 1650.

The thickset **cathedral** (⊘ 10.00–17.00 Mon–Sat), which was modelled on a Seville church, comprises several buildings, the earliest built in 1555 over an Inca temple dedicated to a puma deity. The earthquake in 1746 badly damaged the cathedral, which was rebuilt along original lines in 1755. The massive nave, towering columns and ornate interior are striking, while the carefully carved stalls, silver-coated altars and mosaic-decorated walls are also impressive. A chapel here is also the final resting place of Francisco Pizarro, the conquistador leader and founder of Lima, who was assassinated in the Plaza Mayor in 1541.

Plaza Bolívar was where General José de San Martín proclaimed Peru's independence. A statue of the Liberator astride his horse now dominates the square. Behind him is the Congress building, which stands on the site of the former first university of the Americas.

A huge sculpture dominates Parque del Amor in Miraflores. (SS)

Imposing colonial architecture in the Plaza de Armas (SS)

There are attractive **clifftop gardens** in Miraflores to stroll through. The compact but lively **Parque del Amor** (Park of Love), designed by Victor Delfín with a nod to Parque Güell in Barcelona, features good views that can be enjoyed from benches decorated with mosaics and littered with hearts and romantic writings; a huge sculpture of two entwined people stands over the park and the modern-day couples who stroll here. In the centre, look out for **Parque de la Cultura** (Park of Culture), which hosts occasional music performances. South of here is **El Circuito Mágico del Agua** (Magic Water Tour), an extraordinary collection of fountains that are backed by an evening light show.

For a change of pace, stroll around the largely residential district of **Barranco**. Quieter and more laidback than most other parts of the city, it is a welcome contrast to the hurly burly of the centre. Look out for a pretty wooden footbridge, the **Puente de los Suspiros** ('Bridge of Sighs') and a small passageway, **La Bajada de Baños** ('The Bathing Path'), which is lined with attractive houses and leads to a sea lookout. There are also steep steps down to the beach below.

Lima has a selection of **beaches** although the water offshore is polluted, cold and plagued by strong currents. Nonetheless they are popular with the locals, who flock to them during the summer months. Join them but be aware that opportunistic thieves will make off with anything left even briefly unattended. Further south are some better spots, including **El Silencio**, **Punta Hermosa**, the surf beach of **Santa Maria**, **Punta Negra** and the fishing village of **Pucusana**.

An adobe pyramid stands at the heart of Huaca Pucllana. (e/S)

when turning the corner of a street, making it a superb counterpoint to contemporary Lima. The site was a ceremonial centre and dates back to AD400, it used to be one of many *huacas* and ceremonial centres that stretched across this section of the valley. The temple was occupied over the centuries by a native group known simply as the Lima, and later by the Huari, Ichma and Inca peoples. A large **adobe pyramid**, which originally stood 23m high, dominates the site, even though it has been eroded over the centuries by the wind and rain. Extensive excavations are ongoing. On site is one of the top restaurants in Lima, **Restaurant Huaca Pucllana** (see *Eating out*, page 104), where you can dine on tapas while enjoying the view and the open air.

Fundación Museo Amano

C Retiro 160 ⓦ www.fundacionmuseoamano.org.pe ⊘ By appointment 15.00–17.00 Mon-Fri

The **Amano Museum Foundation** houses an exemplary, privately owned collection of ceramics and textiles created by the Chimú, Nazca and Chancay cultures which can only be viewed by appointment. It is worth making an effort to see inside.

Barranco

Further south down the coast from Miraflores is Barranco, a one-time Spanish coastal retreat that has been swallowed up by the expanding city. These days it is Lima's most bohemian suburb; art galleries and workshops stand alongside cafés, bars and live music venues that come to life in the evenings and which host the capital's most vibrant nightlife. For more on entertainment in Lima, see box on page 104.

Museo de Pedro Osma

Av Pedro de Osma 421 ⓦ www.museopedrodeosma.org ⊘ 10.00–13.30 & 14.30–18.00 Tue-Sun

Hidden within a historic house, the **Pedro de Osma Museum**'s private collection of colonial art includes sculptures, altarpieces and paintings from the Cusco School. There's also a small collection of silver from the 16th to 19th centuries. The building itself, the **Palacio de Osma**, is attractive and ornate and is worth taking time to admire as well.

Around Lima highlights

Pachacámac

⊘ 09.00–17.00 Mon–Fri

Thirty kilometres south of Lima stands the **ancient shrine and oracle** of Pachacámac, which looms over the coastline. The site dates from the 1st century AD but reached its apex under the Huari culture during the 10th century. The name derives from the Huari god Pachacámac, whose two-faced image can be seen on a sacred wooden carved staff in the **on-site museum**; he was reputed to control earthquakes and tremors and these demonstrated his displeasure. The site was later captured by the Incas and became a significant place of pilgrimage during their rule.

The **pyramids** are poorly preserved and may appear like mounds of dried mud to the untrained eye, but some sections have been reconstructed. In their heyday the shrine was richly decorated with precious stones and other valuable commodities such as coral and crystals, but was stripped by priests prior to the arrival of the Spanish,

The train ride into the highlands is spectacular. (RS/S)

The central highlands

The central highlands stretch from the southern end of the Cordillera Blanca down to the department of Cusco. A spectacular region full of dramatic landscapes and history, it is little visited by tour groups as the towns tend to be harder to reach. That said, those that do make the effort are amply rewarded.

The main highlights are the traditional centres of Huancayo, Huancavelica and Ayacucho. **Huancayo** can be reached by rail from Lima; an extraordinary high-altitude train trip, the service is intermittent and occasionally unreliable. The Carreterra Central makes approaching the region by road relatively quick and easy though. The journey is worth it to discover the attractive **Mantaro Valley**, where **traditional villages** such as Cochas Chico, Hualahoyo, San Pedro and San Jerónimo, practise authentic crafts and still celebrate original festivals with great gusto.

Some 150km south of Huancayo is **Huancavelica**, a compact town hidden amidst craggy peaks. Once a strategic Inca centre, it came to prominence when the Spanish conquistadors discovered silver and mercury here. These days it's a relaxed place to enjoy the dramatic landscapes and bracing mountain air.

Ayacucho, 250km further south, is similarly off-the-beaten path even though it's just an hour's flight from Lima. Having been terrorised by the Shining Path, who made this region their heartland, for much of the 1980s and early 1990s, this beautiful colonial town, one of the most architecturally impressive in the Andes, has recovered from the conflict and is again increasingly associated with textiles, handicrafts and the largest and most devout Semana Santa Holy Week celebration in South America. The town boasts some exceptional colonial architecture and mansions, as well as 33 churches, including a 17th-century Baroque cathedral which conceals several gold-leaf altars, the Templo de San Cristobal, which dates from 1540 and the fabulous, photogenic Iglesia de Santo Domingo.

Close by are the **archaeological ruins of Huari** (⊘ 08.00–17.00 daily). Some 20km north of the city, these ruins date from AD600–1000 and are considered to be the first walled city in the Andes. The Huari are best known though for their extensive ceramic production and for the skill with which they manipulated gold, silver and other metals.

Traditional events and festivals are celebrated enthusiastically in the central highlands. Semana Santa in Ayacucho is considered the largest and most devout in South America. (GT/PP)

led by Francisco Pizarro's brother Hernando, who would have certainly pillaged what was left.

These days you can see the reconstructed **Templo de la Luna** ('Temple of the Moon') and climb to the top of the **Templo del Sol** ('Temple of the Sun'), which was added to the earlier citadel by the Incas. From the top it's possible to see the whole site and catch a glimpse of the coast and beach at Playa San Pedro. Alternatively, admire the **Palacio de las Mamacuna** ('House of the Chosen Women'), which features a number of Inca-style architectural elements. You can't get too close to the structure, however, as earthquake damage has weakened it.

Caral

⊘ 09.00–17.00 daily

Caral, roughly 240km north of Lima, is the **oldest settlement in the Americas**, having been established around 2600BC, 4,000 years before the emergence of the Incas. First discovered in 1905, the site was initially largely ignored by archaeologists as they didn't discover any pottery or gold here. In fact, Caral is a pre-ceramic site, most important for the scale of its construction at this time and for the domestication of plants, which allowed the inhabitants to grow crops and farm cotton.

Six **stone pyramids** still stand adjacent to amphitheatres, ceremonial rooms, altars, adobe complexes and sunken plazas. The residential buildings are thought to have been home to up to 3,000 residents during the site's heyday. The largest pyramid is 18m, making it one of the tallest in Peru. Artefacts found in the pyramids include flutes made from animal and bird bones and some of Peru's most ancient *quipus*, the rope and knot system of recording information used by people without a written language (see box, page 8). The site functioned for about 500 years before a harsh drought probably forced the culture to move on in search of water and more fertile soils.

A sunken plaza surrounded by pyramids at Caral. (DB)

In conversation with ...
SouthAmerica.travel

www.
SouthAmerica.*travel*
Our name is our passion...

Can you describe an itinerary that gives a good range of what Peru has to offer?

Our Essence of Peru tour includes several amazing sights with each day more fascinating than the last: Lima, Paracas Bay and the Ballestas Islands, the mysterious Nazca Lines, the 'white city' Arequipa, Colca Canyon, Lake Titicaca, Cusco, the Sacred Valley and Machu Picchu. You'll need about two weeks to see all these highlights, though we'll tailor your itinerary perfectly to the time you have.

Besides Machu Picchu, Peru offers several amazing sights and experiences. How can a traveller choose?

We make recommendations based upon the traveller's interests. Do you like archaeology? Visit the northern region of Peru, or focus on the Inca ruins in Cusco and the Sacred Valley. If you prefer natural beauty, you'll want to see the Paracas Bay National Reserve, Colca Canyon, Lake Titicaca and the Amazon rainforest. The best way to maximise your Peru holiday is to speak with a travel expert who knows Peru well and can prepare the perfect personal itinerary based on your travel style.

What insider tips can you give to a first-timer to Peru?

Many visitors think Lima is only worthwhile as a short stopover on the way to Cusco and Machu Picchu. But the city is alive with world-class cuisine, fascinating museums, a beautifully restored historic district, and a monastery housing Latin America's oldest library. Consider spending several days exploring the historic capital of the Spanish Empire, founded in 1542.

SouthAmerica.travel is the expert in four-star and five-star South America tours. Licensed and bonded in the US, they have been sharing their passion for South American travel since 1999. They have offices in Seattle, Buenos Aires, Lima, Rio de Janeiro and Stuttgart. We spoke to CEO Juergen Keller.

ⓣ +1 800 747 4540
ⓔ bradt@SouthAmerica.travel ⓦ www.SouthAmerica.travel

6 The North

The Pan-American Highway north of Lima quickly takes you into a region rich in pre-Columbian history. Highlights include significant archaeological sites such as the Huacas de Sol and de la Luna, the vast adobe city of Chan Chan, pyramids that tower over the desert sands, and troves of spectacular treasure displayed in contemporary museums, which are almost unparalleled in the rest of the country.

Along the way are some of Peru's best outdoor centres and exquisite alpine scenery, including the world-renowned Cordillera Blanca, which can be explored on simple or more challenging treks. Elsewhere, fine colonial centres such as Trujillo are full of conquistador history and serve up sublime seafood and relaxed history lessons. Then there's the option to just unwind at Huanchaco or Máncora, enjoy still-empty beaches where it's warm enough to swim, or catch a wave and celebrate this varied region.

Touring the north

Snow-capped mountains provide a breathtaking backdrop to outdoor activities in the Andes. (MF/C)

The north comprises a vast and varied area that requires some time and planning to explore properly – a tour operator will be able to pick out the highlights for you, but will probably focus on the Cordillera Blanca and region around Trujillo. You may be able to tailor your itinerary, however, to visit Chachapoyas or Máncora. In essence, it's possible to drive the entire length of the long, dusty coast on the Pan-American Highway, and there are good-quality roads leading inland to each of the towns discussed. Distances, however, can be daunting. With time precious, it may be better to fly to Huaraz, Trujillo or Chiclayo and then take to the roads.

If you make it as far as Máncora, try to allow enough time to enjoy the beaches and relax properly. Allow ten days to satisfy cravings for culture and activity by travelling from Trujillo to Chiclayo and on to Máncora, before flying back to Lima.

Huaraz to Caraz

Huaraz and around

Huaraz, dubbed the 'Chamonix of the Andes', is the main hub for people looking to access and explore the pair of rugged mountain ranges (*cordilleras*) that make this area such a popular stop. To the east lies the stunning snow-capped Cordillera Blanca, whilst to the west stands the dry, barren Cordillera Negra. Standing at 3,100m, the town has a spectacular setting in a valley, the Callejón de Huaylas, which runs north–south and separates the two mountain ranges. Whichever way you look, Huaraz is surrounded by stunning scenery and boasts picture-postcard views of 20 snow-capped summits over 6,000m to awe and inspire visitors. Churup, Rima Rima and Vallunaraju could almost

be touched if you reached out, whilst the monolithic Huandoy and Huascarán (the highest peak in Peru) are also visible. This, along with the town's character and attitude, more than make up for its somewhat scruffy appearance and concrete buildings, which are largely down to the city having to be rebuilt following the devastation caused by an enormous earthquake in 1970. Above all, Huaraz is a mecca for trekkers and climbers who come to pitch themselves against the peaks; during the high season from June to October, you won't be able to move for big boots and Gore-Tex but the buzz is undeniable. However, it's also an excellent base for exploring nearby archaeological sites, including the ancient and enigmatic Chavín de Huántar.

Practicalities

Huaraz, 425km from the capital, is the main centre of the region and an established base for trekkers and climbers; you'll find all the necessary amenities here. It's possible to **fly** to Huaraz from Lima; there's a daily flight with LC Busre. The **airport**, Aeropuerto de Anta, is some 22km north of Huaraz in Anta. Alternatively, there are several **overland** routes, the most straightforward of which branches off the Pan-American Highway as it makes its way north. The town itself is compact and easy to explore **on foot**. The main street, Avenida Luzuriaga, is home to trekking agencies and equipment shops, bars and restaurants, whilst hotels tend to fan out from the Plaza. There are plenty of places to stay but good quality hotels fill up early during high season and around **festivals** such as El Señor de le Soledad, the town's patron saint's day on 3 May; the Semana del Andinismo, a week-long climbing

Accommodation

Upmarket

Andino Club Hotel (Huaraz) ⓦ www.hotelandino.com
El Patio (Monterrey) ⓦ www.elpatio.com.pe
Lazy Dog Inn (Huascarán National Park) ⓦ www.thelazydoginn.com

Moderate

Casa de Pocha (Carhuaz) ⓦ www.socialwellbeing.org/lacasadepocha.htm
Hotel Baños Termales (Monterrey) ⓔ realhotelmonterrey@yahoo.com
Llanganuco Mountain Lodge (Yungay) ⓦ www.llanganucolodge.com
Olaza's Bed and Breakfast (Huaraz) ⓦ www.olazas.com
O'Pal Inn (Caraz) ⓦ www.opalsierraresort.com
San Sebastian (Huaraz) ⓦ www.sansebastianhuaraz.com
Way Inn Lodge (Huaraz) ⓦ www.thewayinn.com/lodge.htm

Huaraz and around highlights
Museo Arqueológico de Ancash
Plaza de Armas ⊘ 09.00-18.00 Mon-Sat, 09.00-14.00 Sun
The small **Ancash Archaeological Museum** has collected together a number of exhibits to bring to life the long history of the region. Mummies, trepanned skulls (where holes are surgically drilled into the skull), textiles and ceramics from the Chavín, Huaraz and Moche cultures hint at the 12,000 years of habitation in this region.

and skiing celebration in June; and over the Inkafest Mountain Film Festival, which takes place in August. There are plenty of small shops and craft stalls selling **handicrafts**, as well as an artisans market off the main plaza. **Banks** can be found on Avenida Luzuriaga, along with numerous **internet cafés**. **iPerú** maintain a tourist office on the Plaza de Armas (⊘ 09.00-18.00 Mon-Sat, 09.00-14.00 Sun).

Further north, **Carhuaz**, **Yungay** and **Caraz** provide alternatives from where to set out on foot, on two wheels or on horseback. These smaller towns are well connected by **road**. They are relatively basic, however, and do not have many of the amenities found in Huaraz. There are **banks** and an **ATM** in Caraz; **internet** access is available in most places. In Yungay, the **tourist office** is on the Plaza de Armas (⊘ 08.00-13.00 & 14.00-18.00 Mon-Fri), and it's the same in Caraz (⊘ 08.00-13.00 & 14.30-17.00 Mon-Fri).

Budget

Albergue Churup (Huaraz) ⑳ www.churup.com
Caraz Dulzura (Caraz) Ⓔ hostalcarazdulzura@hotmail.com
Chamanna (Caraz) ⑳ www.chamanna.com
La Perla de los Andes (Caraz) ⑦ 043 392 007
Los Pinos (Caraz) Ⓔ lospinos@apuaventura.com
Monte Blanco (Huaraz) ⑳ http://monteblancohotel.com

Eating out

Bistro de los Andes (Huaraz, international) Jr de Morales 823 ⑦ 426 249
Café Andino (Huaraz, international) Lucar and Torre 530 ⑦ 421 203
California Café (Huaraz, international) Calle 28 de Julio ⑦ 428 354
El Fogon (Huaraz, Peruvian) Luzuriaga 928 ⑦ 421 267
El Horno (Huaraz, Peruvian) Parque de Periodista ⑦ 424 617

There's also a collection of monoliths in the garden, attributed to the Recuay and Huari cultures, along with scale models of nearby archaeological sites.

Mirador de Rataquena

Around 6km south of Huaraz, about an hour's walk and atop a 3,650m pass, is the exceptional **Rataquena viewpoint**. The trail is quite steep if you climb straight up, although an alternative dirt road zigzags to the same place, where you'll be rewarded with breathtaking panoramic vistas. Sadly the area has been affected by crime so go in a group or take a taxi.

Baños Termales de Monterrey
⊘ 06.00–18.00 daily

Monterrey Hot Springs can be found 6km north of Huaraz. They are a series of hot springs and thermal baths, run by the Hotel Baños Termales Monterrey. Although the water is an unappealing brown colour because of its high iron content, it is pleasant to soak in, especially if you've been out trekking. Go early rather than late as the pools get very busy, particularly at weekends and holidays, and head for the upper pool; it's the most pleasant, although there are also family pools and several small wells.

Wilkahuaín
⊘ daily, hours not fixed

Some 8km north of Huaraz stand a set of **well-preserved ruins**, Wilkahuaín (sometimes shown as Willkawain). It's possible to walk here from Huaraz, through an attractive stretch of valley. The ruins are attributed to the Huari culture and date from the 8th to the 11th century, when the group were at their most influential and commanding. The main site is a large, multi-storeyed structure with some intricate stonework. A number of smaller structures stand close by.

The cordilleras
Cordillera Blanca

Most people come to Huaraz to see and do, with the emphasis on mountains. The focus may be on trekking or climbing, horseriding or mountain biking, parapenting or hang gliding, river rafting or canoeing, but it's all possible and all exceptional in the Cordillera Blanca, the 240km long **mountain range** to the east of Huaraz. Not all activities are extreme or excessively physical though, and there are also some superb day walks, traditional communities and interesting archaeological sites around the mountains, which rise to form an impressive array of ridges,

The beautiful waters of Lagunas de Llanganuco are popular with locals and visitors alike. (SS)

spires and summits. There are more than 50 peaks here higher than 5,700m – to put this in context, there are just three in North America and none in Europe.

Lagunas de Llanganuco

There are a number of gorgeous, glacier-fed **lakes** sprinkled amongst the mountains, which can be accessed from Huaraz or nearby towns such as Yungay. The two brilliant turquoise pools known as the Lagunas de Llanganuco, some 64km north of Huaraz, stand at almost 4,000m, below some soaring peaks that include Huandoy and Huascarán. The lakes are beautiful in their own right, especially in the correct light, and the views of the summits nearby provide a superlative backdrop. Visit the lakes to admire the landscape, take a gentle cruise, stroll along the shore or spot birds, especially water birds such as mountain ducks, Andean geese, puna ibis and, occasionally, rare torrent ducks.

Towns north of Huaraz

Beyond Huaraz there are a number of smaller towns in the **Callejón de Huaylas** that can also be good bases for exploring the mountains, and several are also worth visiting in their own right. Spend up to a week trekking and taking in the sublime landscapes, and make time to see the equally breathtaking archaeological site of Chavín de Huántar. If you plan on tackling one of the splendid multi-day treks here obviously factor in more time for acclimatisation and the trek itself.

Rather more peaceful than Huaraz, **Carhuaz** (32km north) is a developing base for trekkers and climbers who want to escape the hurly burly in the main centre. Pleasant if not especially attractive, the town is also close to an ancient cave containing rock paintings as well as some hot springs. Continue another 19km north to **Yungay**, a small town remembered for a horrific natural disaster; 20,000 people died when a huge rush of rock and mud from high on Huascarán was loosened by a massive earthquake in 1970. The speeding rubble arrived before anyone could react and buried the entire town, leaving just a handful of survivors. It's possible to visit the sombre site and see the scars on the slopes above. Undeterred, however, the locals have rebuilt the town a little further up the valley. Further towards the head of the valley is **Caraz**, a lower but more attractive base for exploring the Cordillera Blanca and which is often used as a rest stop after the Llanganuco to Santa Cruz trek. There's a basic archaeological museum here and the pre-Chavín ruin of Tunshukaiko is close by, it is thought to date from 2000 to 1800BC.

The lakes also feature on the four to five day, 61km-long Llanganuco to Santa Cruz Trek, considered one of the prettiest and most popular routes in Peru.

Pachacoto

Around 56km south of Huaraz is Pachacoto, a **valley** where it's possible to find the bizarre, towering ***Puya raimondii*** plant. Found only in a handful of remote highland spots, this giant bromeliad is a relative of the pineapple but looks more like a giant cactus and flowers just once before it dies. The low, bushy rosette of spiky leaves gives rise to a tall central stem that can grow up to 12m tall and which, when flowering, is covered in thousands of small blooms. *Puya raimondii* can live to 100 years though, so you have to be lucky to see the bloom and your best bet is to visit in May if you're intent on catching a fleeting glimpse of this ancient plant (see pages 30–31).

Glaciar Pastoruri

Pastoruri Glacier, 8km further south, can be reached on a day trip. Unlike many of the mountain highlights here, people without climbing skills can clamber up the glacier to get an impression of what lies higher up, although at 5,240m you will need to be properly acclimatised before you visit and take it slowly while exploring. This is also Peru's only **ski slope**, although facilities are basic and can't compete with those found elsewhere in South America.

Chavín de Huántar

⊘ 08.00-17.00 daily

Chavín de Huántar stands on the eastern slopes of the Cordillera Blanca, at an altitude of 3,250m, 112km from Huaraz and just south of the town of Chavín. These extraordinary **ruins** are 3,000 years old and are the finest example of architecture belonging to the Chavín culture and the largest remaining structure attributed to them. The Chavín dominated the region for almost 1,000 years from around 1200BC. The oldest major culture in Peru, the Chavín were massively influential in terms of unifying tribes and disseminating ideas.

The spectacularly located main site is a religious centre, decorated with skilled stonework that's thought to date from around 800BC. Below this lie a dozen labyrinthine chambers, some of which can be visited. A U-shaped plaza is centred on a sunken central court, which was used as a focal point for people living here. Stairs lead up to a large flat-topped pyramid, **El Castillo,** which stands over carefully constructed water channels. At one time the sides of the pyramid would have been decorated with projecting blocks (*tenons*) carved to resemble human heads, examples of the site.

Reproduction of the Lanzon carving found underground at Chavín de Huántar. (A/D)

As well as these impressive carved heads several key artefacts have been found at the ruins; the **Lanzón** is a stunning white granite carving standing 4.5m high, which looks like a lance or broad dagger and depicts three central deities worshipped by the Chavín, thought to represent a belief in a universe made up of heavens, earth and an underworld. The main figure has a feline head and a human body, whilst serpents radiate from the snarling head and birds are also visible on the sculpture. Still standing underground at the heart of the

Parque Nacional Huascarán

Huascarán National Park is home to plants, animals and spectacular scenery. (I/FB-F/I/FLPA)

Virtually the entire Cordillera Blanca, including the entire area above 4,000m, is contained within the **Huascarán National Park**, a vast UNESCO Biosphere Reserve and World Heritage Site. Created in 1975, the Reserve was established to protect the region's fragile natural resources. The park features 32 summits higher than 6,000m and first among these is **Nevado Huascarán** itself, a muscular mountain that at 6,768m is the highest in Peru and the fourth highest in the Americas. Nearby, **Alpamayo**, although just 5,957m high, is considered to have one of the most stark and beautiful faces in the world.

The park also numbers more than 600 glaciers, 250 lakes and 40 rivers in its roster of natural attractions. Living amidst this natural playground are 100 species of bird, including condors, as well as deer, vicuñas and the odd puma. There are also 800 species of plant surviving here, with the rare *Puya raimondii* and ancient *queñual* forests amongst the highlights.

complex, the monolith is strangely mesmerising. It is thought that devotees would have been brought to see it through the maze, possibly after taking cactus-based hallucinogens, for maximum impact.

Other major artefacts found here have, however, been relocated. The **Tello Obelisk**, named after a Peruvian archaeologist, features a caiman-like deity whose body is decorated with stylised figures, felines, serpents and birds; it can be seen at the **Museo Nacional de Chavín** (☉ 09.00–17.00 Tue–Sun) adjacent to the site. The **Raimondi Stela**, named after an Italian naturalist, shows another feline-faced deity with snakes radiating from his head, standing with his arms open, clutching a staff in each hand. You'll have to look for it in the Museo Naciónal de Antropología, Arqueología y Historia in Lima though (see page 109).

Cordillera Negra

The Cordillera Negra is the Blanca's little brother. Lying to the west of Huaraz, it's lower down, with dry summits and no snow. There are some good walking routes here, although they are neither as spectacular nor as popular as those in the Cordillera Blanca. To get a good idea of what the range looks like, you can walk from Punta Callan back to Huaraz along trails and tracks, it takes around five hours and you can enjoy unparalleled views of the Negra and of Huaraz in the valley below.

Cordillera Huayhuash

The compact Cordillera Huayhuash, nicknamed the 'American Himalayas', is the intimidating cousin that sits to the south of the Cordillera Blanca. Just 32km long, it's wilder and more remote, with vertiginous ice faces and jagged peaks. It was made famous by mountaineers Joe Simpson and Simon Yates, after their near-fatal expedition to conquer Siula Grande was recounted in the book and film *Touching the Void*.

Although a favourite with *Andinistas*, the Huayhuash receives far less traffic than the Cordillera Blanca but is home to Peru's second-highest summit, **Yerupajá** (6,634m), and boasts the best wilderness outing in the region. Intrepid trekkers looking to escape some of the crowds on more popular routes tackle the 160km **Cordillera Huayhuash Circuit**, a challenging multi-day trek that takes as long as 12 days and crosses eight passes higher than 4,600m. Although not technical, the trek does require good fitness as there are regular ascents of between 500m and 1,000m, and you will walk on average four to eight hours a day. For those with less stamina, there's also a tamer half-circuit.

Trujillo to Chiclayo

Trujillo and around

Trujillo is the capital city of the department of La Libertad. Technically the third-largest city in Peru, it has always vied with Arequipa for the second spot and has a history of alternative thinking. Trujillo was the first city to declare independence from Spain and it was the birthplace of the populist workers political party, APRA, which has had a sometimes controversial and significant impact on the country's politics. The city's position on the coast makes it commercially important but it is better known as an attractive colonial city.

Founded in 1534 by Diego Almagro on the orders of Pizarro, it retains a distinctly Spanish flavour. Glamorous, grand and well preserved, it has wide plazas, elegant mansions with wrought-iron grilles and wooden balconies, and a colourful atmosphere enlivened by the bright

Trujillo's attractive colonial centre (SS)

Archaeology tours

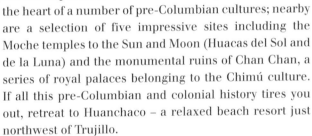

Discover the archaeological treasures of the Chimú, Moche, and other pre-Inca cultures on a northern Peru archaeology tour. Follow the Trujillo circuit to Trujillo, Chiclayo and Chachapoyas, or add Cajamarca, where the last Inca emperor was slain by the conquistadors. Owing to the dry climate, many cities, temples, aqueducts, and artefacts remain remarkably well preserved. Highlights include the Moche Temples of the Sun and Moon and royal tombs of Sipán and Sicán.

pastel paint of most of its buildings. However, the Spanish were just the latest to recognise the importance of the area and Trujillo was in fact at the heart of a number of pre-Columbian cultures; nearby are a selection of five impressive sites including the Moche temples to the Sun and Moon (Huacas del Sol and de la Luna) and the monumental ruins of Chan Chan, a series of royal palaces belonging to the Chimú culture. If all this pre-Columbian and colonial history tires you out, retreat to Huanchaco – a relaxed beach resort just northwest of Trujillo.

Trujillo highlights
The city centre
The city is an attractive place to walk around and there are countless examples of **colonial architecture**, including the **Casa de Uruquiaga** at Pizzaro 446, which is now a bank, **Casona Orbegoso** at Orbegoso 553 and **Casona Ganoza Chopitea** at Independencia 630. Look out too for the gaudily yellow, Neoclassical **Palacio Iturregui** at Pizzaro 688, which is now the home of a social club. The Plaza Mayor is dominated by **Catedral de Trujillo la Merced** (⊘ 07.00–21.00 daily) full of colonial and religious art that dates from 1647, while the Baroque 17th-century **Iglesia de la Merced** (⊘ 08.00–12.00 & 16.00–20.00 daily) on the corner of Pizzaro and Gamarra and **Iglesia del Carmen** (⊘ 09.00–13.00 Mon–Sat) on the corner of Colón and Bolívar are both churches worth ducking into for their interesting art and features.

Practicalities

Eight hours drive and 560km from Lima lies **Trujillo**, a good place from which to explore the area. It's not all old ruins though, **Huanchaco** has both beaches and surf breaks. Although Trujillo is well connected to elsewhere on the coast by **road** – it stands on the Pan-American Highway – it is preferable if time is tight to **fly** to Trujillo from Lima. A number of airlines have daily connections to and from the capital (flight time one hour). The **airport**, Aeropuerto Carlos Martínez de Pinillos, is 10km northwest of the centre. The city itself is laid out on a grid, at the heart of which stands the Plaza de Armas. The main sights are all on adjacent streets making exploring **on foot** easy, although street names can be confusing as almost everywhere is named twice. To see the main archaeological sites you're best off taking a taxi or group tour. There's an **iPerú** tourist office in the airport and at Jirón Diego de Almagro in town (☉ 09.00-19.00 Mon-Sat, 09.00-14.00 Sun). **Banks** can be found in the centre, especially on Jirón Gamarra and Jirón Pizarro, where there are also **ATMs**. **Internet** access is widespread.

About 200km further up the coast is **Chiclayo**, which lies on the main **road** but also has an **airport**, Aeropuerto José Quiñones González, 1.5km east of town. LAN and StarPeru both operate daily flights to Lima. As ever, the centre of town is the Plaza de Armas, although here it is more often known as the

Accommodation

Upmarket
Costa del Sol (Cajamarca) ⓦ www.costadelsolperu.com
Costa del Sol (Chiclayo) ⓦ www.costadelsolperu.com
Garza (Chiclayo) ⓦ www.garzahotel.com
Gran Hotel Chiclayo (Chiclayo) ⓦ www.granhotelchiclayo.com.pe
Hotel & Spa Laguna Seca (Cajamarca) ⓦ www.lagunaseca.com.pe
Hotel El Gran Marqués (Trujillo) ⓦ www.elgranmarques.com
Hotel Libertador (Trujillo) ⓦ www.libertador.com.pe
Los Conquistadores (Trujillo) ⓦ www.losconquistadoreshotel.com

Moderate
Casa Vieja (Chachapoyas) ⓦ www.casaviejaperu.com
El Ingenio (Cajamarca) ⓦ www.elingenio.com
El Portal de Márques (Cajamarca) ⓦ www.portaldemarques.com
El Sol (Chiclayo) ⓦ www.hotelelsoltresestrellas.com
Gran Bolívar (Trujillo) ⓦ www.granbolivarhotel.net
Gran Vilaya (Chachapoyas) ⓔ vilaya@wayna.rcp.net.pe

Parque Principal. Hotels and restaurants spread out from here. Despite being busy and congested, it's relatively straightforward to get around the centre **on foot**, but take a taxi or group tour to get to Lambeyque or the archaeological sites. **Banks** can be found on Jirón Balta or gathered around the Parque Principal. There are a number of **internet cafés** across the centre of town. For **information**, visit the Centro de Información Turistico at Sáenz Peña 838.

It takes around 12 hours to **drive** to **Cajamarca** from Lima or there are daily **flights** with LAN and LC Busre that take just a couple of hours. The **airport**, Armando Revoredo Aeropuerto de Cajamarca, is 3km east of the town centre. The Plaza de Armas is the town's focal point and the place where Pizarro killed the Inca Atahualpa (see page 11). Most of the main attractions are close by. **Information** can be found at the Regional Tourist Office at Jirón Belén 600 and the Oficina de Información Turística at Batán 289. There are **banks** off the Plaza de Armas and on Jirón del Comercio, where there are also **internet cafés**.

There's no airport in **Chachapoyas** so it's necessary to approach the city **overland** from Trujillo or Chiclayo; the journey is long and slow from either start point. There are a couple of **banks** and **internet cafés** on the Plaza de Armas. Kuélep is close to Chachapoyas (reached overland from Chiclayo or Cajamarca) and the town is a good base for discovering the pre-Inca sites inland and the surrounding forested landscapes.

Hotel Bracamonte (Huanchaco) ⓦ www.hotelbracamonte.com.pe
Hotel las Musas (Chiclayo) Ⓔ nazih@viabpc.com
Inti (Chiclayo) ⓦ www.intihotel.com.pe
La Casona Monsante (Chachapoyas) ⓦ www.lacasonamonsante.com
Las Palmeras (Huanchaco) ⓦ www.laspalmerasdehuanchaco.com
Los Horcones de Túcume (Túcume) ⓦ www.loshorconesdetucume.com
Posada del Puruay (Cajamarca) ⓦ www.posadapuruay.com.pe
Saint Germain Hotel (Trujillo) ⓦ www.saintgermainhotel.net

Budget

Hostal Colonial (Trujillo) Ⓔ hostalcolonialtruji@hotmail.com
Hostal Portada del Sol (Cajamarca) Ⓔ portasol@amet.com.pe
Kuélap (Chachapoyas) Ⓣ 041 477 136
La Casa Suiza (Huanchaco) ⓦ www.lacasasuiza.com
Latinos Hostal (Chiclayo) Ⓣ 255 437
Los Balcones de la Recoleta (Cajamarca) Ⓣ 076 363 302
Naylamp (Huanchaco) ⓦ www.hostalnaylamp.com
Revash (Chachapoyas) ⓦ www.chachapoyaskuelap.com.pe
San Martín (Trujillo) ⓦ www.deperu.com/sanmartin

Surf the waves on a traditional totora reed boat. (SS)

Huanchaco and Puerto Chicama

Laidback and youthful, **Huanchaco**, 13km north of Trujillo, is an ideal spot to step away from the bustle of the bigger city. Close enough to the ruins to be used as a base, this traditional fishing community also has several brilliant beaches to the south and a range of breaks popular with surfers. Look out for the traditional boats made from tortora reeds nicknamed 'little horses' (*caballitos*) that are still ridden by fishermen in a style similar to a surfboard. There are decent hotels, good-value hostels and fine fish or seafood restaurants as well, overlooked by one of the oldest churches in Peru, thought to date from about 1535; climb the belfry for some splendid views.

More experienced wave riders might like to head up the coast another 56km to **Puerto Chicama**, where they'll find one of the longest left-hand point breaks in the world; the Peruvian National Surfing Championships are held here in March. The water off the beaches here and at Huanchaco is warm enough for swimming in during the summer months of December to April.

Around Trujillo highlights
Huaca del Sol and Huaca de la Luna
Valle de Moche ⓦ www.huacadelaluna.org.pe ☺ 09.00–16.00 daily
The arid Valle de Moche, 8km south of Trujillo, is home to a fascinating pair of badly weathered but still imposing **pyramids**. Constructed by the Moche culture around AD500, they were part of a substantial religious centre here. The **Huaca del Sol** ('**Temple of the Sun**') is the larger pyramid; it stands 20m high despite being both badly eroded

Eating out

Big Ben (Huanchaco, International) Av Larco 1182 ⓣ 461 869
Café Oviedo (Trujillo, Peruvian and international) Pizarro 737 ⓣ 223 305
Club Colonial (Huanchaco, Peruvian and international) La Rivera 514 ⓣ 461 015
El Mochica (Trujillo, international) Bolivar 462
Demarco (Trujillo, international) Pizarro 725 ⓣ 234 251
Romano (Trujillo, international) Pizarro 747 ⓣ 252 251

by weather and also the Spanish attempt to divert the Moche River to wash away the sand in search of plunder. At its zenith, the pyramid was probably two-thirds larger, making it one of the biggest manmade structures in the Americas at the time of its creation. Unexcavated and rather fragile, it requires a bit of imagination to picture the pyramid in all its pomp, when multiple staircases would have ascended to seven different levels and platforms. These days, you mustn't climb on it as this adds to the erosion.

The **Huaca de la Luna** ('**Temple of the Moon**') is the sister site, which stands 500m away across an open patch of sand. Burial sites and the remains of a large settlement have been discovered here. Made up of five levels, it's smaller than the Huaca del Sol, but better preserved and more interesting; the pyramid has been excavated to reveal some significant finds including spectacular friezes on the adobe walls repeatedly featuring a frightening figure, Ai-Apaek or the Decapitator. The original colours are still vibrant and the effect of the yellow, red, white and black designs is dramatic.

Chan Chan
Valle de Moche ⊘ 09.00–17.00 daily

Five kilometres northwest of Trujillo stands Chan Chan, considered **one of the most important archaeological sites** in Peru and the largest **adobe city** in the world. A vast city complex covering almost 16km², it was the centre of the Chimú culture, which rose to prominence during the 11th century, peaking in the 15th century before succumbing to the Incas in a protracted struggle around 1471. Dating from around 1300, Chan Chan is some eight centuries younger than the Huacas del Sol and de la Luna but far more substantial. At its height it would have housed up to 60,000 people and operating as the capital of a sophisticated society. The complex has been badly damaged by El Niño rains and strong

The vast complex of Chan Chan (MZ/D)

winds, meaning the mud walls have been eroded. Little reconstruction has taken place here so the site isn't as 'complete' as some of the Inca ruins elsewhere, but its sheer size is impressive and it's possible to pick out citadels, pyramids, living quarters, streets, a reservoir and a royal cemetery. Walls are decorated with stylised figures, birds, fish and motifs representing the sea.

Nine **palaces**, protected by huge 9m-high walls, stand amongst the narrow streets; each belonged to a Chimú ruler who would be buried in the palace upon his death and a new royal structure built for his heir. The palaces would have been lavishly decorated with precious metals and ceramics but these were pillaged first by the Spanish conquistadors then by grave robbers (*huaqueros*). One of the palaces, the **Tschudi Palace**, named after a Swiss explorer, has been partially restored to give an indication of what it would have originally looked like. Employ a guide or follow a series of arrows on a walking tour to discover a ceremonial courtyard with 4m-thick walls covered in recreated ocean motifs. Outer walls are covered in restored seabird and fish friezes.

A large **assembly room** has 24 niches containing seats, and boasts acoustics that allow people sitting in the niches to be clearly heard from all over the room.

On the approach road to the ruins stands the **Museo de Sitio de Chan Chan** (Chan Chan Site Museum), where you can see a small collection of ceramics, aerial photos of the site and some displays giving a bit of background to the ruins.

Huaca Esmeralda
Mansiche ⊘ 09.00–17.00 daily

Halfway between Trujillo and Chan Chan stands the **Emerald Temple**. The **pyramid**, partially buried in the surrounding sand, hasn't been excavated but it is possible to explore and there are some interesting, original Chimú friezes to find.

Huaca Arco Iris
La Esperanza ⊘ 09.00–17.00 daily

West of the Pan-American Highway and several kilometres from Trujillo stands the **Rainbow Temple**, a **pyramid** dating from the 12th century and so named for the well-preserved repeated rainbow-like arches that decorate the walls. The main pyramid stands within a giant defensive wall some 2m thick. It was once coloured yellow but this has faded. Along with the rainbow patterns, there are friezes of lizards, snakes and what has been described as a dragon.

Complejo Arqueológico La Huaca El Brujo
Valle de Chicama ☉ 09.00-17.00 daily
Further afield and harder to access, **El Brujo Temple Archaeological Complex** lies 64km north of Trujillo. Ongoing excavations at the archaeological complex suggest that a number of cultures lived in the Chicama Valley and used it as a ceremonial centre. The main points of interest are the giant and well-preserved friezes at **Huaca Cao Viejo**, a flat-topped Moche-era **pyramid** decorated with colourful depictions of warriors, priests and people being sacrificed. Also worth seeking out are the warlike figures on the walls of **Huaca Cortada**, one of which wields a knife and a decapitated head.

Chiclayo and around
What was a small Spanish settlement in the 16th century has developed into Peru's fourth-largest city and capital of the Lambayeque department. These days Chiclayo, 200km north of Trujillo and some 800km north of Lima, is a bustling commercial hub grown fat on the trade of sugar cane and rice, with little in town to cause you to pause.

It has another side, however, and the primary reason for visiting is to access the archaeological sites nearby belonging to the Moche and Lambayeque (sometimes known as Sicán) cultures and to see the extraordinary tomb of the Lord of Sipán.

Chiclayo highlights
The city centre
The Plaza de Armas, or **Parque Principal**, is a lively centre, overlooked by a Neoclassical cathedral. Several blocks to the south is **Paseo de las Musas** ('Street of Muses'), a pretty park packed, rather confusingly, with statues of Greek mythological figures and muses. To the north of the centre on the corner of Arica and Balta is **Mercado Modelo**, a sprawling daily market (☉ 09.00–17.00) where you'll find everything from fresh produce and animals to handicrafts and woven goods. In a corner is the **Mercado de Brujos** (Witch Doctors' Market), where you can pick up an amulet, vials of potions, ritual paraphernalia, religious charms (*seguros*) and seeds designed to bring good fortune (*huayruros*).

Eating out

El Huaralino (Peruvian) Libertad 155 ① 27 0330
La Fiesta (Peruvian) Salaverry 1820 ① 20 1970

Lambayeque

Thirteen kilometres northwest of Chiclayo, Lambayeque was once the more important town but these days it is overshadowed by its neighbour and has become a bit quiet. Nonetheless, there are plenty of reasons to visit and two of the region's best museums are found here.

Museo Nacional de Arqueología y Ethnografía Heinrich Brüning
Av Huamachuco Ⓦ www.museobruning.com ⊘ 09.00-17.00 daily
The original home for the treasures of Sipán, the **Heinrich Brüning Archaeological Museum** has faltered since losing its star attraction; the tomb of the Lord of Sipán, and is overshadowed by the Lord's latest resting place in the newer Museo Tumbas Reales (see below). Nonetheless, it merits a visit for the 1,500 pieces still on display, including Sicán gold and masks, Moche ceramics and artefacts found at Túcume. Models of the nearby sites also help put the places and the discoveries made there into context.

Museo Tumbas Reales de Sipán
Juan Pablo Vizcardo y Guzman Ⓦ www.museotumbasrealessipan.pe ⊘ 08.00-17.00 daily
The pre-eminent museum in northern Peru, **Museum Tumbas Reales** is a modern structure of contemporary glass, sharp angles and orange-red concrete that mimics the Moche pyramids found close by. Created to house the tomb of the Lord of Sipán and all the main discoveries found at the Sipán site, it is an essential stop, especially if the eroded pyramids and weathered ruins in the desert have left you wondering what all the fuss is about. Climb to the third floor and descend chronologically.

The Lord was Moche royalty and he died more than 1,700 years ago. Buried with a wealth of ceremonial objects and rich treasures, the king was interred alongside a warrior, a priest, three female concubines and a child. Also joining him on his journey to the afterlife were a dog and two llamas. The group's luggage included 212 vessels for food and drink; headdresses; clothes; breastplates made from silver, gold and precious stones; and jewellery and beadwork that tell of position and power. Other recreated tombs showcase what was found with the spiritual leader, El Viejo.

Around Chiclayo highlights
Sipán
Huaca Rajada Ⓦ www.huacarajadasipan.cb.pe ⊘ 08.00-18.00 daily
Sipán, 32km southeast of Chiclayo, was a Moche **burial ground**. Long

The tomb of the Lord of Sipán was one of the richest ever found. (SS)

overlooked, it wasn't found until 1987, when grave robbers selling artefacts inadvertently alerted a Peruvian archaeologist, Walter Alva, to the existence of the site. He was able to secure the area and in so doing preserved some of the most bountiful treasure and funerary objects found in Peru. Two dusty mounds turned out to be twin adobe **pyramids**, dating from the first centuries AD, and concealing a number of **tombs**. The most impressive belonged to **El Señor de Sipán** (the Lord of Sipán) who was found decked out in gold and turquoise armour and jewellery. A deeper tomb, suggesting its incumbent died earlier, was the final resting place of a spiritual leader now known as **El Viejo Señor**. The fantastic finds from the tombs are displayed at the Museo Tumbas Reales in Lambayeque (see page 141), whilst on site there is a rather **small museum** showing replicas of the tombs and some photographs.

Sicán

Some 32km north of Chiclayo are the enigmatic **burial tombs** of Sicán, lost amongst an arid wilderness that can make exploring difficult. A dozen pyramids up to 40m tall stand amongst a dry carob forest; there's a viewing tower that lets you look over the scrubby canopy and see the pyramids rise above the treetops. Additionally, tombs up to 12m deep were discovered here belonging to the Sicán culture, who achieved pre-eminence in the area from AD750 to 1375. Most striking is the tomb of the **Lord of Sicán**, who was interred upside down, in a foetal position. Other significant finds include the oldest ceremonial knife (*tumi*) in Peru and some exquisite gold artefacts.

The **Museo Nacional Sicán** (⊘ daily) on Avenida Batán Grande in Ferreñafe, 18km north of Chiclayo but 14km south of the tombs of Sicán, features replicas of the tombs and contains a number of fascinating and unusual exhibits from the site.

Túcume
⊘ 08.00-16.00 daily

Found 32km north of Chiclayo but to the west of Sicán lies the **Valley of the Pyramids**, El Valle de las Pirámides, so called because of the 26 adobe structures built here by the Lambayeque culture around the year AD1000. Later the area was inhabited and developed by the Chimú, before the Inca took over in the 15th century. Túcume is considered the most important centre in the region.

It's possible to walk amongst the pyramids and even ascend a couple to get a sense of the scale of the centre. At the back of the complex stands **Huaca Larga** which, at 30m high and 700m long, is reputed to be the largest adobe brick structure in South America. Originally built by the Lambayeque, it was increased in size by the Chimú and then added to by the Inca; in the Inca structure 22 bodies were found interred, including a local ruler and warrior. Look out for red, white and black murals that colour the walls as you wander up and down ramps and corridors connecting courtyards and patios. There's a small **site museum** as well, with photographs of excavations carried out by Thor Heyerdahl, the Norwegian explorer and director of the dig from 1989 to 1994, who attempted to connect Peruvian culture to Polynesia.

Cajamarca and around
Inland from the coast, around 130km northeast of Trujillo and about 240km southeast of Chiclayo, stands Cajamarca, a historic mountain town that's surrounded by impressive Andean peaks but retains a traditional, low-key air. The area is very fertile and consequently the countryside is impressively lush and also perfect for dairy farming. It's a good place to detour in order to uncover some of Peru's Inca history and explore the attractive landscapes.

Cajamarca highlights
The town centre

The most famous building in Cajamarca is **El Cuarto del Rescate** (The Ransom Room; ⊘ 09.00–1300 & 15.00–18.00 Mon, Wed–Fri, 09.00–13.00 Sat–Sun), the building Francisco Pizarro used to imprison the Inca Atahualpa in 1532. Atahualpa famously promised to fill his cell with gold and silver several times over in return for his freedom (see

Cajamarca is a perfect place to pick up a traditional souvenir. (SS)

History, page 11). The actual cell is a bare Inca-walled room at the back of a courtyard; it nonetheless, represents a very important event in Peruvian history.

There are also a number of colonial mansions and large houses to see in town, as well as ornate churches, including the **Iglesia de San Francisco** (Church of Saint Francis), which is built from volcanic rock. There are also several museums to explore in the centre. Cajamarca is famous for its **handicrafts**, including gilded mirrors, cotton and wool bags, straw hats and painted ceramics, which can be purchased from markets and stalls in the town, including the **Mercado Central** (⊙ 06.00–19.00 daily) on Amazonas.

Around Cajamarca highlights
Los Baños del Inca
⊙ 06.00–19.00 daily
The **Inca Baths**, 6km southeast of Cajamarca, are a series of sulphurous hot springs and pools that have been in use since the Inca controlled this section of the country. There are both indoor and outdoor pools as

Festivals

Cajamarca is a traditional and slightly conservative place but it lets its hair down for **Carnival** just before Lent in February or March. Celebrations are raucous and involve the flinging of paint and water over everyone. Embrace the chaos and you'll be fine. Popular with Peruvians, it means the city's accommodation gets booked up at this time of year. **Corpus Christi** in either May or June is equally popular although a little more refined, featuring processions, live music, bullfights and horse demonstrations.

well as a sauna. Clean and revitalising, they have excellent views and are said to be effective at treating bronchial conditions. The baths are popular with locals, however, and so can be busy; go in the mornings to avoid crowds. Bear in mind that the water can reach temperatures of more than 70°C.

Cumbe Mayo
⊘ 08.00–17.00 daily
Nineteen kilometres southwest of Cajamarca is Cumbe Mayo, a surreal landscape of **rock formations** that stand amidst rolling hills. Trek through the stone forest to find caves decorated with petroglyphs, sacrificial stones and an ancient aqueduct. The aqueduct flows for more than 8km and dates from as early as 1000BC, making it one of the oldest manmade constructions in the Americas.

Chachapoyas and around
The city of Chachapoyas was founded in 1538 as an important junction between the coast and the jungle but it has been an important centre far longer than that. The city itself retains a little of its colonial charm, with pretty houses and patios, overlooked by wooden balconies. Ascend the **Guayamil viewpoint** for vistas over the city and beyond.

Amongst the archaeological highlights scattered around the city and attributed to the Chachapoyas culture (known as the Cloud Forest people), Kuélap is the obvious highlight. Buried amongst dense vegetation with huge trees, bromeliads and orchids adding to its appeal, the site was brought to the world's attention in 1843 but has remained off-the-beaten track and less visited than many of Peru's other spectacular sites as a result of the remoteness of the region and a lack of easy access by plane.

Chachapoyas and around highlights
Kuélap lost city
⊘ 08.00–17.00 daily
Kuélap is Peru's mightiest secret and the most important site around Chachapoyas. A formidable lost city that pre-dates Machu Picchu, straggling almost a kilometre along an Andean mountain ridge at 3,000m and hidden under highland cloud, it comprises a vast set of ruins – and yet few people visit. Features include an impressively fortified entrance, temples, a large castle and some 400 buildings, most of them circular, set within a 30m-high defensive wall. The scale of the place is dizzying. Furthermore, almost all the ruin is original with little restoration having been done.

The spectacularly sited funerary site of Karajía (D)

Built over two centuries from AD900 to 1100, some 3,000 people lived here between AD1100 and 1300, although little is known about them. It is thought that the ruins were constructed at enormous effort by the Chachapoyans – the most advanced jungle civilisation – who were later assimilated by the Incas. The Inca went on to occupy the fortress at the heart of the site. The ruins were never uncovered by the Spanish, however, and so escaped destruction.

Karajía sarcophagi

Northwest of Chachapoyas are some more extraordinary archaeological remains. Karajía is home to a series of strange **sarcophagi** cut into the cliffs, which date from about 1200. The sarcophagi are 2.5m tall and boast elaborate effigies. They're still intact, although grave robbers have long since broken into the tombs from the back and plundered them of the mummies and treasure they once contained. The road to the valley where the impressive cliff featuring these tombs stands is rough, meaning that in some conditions the easiest way to access the site is to walk in with a guide.

Máncora to Tumbes

The long northern coast is the place to find Peru's best beaches. Once considered remote and too much of an effort to access, the long sandy stretches around Máncora, originally favoured by locals lured here by the big breaks and spectacular swell, have evolved into world-class stop-offs for travellers moving around the region or crossing over

Practicalities

It's a very long **drive** from Lima along the Pan-American Highway, some 16 hours, meaning that the trip is often done overnight. It is possible to **fly** though, with daily flights to Piura and Tumbes, which necessitate a $2\frac{1}{2}$ and one hour transfer respectively.

Máncora comprises little more than a single street, Avenida Piura. On one side is the dry desert, on the other the Pacific Ocean. Most of the main restaurants and bars can be found here, with the majority of tourist services to the south of the strip. If you want to access the beaches a little further afield, jump in a **mototaxi**. Popular during the Peruvian summer (December to April), Máncora can be busy with locals as well as visitors. For crafts and souvenirs head to the **market** on the main drag. If you're after surf gear, board hire or lessons then you'll find outfitters here too. There are also a couple of **banks** and several **internet cafés** along the short stretch.

Accommodation

Upmarket
DCO Suites ⓦ www.hoteldco.com
Hotelier Arte y Cocina ⓦ www.hotelier.pe
La Casita de Sueños ⓦ www.mancora-peru.com

Moderate
Casa del Muelle ⓦ www.casadelmuellemancora.com
Del Wawa ⓦ www.delwawa.com
Vichayito Bungalows ⓦ www.vichayito.com

Budget
Hospedaje Crillon ⓣ 073 258 001
Hostal Sol y Mar ⓔ hsolymar@hotmail.com
Punta Ballenas ⓦ www.puntaballenas.com

Eating out

Cafeteria de Angela (café) Piura 396 ⓣ 258 603
Chan Chan (international) Piura 384 ⓣ 258 146
El Tuno (international) Piura 233

from Ecuador. Hip beachside hotels now sit alongside good value cottages meaning that everyone from seasoned surfers to chic *Limeños* can find something here to suit.

Máncora

The heart of the burgeoning beach scene is Máncora, more than 1,100km north of Lima and just 120km south of the border with Ecuador. A little rough and ready, this one-time tiny fishing village still has an authentic feel despite its expansion and gentle gentrification. People forgive its rough edges because of the beaches; 24km of sand stretch north and south, with safe swimming along the length. Surfing is well established here and kite- and windsurfing are taking off, too. The water is warm, as the cold Humboldt Current veers off into the Pacific, and the sun shines most of the time, in contrast with the beaches further south that are frequently cloaked in sea mist, *gárua*. The currents create superb waves, big swell, long left-hand breaks and some perfect barrels for people who know about such things. Between Mancora and Tumbes close to the border with Ecuador there are also nature reserves, national parks and some habitats not found anywhere else in Peru.

Máncora beaches

The most accessible areas for visitors interested in relaxing or swimming include **Cabo Blanco**, **Los Organos**, **Vichayito** and **Los Pocitas** in the south, and **Punta Sal**, **Cancas** and **Zorritos** in the north. **Surfers** should head to Lobitos, Cabo Blanco, Organos, and Punta Ballenas but do check the surf against your skill level before taking the plunge.

Tumbes

Tumbes marks the northern end of Peru's stretch of beaches. Just 30km from the border with Ecuador, it's the last major provincial town of note before the border and as such is the place where people crossing to and from Ecuador congregate. It's also the point where Pizarro landed in 1532 to start his conquest of the Incas.

The beaches and surf around Máncora are popular playgrounds. (JW-LP/A)

Other than entering or exiting the country, the city is the access point for three **interesting protected areas** including Peru's only mangrove swamps and an ecological corridor critical for conservation. The **Santuario Nacional los Manglares de Tumbes** (National Sanctuary of Tumbes Mangoves), on the coast and adjacent to the border, preserves the mangrove swamps that are home to 200 species of bird; the **Zona Reservada de Tumbes** (Tumbes Reserve), inland and which abuts the border, was established to preserve a section of rainforest where the wildlife includes wild boar, primates, otters and caiman; the **Parque Nacional Cerros de Amotape** (Cerros de Amotape National Park) conserves a swathe of equatorial forest that's home to deer, fox, puma, otter and crocodile as well as birds including parrots and guans. Be aware that roads are often closed or impassable during the rainy season from January to mid-April.

7 Coastal Peru south of Lima

Follow the Pan-American Highway south from Lima and you quickly enter a dry, seemingly barren stretch of unspoiled coast. Historically home to three important cultures - the Paracas, Nazca and Ica - the area hides a number of interesting towns along with archaeological sites, including the enigmatic Nazca Lines. There are also marine and wildlife reserves, sand dunes and tranquil oases, colonial centres, and traditional bodegas producing *pisco* (Peru's national drink) to discover. In addition, the coast is considered a cultural hub for Afro-Peruvian traditions.

On the evening of 15 August 2007, the region was rocked by a devastating earthquake, measuring 7.9 on the Richter scale. The tremor destroyed almost 60,000 homes, and more than 500 people were killed and a further 1,350 injured, making this one of the worst natural disasters to affect the region. Since the devastation though, the area has slowly recovered and you can easily take a week or two to travel south down the coast.

Cañete

Almost 160km south of Lima, amidst the desert, stands the bustling market town of Cañete, sometimes referred to as San Vicente de Cañete. Blessed with sunshine for much of the year, it is a good base for visiting the surf beaches close to the nearby village of **Cerro Azul** or exploring the scenic, rural Lunahuana Valley.

Lunahuana Valley

The valley has some good trekking and mountain biking, and is well set up for eco-adventure. It is also popular for kayaking and **white-water rafting** from December to April when the Cañete River is high; San Jerónimo is the rafting centre and at their most intimidating, rapids can reach Grade IV.

The valley is also home to a traditional *caballos de paso* horse centre, where some of Peru's famous stepping horses are trained, and a number of vineyards; visit bodegas such as **Los Reyes** (☉ 09.00–16.00 daily) and **Viña Santa Marta** (☉ 09.00–16.00 daily) in Condoray to be able to sample wine, *pisco* and *manzanilla*. There is also an Inca archaeological site at **Incawasi**, a substantial city built by Pachacutec, the Inca who also commissioned Machu Picchu.

Pisco and around

As you travel south from Lima, Pisco, 240km away, is the first place of any real size or importance and is a pleasant intermediary base before you reach Nazca or Arequipa.

Initially known as San Clemente de Macera by the Spanish, who considered making it the coastal capital prior to choosing Lima, Pisco quickly reverted to its current name, in recognition of the grape brandy and national beverage produced in the region. Later, the town became the initial base for the Liberator San Martín when he made landfall at Paracas in 1819; his **statue** still dominates the main plaza and there is a concrete **obelisk** on the road to the Paracas Peninsula marking his entry point. These days, although the town functions as a port and fishing community, it is most regularly used as a base for people visiting Paracas (see page 156) and the Ballestas Islands (see page 157) nearby.

In 2007, the earthquake that struck the region devastated Pisco; some 20,000 houses (about half the town) were destroyed, as the adobe buildings couldn't stand up to the shocks. Pisco's major church was also levelled, killing a large proportion of the congregation present for a service. Years later, the city is still recovering and slowly rebuilding although the scars of the earthquake are still visible.

Eating out

As de Oro (Pisco, international) San Martín 472 ☎ 532 010
El Chorito (Paracas, Peruvian) El Chaco ☎ 545 045
Juan Pablo (Paracas, Peruvian) Bld Turistico ☎ 797 240
Anita (Ica, Peruvian) Libertad 133
El Huarango (Nazca, Peruvian) Arica 602 ☎ 522 141
El Portón (Nazca, Peruvian) Moresky 120
La Carreta (Nazca, Nuevo Andino) Bolognesi 265
La Taberna (Nazca, international) Lima 321 ☎ 521 411
Plaza Mayor (Nazca, barbecue) On the plaza

Practicalities

An **organised tour** is the most comfortable way to see the majority of sights in this area and given the lack of an airport at any of the main towns, the only feasible way to travel other than **self-drive**. The highway is in good condition and traffic is light, making it a smooth drive. Distances are manageable: Ica is 298km from Lima, and Nazca some 440km. Bear in mind, for short forays you may spend a significant proportion of time driving, either from and to Lima or from Lima and then onwards to Arequipa or an alternative destination.

Pisco is easy to navigate **on foot**, as all of its places of interest are adjacent to the main Plaza de Armas. There are **banks** on the Plaza de Armas, and **internet** services throughout the town. The beach should be avoided after dark as tourists have been robbed there in the past.

Ica is a sprawling city and you'll need a taxi to get about, especially to visit the bodegas outside the centre. You can pick up tourist information from Directeur on Avenida Grau (⊙ 08.00–19.00 Mon–Sat, 09.00–18.00 Sun) and there are banks in the centre. It is possible to arrange flights over the Nazca Lines from Ica but they will be more expensive than corresponding trips from Nazca itself.

Within **Nazca** town there are **banks** and **internet cafés** on Jirón Bolognesi. There is also a small **airport**, where sightseeing flights take off and land. Flights over the Lines last approximately half an hour and take place on small planes that seat up to five or six people. The planes have to bank hard left and right to show passengers the Lines and flights can be bumpy due to turbulence,

Accommodation

Upmarket
Casa Andina Classic (Nazca) ⓦ www.casa-andina.com
Doubletree Guest Suites by Hilton (Paracas) ⓦ www.doubletree.com
Hotel Cantayo Spa and Resort (Nazca) ⓦ www.hotelcantayo.com
Hotel Hacienda Ocucaje (Ica) ⓦ www.hotelocucaje.com
Hotel Paracas Luxury Collection Resort (Paracas) ⓦ www.libertador.com.pe
Las Dunas (Ica) ⓦ www.lasdunashotel.com
Maison Suisse (Nazca) ⓦ www.aeroica.net
Majoro (Nazca) ⓦ www.hotelmajoro.com
Nazca Lines Hotel (Nazca) ⓦ www.dematourshoteles.com

which is worse during the midday heat; the best time to fly is first thing in the morning from 08.00 to 10.00. If it is foggy, flights will be cancelled. You may be able to combine a flight over the Nazca Lines with a flight over the symbols close to Palpa. **Taxis** will ferry you to Nazca's outlying sites if your tour doesn't include them.

There are a couple of **places to eat** in tiny fishing communities such as Lagunillas around the **Paracas Peninsula**, and you're allowed to camp on the beaches. Excursions to the **Islas Ballestas** depart from Pisco from December to March; **boats** actually leave from El Chaco, close to Paracas. Tours generally depart early in the morning to make the most of the calmer waters but can be cancelled if conditions are too rough. They generally take a couple of hours and allow you to see the Candelabra and circle the atolls. There is no cover on the boats and you will need to dress appropriately for spray and sun.

Depending on time, you may spend three days travelling through the coastal area, firstly taking a cruise to explore the Ballestas Islands and see the marine birds and wildlife, before discovering the traditional bodegas around Ica, and then flying over the Nazca Lines, one of Peru's strangest archaeological sites. If time is pressing, then the Paracas Peninsula National Reserve including the Ballestas Islands are the stand-out attractions. With more time, it's easy to spend a week in the area, spending longer on Paracas Peninsula, and the wildlife and pre-Columbian sites here, ahead of relaxing in Huacachina and trying your hand at sandboarding on the dunes, then travelling inland from Nazca to the Pampas Galeras Reserve, to see vicuña in a stunning setting.

Moderate
Hostería Suiza (Huacachina) Ⓦ www.hostesuiza.5u.com
Hotel Alegría (Nazca) Ⓦ www.hostalalegria.net
Hotel El Mirador (Paracas) Ⓦ www.elmiradorhotel.com
Hotel Mossone, Huacachina (Ica) Ⓦ www.dematourshoteles.com
Paradones Inn (Nazca) Ⓦ www.paredonesinn.com
Posada Hispana Hotel (Pisco) Ⓦ www.posadahispana.com
Santa María (Paracas) Ⓦ www.santamariahostal.com
Villa Jazmín (Ica) Ⓦ www.villajazmin.net

Budget
Hostal Huacachinero (Ica) Ⓦ http://elhuacachinero.com
Hostal Las Lineas (Nazca) Jr Arica 299 Ⓔ laslineashotel@hotmail.com
Hostal Tambo Colorado (Pisco) Ⓦ www.hostaltambocolorado.com
The WalkOn Inn (Nazca) Ⓦ www.walkoninn.com

The well-preserved Inca adobe complex at Tambo Colorado (SS)

Tambo Colorado

⊘ 09.00–17.00 daily

Northeast of Pisco, 48km away, these **ruins** are considered some of the best-preserved lowland Inca ruins along the coast and once would have been a fortified administrative centre and would also have hosted the Inca as he moved around the empire. They still retain an air of grandeur today. Although roofless, the structures, including places to live, offices and storehouses, are largely intact and architectural features associated with the Incas such as **trapezoidal arches** are evident. Many of the adobe walls are still decorated with their original red colouring.

Paracas

Paracas lies about 16km south of Pisco, on the shores of a well-protected bay. Its name derives from the daily wind which gets up every afternoon and in August can generate sandstorms that last up to three days. The bay is guarded by the **Paracas Peninsula** which, along with the Ballestas Islands, forms a substantial national reserve that is internationally important due to its large number of marine birds. The region is also known for the Paracas people that used to live here.

Paracas highlights
Reserva Nacional de Paracas
⊘ 07.00–18.00 daily

The **Paracas National Reserve** comprises the desert peninsula, the bay and the Ballestas Islands offshore. Although it is an arid place with some starkly beautiful landscapes to discover, it is essentially a marine park, with large numbers of sea mammals, squid, octopus, fish and marine and migratory birds. You can also see flamingos in Paracas Bay and you may spot condors at certain times of year. Dirt tracks criss-cross the desert and a paved road circles the peninsula.

Although it's possible to walk around the peninsula, you'll need plenty of suncream, water and a realistic sense of how far it actually is; it's very easy to get lost in a large desert area. In reality though, as there is no public transport here, you'll need a guide to explore it properly.

El Candelabro

The **Candelabra** is a giant sculpture measuring 180m tall and 50m wide, cut into the surface of the desert on the north shore of the Paracas Peninsula (see photo, page 159). Described variously as a trident or a candlestick, this giant geoglyph is eye-catching and enigmatic. No-one knows who created it or for what purpose, although archaeologists suspect it may be up to 3,000 years old. Theories variously connect this pre-Columbian sculpture to the Nazca Lines or suggest it represents the hallucinogenic cactus used by shaman during rituals. Others maintain that it was an ancient navigational aid for sailors, based on the constellation of the Southern Cross. Best seen from the sea, the Candelabra has unfortunately been damaged by irresponsible drivers on the dunes, and risks further degradation without proper protection.

Mirador de los Lobos

The **Los Lobos viewpoint**, atop a prominent cliff, has panoramic views of the ocean. There are often lots of barking sea lions close by as well, making it a good place to see these mammals and to spot sea birds circling overhead.

Islas Ballestas

The **Ballestas Islands**, sitting in the middle of the Humboldt Current, are a protected haven for marine animals and birdlife; with more than 100 migratory and resident bird species supported by the plankton that

The Paracas Necropolis

It wasn't until the 1920s that the Paracas culture, which thrived from 1300BC for about 1,500 years, was studied in note with the Peruvian archaeologist Julio C Tello dedicating himself to understanding the culture after discovering the **Paracas Necropolis** sites (**Cabezas Largas** and **Cerro Colorado**). These are the oldest sites in the area dating from 100BC to AD300. Even now little is known, with the latter period best understood.

Tello was able to gain a lot of the knowledge from the Paracas Necropolis which was named after the burial site on the isthmus connecting the Paracas peninsula to the mainland. The sites yielded valuable treasures used to provide vital clues about the culture including impressive textiles, some of which are now held by the Museo de la Nación in Lima (page 110). Others can be seen in Ica's Museo Regional (page 162).

Some 400 funerary bundles and remains were excavated and the culture is these days celebrated for their expertise in mummifying the dead. They also practised trepanning (a type of brain surgery) and there is evidence of this on some of the mummies. Other mummies display signs of how the Paracas people used to shape the skull using weights and boards, the deformed cranium being indicative of rank and status.

Each of the funerary bundles comprised a mummified man wrapped in intricate textiles, known as mantos, embroidered with detailed figures and motifs. The textiles were of extraordinary quality and a significant advance even on those associated with the earlier mid-Paracas period, which were much coarser. The Paracas were also very skilled at embroidery and textiles; some of the most exquisite pre-Columbian textiles, decorated with colourful motifs of birds, fish and flora, date from this era.

Museo de Sitio Julio C Tello
⊘ 09.00-17.00 daily

Just inside the **Paracas National Reserve** stands the small but intelligently curated **Julio C Tello Site Museum**, named after the archaeologist considered responsible for uncovering many of the mysteries associated with the Paracas culture during the mid 1920s. A number of exhibits were lost during the 2007 earthquake but there are still some interesting mummies, weavings and trophy heads on display. The majority of the finds are displayed in Lima, however, at the Museo de la Nación (see page 110) and the Museo Nacional de Anthropolgía, Arcqueología y Historia. A walkway leads from the museum to a *mirador*, which has good views of the bay and the flamingos that congregate there from July to November.

El Candelabro sculpture etched into the desert. (ss)

thrives in the warm shallow waters, they are sometimes generously described as Peru's Galápagos. There are dozens of small islands but tours focus on three main rocky atolls pocked with caves and crannies that rear out of the ocean, with rock arches spanning stretches of sea and providing a surreal sculpted landscape for a wealth of endemic wildlife. The islands are home to hordes of sea otters, Humboldt penguins, pelicans, terns, boobies and cormorants, with more beneath the surface to discover. Pods of dolphins are often seen nearby, whilst humpback whales can also be spotted in the vicinity.

Visitors can't actually walk on the islands, but they can circle them by boat, getting close enough, despite the choppy sea, to hear the noisy bird cries and smell the *guano*. The *guano*, bird droppings, which colours the islands white, adds stability to the birds' nests. Every decade it is

harvested and sold as nitrogen-rich fertiliser; during the mid 1800s the export of *guano* to Europe and America made Peru wealthy, before war with Spain and later over-exploitation took their toll. A former *guano* factory still stands on one of the islands. The sea lions, often present in their hundreds, provide plenty of distraction as they bark and perform close by. Their pups are born during the summer, from January to March, making this a popular time to visit.

Ica

Ica stands on the Ica River and is the capital of the regional department. It was first settled around 10,000 years ago and was home successively to the Paracas, Nazca, Huari and Ica cultures before being assimilated into the Inca Empire. After the conquest, the Spaniard Jerónimo Luis de Cabrera established a commercial centre here, which evolved into

a major centre for the production of cotton and wine. As such it is surprisingly large, despite its location some 48km from the coast, amidst a sea of sand dunes. A bustling place, it is steeped in **colonial history** and has a quantity of attractive colonial architecture to discover. The main attractions, however, are the **wineries and bodegas** around the town that produce a range of wines and *pisco*. The climate is ideal for grape growing and the cultivation of vines took off around Ica following their introduction by the Spanish. Production tends to be small scale and involve traditional methods, whereby the grapes are crushed underfoot and the fermented juice tipped into traditional stills. The Ica valley remains the foremost producer of *pisco* in Peru.

The earthquake of 2007 devastated the city; Ica was the region most seriously affected by the giant tremor. The main church was ruined and many of the residents saw their homes levelled. Since then, a programme of rebuilding and regeneration has seen Ica battle back.

Ica comes to life during early March when the city celebrates a wine-harvest festival, **La Fiesta de la Vendimia**, on the second Friday of the month, which includes concerts, craft fairs, beauty pageants and other shows. If you haven't had your fill of *pisco*, then return on the fourth Sunday in July (the drink's national day) when everyone gets drunk on the stuff.

Traditional clay jars for storing *pisco* are still used in Ica. (RI/D)

Ica highlights
The town centre

Look out in town for **colonial architecture**; there are some sizeable churches and the cathedral, which houses an ornate wooden altar. Amongst the most attractive examples is the **Casona del Marqués de Torre**, which has today been converted into a bank. The smart **Plaza de Armas** was the setting for the 1820 declaration of independence from Spain.

Museo Regional

Ayabaca cuadra 8 ⊘ 08.00–19.00 Mon–Sat, 09.00–18.00 Sun

The small **Regional Museum**, south of the town centre, is known as one of the best regional museums in Peru and gives a good overview of the cultures that inhabited the area. Although a number of objects were stolen in 2004, it's still home to a superlative collection of Paracas textiles, Nazca ceramics and artefacts from the Huari, Ica, Chincha and Incas including mummies, skulls and trophy heads taken from defeated enemy warriors. There's also a selection of colonial art on display. Behind the museum look out for a large scale model of the Nazca Lines.

Bodegas

A trip to Ica inevitably includes the chance to tour a **working winery** or bodega; there are around 85 traditional producers in the region and many of the larger ones are happy to have visitors. Many offer free tours and tastings, explaining the production process and introducing you to their produce. To see the bodegas at their best, visit during harvest time which runs from the end of February to April.

The oasis town Huacachina is an ideal base for enjoying the desert. (Ch/D)

Some of the recommended ones, set in colonial haciendas, include **Bodega Catador** (⊙ 10.00–18.00 daily), in the Subtanjalla district some 8km from Ica, and **Bodega Vista Alegre** (⊙ 09.00–14.00 Mon–Fri), which is just 3km north of the city. Further afield is **Hacienda Tacama** (⊙ 09.00–15.00 daily), which is one of the best-known international exporters of *pisco*. The vineyards here are watered by original Inca irrigation channels, although the bodega uses modern production techniques. Worth making the trek to is **Bodega Ocucaje** (⊙ 09.00–12.00 & 14.00–17.00 Mon–Fri, 09.00–12.00 Sat), some 32km south of Ica, which produces both *pisco* and wine.

Around Ica highlights

Huacachina

Amidst the scorching desert and sand dunes 5km southwest of Ica stands this attractive, unexpected **oasis**, with a relaxing resort village built around a pretty palm-fringed lagoon. Once a glamorous retreat for the elegant upper echelons of Peruvian society, it is now a more established centre for people looking to see the desert; climb the dunes

at the end of the lake to be able to gaze out over swathes of sand. The lagoon is a good swimming spot and is reputed to have medicinal, curative properties. People looking to be more active should try dune buggying or sand boarding in the surrounding desert. The dunes are high and you can gather impressive speed during the descent. Beware that accidents happen though.

Palpa and around

About 90km south of Ica, the Pan-American Highway passes through Palpa, a small town celebrated for its orange groves. Set amidst the pampa, the town is surrounded by **geoglyphs** similar to those found further south at Nazca. Drawings indelibly marked on the desert include the Reloj Solar (a giant sun dial that measures 150m wide), an enormous whale, a pelican with a 45m wingspan and some humanoid figures standing 30m tall.

There are several sites close to Palpa worth exploring, too. **La Muña** boasts a number of large Nazca tombs, **Los Molinos** was a substantial Nazca site and the **Ciudad Perdida de Hualluri** was an Inca settlement. From Palpa, a road rises onto the Nazca plain where the better-known Nazca Lines are scored into the surface of the desert (see page 166).

Nazca

A dusty desert town roughly mid-way between Lima and Arequipa with little to initially recommend it, Nazca was largely overlooked until the discovery of extraordinary, enormous etchings in the sand of the pampas close by in 1927. These mysterious drawings, known as the **Nazca Lines**, make up a massive tapestry and cover vast tracts of the bleak, wind-lashed Pampa de San José. Their creation and purpose has baffled people since they were first spotted but they have helped to put the town and the Nazca people firmly on the map.

The Lines were declared a UNESCO World Heritage Site in 1994 in a bid to help preserve them, although by this time the Pan-American Highway had been built right across the tail of the giant lizard found close to the observation tower. The fragile site was added to the World Monuments Fund Global Watch List in 2012 amidst concerns that unregulated tourism constituted a threat to its preservation.

Nazca town was almost destroyed by a huge earthquake in 1996 but has struggled on, boosted by tourism as people continue to flock to see these unique, enigmatic drawings.

Nazca highlights
Planetarium Maria Reiche

Nazca Lines Hotel Ⓦ www.concytec.gob.pe/ipa/inicio_ingles.htm ⊘ daily talks at 19.00 & 21.00

The Nazca Lines Hotel is home to this small planetarium, which hosts nightly talks on the Nazca Lines. The lectures are in English, last about 45 minutes and expand on the theories of Maria Reiche (see pages 166–7), taking into account her archaeological and astronomical observations. There are also some impressive telescopes here for viewing the heavens.

Museo Antonini

Av de la Cultura 600 Ⓦ http://digilander. libero.it/ ⊘ 09.00–19.00 daily

Visit the interesting **Antonini Museum** to gain an overview of the Nazca culture and to put some of their archaeological sites into context. In this private museum there's a scale model of the Nazca Lines, models of tombs that would have held mummies, and a small collection of artefacts including textiles, ceramics and musical instruments such as flutes and pipes, many of which came

A colourful Nazca textile exhibited at the Museo Antonini. (SS)

from Cahuachi. A number of well-preserved mummies can also be seen on site. A pre-Hispanic aqueduct runs through the back garden and is thought to be an ancient irrigation canal.

The enigmatic etchings of the Nazca Lines decorate the desert; pictured here - the monkey. (TK/S)

Around Nazca highlights
Las Lineas de Nazca

Nazca's main attraction are the extraordinary and baffling **Nazca Lines** that are cut into the desert surface of the Pampa de San José, some 24km north of the city. They are easy to access. The Lines, created by the Nazca culture, include anthropomorphic and zoomorphic drawings all executed as a single, continuous line, as well as geoglyphs, triangles and hundreds of lines. Some of the 70 or so plant and animal figures measure almost 300m long, meaning that they are hard to appreciate from the desert floor and can only really be put in context from the air.

Best known are the giant monkey measuring 93m by 58m, the 93m-long hummingbird, the huge spider, the killer whale and the tree.

Mirador

Around 24km north of Nazca stands this metal tower, built by Maria Reiche (see below) at her own expense in 1976 to provide a **viewpoint** from which to look down on a number of the Nazca Lines. Climb the 12m-tall tower to see the lizard, tree and hands, although the tower is not high enough to let you truly look down on the designs. There is another viewpoint, from the slopes of a hill, some 500m further back.

Museo Maria Reiche
⊘ 09.00-18.30 Mon-Sat, 09.00-13.00 Sun

This was the simple house, just outside Nazca, of the German mathematician and researcher Maria Reiche, who dedicated much of her life to investigating the Nazca Lines and subsequently became the leading authority on the subject. Upon her death in 1988, it was turned

Nazca Lines

The Nazca etched the lines into the desert from about 400bc to ad600. The shallow designs – 10-15cm deep – were made by removing the top, red-coloured rocks of the desert to reveal the white-grey ground below. Because the conditions are arid and stable and there's little wind to disturb things, the drawings have endured. They remained unknown until spotted in 1927 by a Peruvian archaeologist. The first explanation of their function came in 1941, when an American scholar was the first to fly over the Lines and noticed the shapes. He also observed that one of the lines was aligned with the sunrise on the winter solstice, suggesting they had connections to astronomy.

Much of our understanding of the Lines is due to the work of **Maria Reiche**, a German mathematician and researcher who began studying the lines during the 1930s and spent more than 50 years investigating them. Her detailed study led her to believe that the lines were part of a vast astronomical calendar. She also believed that the lines had a practical day-to-day purpose that meant that people could measure when to harvest crops, or hold festivals. Reiche supposed that the Lines were drawn using long cords attached to stakes embedded in the desert, which allowed the artist to create a series of arcs of varying length. Scholars have since replicated the technique to demonstrate that with simple technologies even a small group could draw the designs without aerial assistance.

Alternative theories include suggestions that the Lines were running tracks, weaving patterns, ceremonial walking routes, a map of the empire, inspiration for shaman or even landing sites for alien spacecraft, as advocated by the eccentric Eric von Daniken. More recent suggestions include the idea that the Lines were sites for offerings and the worship of water and fertility, essential elements for a desert culture like the Nazca. Regardless of your view point, they remain one of South America's most enigmatic mysteries.

into the basic **Maria Reiche Museum**. Rooms have been preserved as they were when she was alive, allowing visitors to see how she worked amidst maps, models and photographs. It's a good way of glimpsing the daily life of the 'Dame of the Desert' as she expanded theories, debunked myths and brought the lines to the attention of a wider audience. Reiche's tomb has been placed next to her room.

Cerro Blanco sand dune

Cerro Blanco, at 2,070m tall, is considered the tallest sand dune in the world. Travel some 10km southeast of Nazca into the desert to visit this vast behemoth, which sits amidst a series of folds and ridges in the sand. Trek to the top and sandboard down its slopes or paraglide from its summit for an adrenaline-fuelled alternative to the cultural sites elsewhere.

Cahuachi

About 24km west of Nazca stands this substantial, **important ruin**, attributed to the Nazca culture and considered one of their most important sites. The site is still being excavated but archaeologists have so far identified around 30 **pyramids**, a graveyard and a place known as **El Estequieria**, the Place of the Stakes, which includes a dozen rows of hard wood pillars and where it is thought the deceased were dried and mummified. Archaeologist Giuseppe Orefici explored Cahuachi for almost 20 years, uncovering hundreds of graves. Artefacts from the site are displayed in the Museo Antonini (see page 165).

Cementerio de Chauchilla
⊘ 08.00–17.00 daily

There are literally dozens of cemeteries in the Nazca region, and the dry air free from any moisture has preserved the bodies and material they were shrouded in perfectly. About 32km southeast of Nazca lies the atmospheric **Chauchilla Cemetery**, an extraordinary expanse of desert that was the final resting place for countless mummies that date back to the Ica-Chincha culture, which inhabited the region around AD1000. Grave robbers (*huaqueros*) plundered this enormous necropolis once word of its discovery got out, and left skulls, bones and bits of pottery

Nazca culture

The Nazca succeeded the Paracas culture in this region. Along with their artistry, the Nazca are now celebrated for their pottery (which is amongst the finest from pre-Columbian Peru) and for their engineers, who built complex irrigation canals to bring water to the desert enabling crops to grow here. Their name derives from the Quechua word *nanasca*, meaning 'suffering', which is symbolic of their struggle to exist in the harsh conditions of the desert. It is thought that the felling of huarango trees and the gradual deforestation of the region for the purpose of planting crops meant that when a substantial El Niño hit, the land was badly damaged by floods and the Nazca's irrigation canals were washed away. This made farming impractical and caused the Nazca to abandon their territory.

See vicuña up close and watch a traditional shearing at the Reserva Nacional Pampas Galeras. (IK/C)

strewn across the desert. These relics have subsequently been gathered up and arranged as they once would have sat, in a sequence of tombs, which can now be visited and present a vivid impression of life in this desert culture.

Reserva Nacional Pampas Galeras

⊘ 09.00–18.00 daily

The **Pampas Galeras National Reserve** is 88km east of Nazca on the road to Cusco, and is a protected reserve for vicuña, a small relative of the llama. The reserve, high in the mountains at 4,100m, is home to around 8,000 of these endangered animals and represents your best chance to see them in the wild. Every year, in late May or early June, is the *chaccu*, a three-day festival packed with dancing and drinking that marks the start of the season when the vicuña are rounded up and sheared for their very high-quality wool.

Museo de Sacaco

⊘ 09.00–15.00 daily

In the middle of the desert, 96km south of Nazca, stands the unlikely **Sacaco Museum**. The small structure stands over the fossilised skeleton of a whale, which still lies partially interred in the sands, kilometres from the current coastline.

8 The South

Having travelled down the south coast and experienced its magnificent cultural heritage, discover the varied natural wonders in the southwest corner and south of Peru. Towering volcanoes, plummeting gorges and vast lakes are the order of the day; it's a landscape designed for adventure and there's myriad opportunities for outdoor activities.

There are two main centres: Arequipa, close to the coast but well above sea level, filled with colonial history and surrounded by mountains, volcanoes and canyons; and Puno, set on the shore of Lake Titicaca and within easy reach of some unusual archaeological ruins amidst a stark, wind-blown landscape. Both cities are fairly isolated from the rest of Peru yet both demand your attention and should be essential stops. Lake Titicaca, held in high esteem by the Incas and at the heart of their central legends, is also a vital place to visit if you are to get a glimpse of traditional life on the islands of Taquile and Amantaní and gain an insight into the communities that continue to thrive here.

Touring the south

If you're only making a brief foray into Peru's southern region, then a round trip from Lima might take five days, allowing you to fly to Arequipa, explore the city and its sights, then travel out to the Colca Canyon or the Toro Muerto petroglyphs, before flying back to the capital. Ideally though you'd want longer to allow you to combine this section of the south with a trip to Puno, just over 160km away, to see Lake Titicaca and get out onto the water there.

To explore more thoroughly the Puno area, expect to spend at least three days visiting the archaeological site of Sillustani nearby and then sailing to the Uros Islands and either the island of Taquile or Amantaní on a day trip. Ideally though, take five days so that you can see these sights but also stay overnight on one of the islands on the lake, preferably Amantaní, before returning to shore and exploring the nearby villages of Lampa and Chucuito, for a fuller impression of what the area is like.

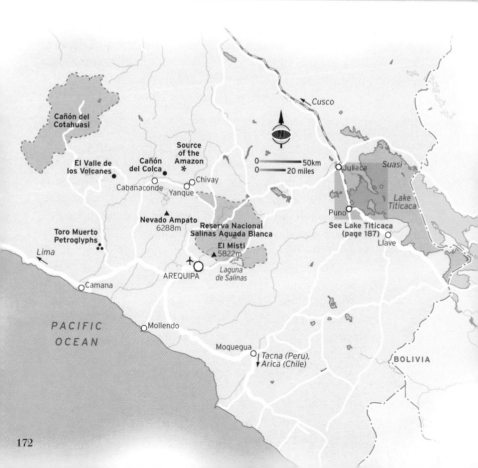

Arequipa and around

Formally founded by the Spanish in 1540, Arequipa has been an important centre since pre-Inca times, with both the Colla and Inca active here. Developing late as a provincial capital and until about 1870 connected to the rest of Peru only by mule track, Arequipa has since established itself as the main commercial centre for the south and is Peru's second city. It has never cared much for the capital and has occasionally hotly contested the right to be the foremost city; two of Peru's major political coups began here in 1930 and 1948. People still cite Arequipa's historic centre, wealth of colonial attractions, handsome architecture and stunning setting – three towering volcanic peaks ring the city – as reasons why the city should be duly recognised.

The nearby volcanoes are testament to the seismic forces that have shaped the region. The most recent natural disaster rocked the city in 2001; a giant earthquake measuring 8.1 on the Richter scale laid waste to the city, killing more than 100 people and injuring another 800. However, the core survived and the city rebuilt itself. Relatively wealthy and independently minded, Arequipa's alumni include intellectuals, artists and writers such as Mario Vargas Llosa and politicians including former President Belaúnde Terry. It has a distinct attitude and atmosphere and people are proud to be Ariquepeños; in a futile attempt at separatism Arequipa once even designed its own passport and flag.

The city is a stand-out destination in its own right, with attractions including attractive colonial architecture, impressive churches and the Santa Catalina Convent, which was closed and cloaked in secrecy for four centuries but is now open to explore. The city is also an ideal base for discovering the region and surrounding countryside. Excursions to the Colca Canyon, Cotahuasi Canyon and Toro Muerto petroglyphs are primary reasons for coming, whilst outdoor enthusiasts will be spoiled for choice here. Trekkers are drawn to climb the perfectly conical volcano that stands sentinel over the city, El Misti, or descend into the deep canyons nearby, which compete for the title of deepest canyon in the world; thrill seekers are lured by the promise of exceptional white-water rafting, while birdwatchers come, keen to spot condors ascending on thermals from the depths of the deep gouges in the sierra.

Arequipa highlights
The city centre
The city centre is attractive and elegant; for a great view climb the elevated *mirador* or **viewpoint**, in the suburb of Yanahuara, and look

Practicalities

Travelling around the south is fairly straightforward although a little time consuming; an **organised tour** takes the hassle out of managing logistics, whether you choose to **fly** into or out of the region, travel **overland** by bus or coach, or take to the rails for one of Peru's most scenic **train** journeys.

Because of the significant increase in altitude between the coast and the sierra around Arequipa and Puno, if you're travelling overland you'll need to spend a couple of days acclimatising. April to October are the prime months to visit; but although pleasant for much of the year, the cities here can get cold at night, so come prepared.

Arequipa is the main hub for journeys in the south – if you're travelling overland from Lima or somewhere along the south coast to Lake Titicaca or Cusco, chances are you'll come this way. It's possible to **fly** daily to Arequipa from Lima or Cusco with LAN. The **airport**, Aeropuerto Rodríquez Ballón, is around 6km northwest of the city. Alternatively, you can drive **overland** to Arequipa along the Pan-American Highway, which takes a full day. More than 960km south of Lima, Arequipa is the southernmost point for most people making a circuitous overland loop to Cusco. From here the typical tour tends to curve northeast and follow the road to Puno and then carry on to Cusco by road or rail, itself 480km north of Arequipa. Arequipa's weather is balmy and

Accommodation

Upmarket

Casa Andina (Chivay) ⓦ www.casa-andina.com
Casa Andina Private Collection (Arequipa) ⓦ www.casa-andina.com
Colca Lodge (Yanque) ⓦ www.colca-lodge.com
Hotel Libertador (Arequipa) ⓦ www.libertador.com.pe
Las Casitas del Colca (Yanque) ⓦ www.lascasitasdelcolca.com
Pozo del Cielo (Chivay) ⓦ www.pozodelcielo.com.pe
Sonesta Posadas del Inca (Arequipa) ⓦ www.sonesta.com/arequipa

Moderate

Casa Andina Classic (Arequipa) ⓦ www.casa-andina.com
Casa Arequipa (Arequipa) ⓦ www.arequipacasa.com
Colca Inn (Chivay) ⓦ www.hotelcolcainn.com
Hostal La Pascana (Chivay) ⓔ hrlapascana@hotmail.com

warm most of the year, with low humidity making it good to visit all year round.

The compact city centre means **exploring on foot** is easy, with the focus on the Plaza de Armas, cathedral and surrounding attractions. The majority of hotels and restaurants are also close by. There are plenty of both but the city can get busy, especially between 6 and 17 August, when locals celebrate Arequipa's founding day with a sequence of music events, parades and exhibitions; on the evening before the actual day, the 15 August, there is a huge celebration and firework display. The city is generally safe although, like most big urban centres, there are reports of muggings; be careful, stay vigilant, don't flaunt your valuables or walk about alone at night, and don't take unlicensed taxis. Should the worst happen, the **tourist police** are based at Jerusalén 315. There's an **iPerú** tourist information booth at the airport (⊘ opening times coincide with arrivals), on the Plaza de Armas (⊘ 08.30–18.00 daily) at Portal de la Municipalidad 112 and at Santa Catalina 210 (⊘ 09.00–19.00 daily) opposite the convent. **Banks** can be found in the centre on San Juan de Dios and General Morán; there are *casas de cambio* on the plaza and an **ATM** in Casa Ricketts at San Francisco 108, where Banco Continental is based. **Internet cafés** are everywhere, especially on Jerusalén.

At **Chivay** there's a **bank**, an **ATM** and **internet cafés**, and the Casa Andina Hotel has a **planetarium** that hosts nightly showings of the night sky, explaining the ancient Andean understanding of constellations.

Hotel Kuntur Wasi (Cabanaconde) Ⓦ www.arequipacolca.com
Hotel La Posada del Monasterio (Arequipa) Ⓦ www.hotelsanagustin.com.pe
La Casa de Mamayacchi (Yanque) Ⓦ www.lacasademamayacchi.com
La Casa de Mi Abuela (Arequipa) Ⓦ www.lacasademiabuela.com
La Maison d'Elise (Arequipa) Ⓦ http://aqplink.com/hotel/maison
La Posada del Conde (Cabanaconde) Ⓦ www.posadadelconde.com
Tradición Colca Albergue (Yanque) Ⓦ www.tradiciocolca.com

Budget
Casablanca Hostal (Arequipa) Ⓦ www.casablancahostal.com
Colonial House Inn (Arequipa) Ⓦ www.colonialhouseinn-arequipa.com
Hostal Núñez (Arequipa) Ⓦ www.hotel-nunez.de
La Casa de Melgar Hostal (Arequipa) Ⓦ www.lacasademelgar.com
Los Balcones de Moral y Santa Catalina (Arequipa) Ⓦ www.balconeshotel.com
Pachamama Hostal (Cabanconde) Ⓦ www.pachamamahome.com

The cathedral in Arequipa's Plaza de Armas is just one of the city's colonial architectural icons. (MG/S)

back across the city. The majority of buildings are built from *sillar*, a porous white volcanic stone described as looking like petrified nougat, which has led to the nickname 'La Ciudad Blanca', or 'the White City'. The grand **Plaza de Armas**, one of the most attractive in Peru, is filled with palms and fountains and is dominated by a substantial Neoclassical **cathedral** (⊘ 07.00–11.30 & 17.00–19.30 Mon–Sat, 07.00–13.00 & 17.00–19.00 Sun) dating from the 17th century, which fills an entire side of the plaza. One of the cathedral's impressive twin towers was destroyed completely by the earthquake in 2001 and the other was reduced to a stub by the giant shock; they have since been restored. Close by on the corner of Alvarez Thomas and General Morán stands the similarly impressive Jesuit church and cloister **La Compañía** (⊘ 09.00–12.30 Mon–Fri, 15.00–18.00 Sat, 17.00–18.00 Sun), which was completed in 1698. Full of attractive features, it's worth exploring.

Colonial architecture

Arequipa is blessed with a wealth of attractive colonial architecture for you to enjoy as you wander around. Look out in particular for the **Casa del Moral** on Avenida Bolívar (⊘ 09.00–17.00 Mon–Sat, 09.00–13.00 Sun), a sumptuous Baroque mansion built in the early 1730s, which provides a glimpse of colonial life in the city. The *moral*, a 200-year-old mulberry tree, stands in a gorgeous courtyard. Inside are smart furnishings, carefully carved furniture and doors, and a large collection of art from the Cusco School of painting. Ascend to the roof for great views of the city and the nearby volcanoes. Elsewhere, **Casa Ricketts** at San Francisco 108 and **Casa Arróspide** on San Agustín are good examples of 18th-century mansions.

Monasterio de Santa Catalina

Santa Catalina 301 ⓦ www.santacatalina.org.pe ⊘ 09.00–17.00 Fri–Mon (last admission 16.00), 19.00–21.00 Tue–Thu

The Dominican **Santa Catalina Convent**, founded in 1579, is an oasis of tranquillity and calm. A self-contained, enigmatic complex covering an entire block, effectively making it a city within a city, it wasn't opened or revealed to the wider world until 1972, but is now considered one of Peru's most important religious icons. A major tourist draw, it is still, in fact, a functioning convent, albeit with just a handful of nuns now in residence. Originally the nuns, who numbered several hundred, were chosen from rich aristocratic families and intended to live a chaste and abstemious life. Within the convent though they had a pretty charmed existence, outnumbered by servants and hosting substantial events, at least until a strict Sister restored order in 1871. Tall, thick walls are coloured terracotta orange, cobalt blue and brick red; labyrinthine cobbled streets conceal small cells, which house antique furniture and art. Pretty plazas hide fountains and secret niches. The streets are

Eating out

Arequipa has a definite food scene and is second only to Lima for its culinary excellence. Regional dishes tend to be spicy; visit a *picantería* (a traditional restaurant) to try *rocoto relleno*, hot stuffed peppers, and *adobo de cerdo*, slow-cooked pork. Look for restaurants in the old quarter or north of the Plaza de Armas to try these. Alternatively embrace the lively café scene and hang out on the colonnaded balconies above gracefully arched colonial façades that line the Plaza de Armas and watch the world go by.

Ary Quepay (Peruvian) Jerusalén 502 ⓣ 204 583
Chicha (fusion) Santa Catalina 210 ⓣ 287 360
Crepisimo (café) Santa Catalina 208 ⓣ 206 620
Paladar 1900 (Peruvian) Villalba 309 ⓣ 226 295
Tradición Ariquipeña (Peruvian) Avenida Dolores 111 ⓣ 246 467
Wayrana (Peruvian) Santa Catalina 200 ⓣ 285 641

Iglesia de San Agustín is famed for its Baroque façade. (M/D)

Colonial churches

Arequipa has an unrivalled collection of colonial churches. The Franciscan **Monasterio de la Recoleta** (☉ 09.00–12.00 & 15.00–17.00 Mon–Sat) at Recoleta 117 dates from 1648 and has a distinctive red-and-white steeple. The monastery also has attractive cloisters and pretty gardens to wander through, and a collection of pre-Inca artefacts to uncover along with mummies and a horde of Amazonian curios picked up by Franciscan missionaries as they attempted to spread the word throughout the region. A library containing 20,000 books and maps is as impressive as it sounds. Elsewhere, **Iglesia de San Francisco** at Zela 103 is a 16th-century *sillar* structure with a silver altar and pretty vaulted ceiling; **Iglesia de San Agustín**, on the corner of San Agustín and Sucre, was rebuilt in the late 1890s after an earthquake but still boasts a superb Baroque façade; **Iglesia de Santo Domingo**, at the junction of Santo Domingo and Piérola, is known for its smart cloisters; whilst **Iglesia de la Merced** at La Merced 103 is home to a huge colonial library.

named after Spanish cities and the place has a distinct Moorish feel, making it seem even more removed from the vibrant South American city outside. Highlights include the **Orange Tree Cloister**, which is decorated with murals, the blackened 17th-century **kitchen**, the **choir room** of the church, and the rooms belonging to the extraordinarily prescient nun Sor Ana. You'll want several hours inside the convent to amble about, get lost, discover quiet corners and splashes of intense colour, or to take a guided tour and have the features described in detail.

Museo Arqueológico Chiribaya
La Merced 117 ⓦ www.museochiribaya.org ⊘ 08.30–19.00 Mon–Sat, 09.00–15.00 Sun

Set in an attractive colonial mansion, **Chiribaya Archaeological Museum** features a range of artefacts attributed to the Chiribaya culture, a pre-Inca civilisation that flourished in the Arequipa region from AD800 to 1350. Exhibits include everyday domestic objects used for fishing and farming, as well as textiles and gold jewellery.

Museo Santurarios Andinos
La Merced 110 ⓦ www.ucsm.edu.pe/santury ⊘ 09.00–18.00 Mon–Sat, 09.00–15.00 Sun

Small but well presented and full of fascinating exhibits, the **museum** houses a range of Inca items that can be seen on an obligatory **guided tour**. It's most famous, however, as the home of Juanita, the Ice Maiden found preserved atop the Ampato volcano (see box overleaf). Sacrificed aged 13, the body had been remarkably well preserved by the ice and is now on display in what looks like a giant freezer cabinet. Sacrificial items, doll offerings and other funerary objects were also found at the site and are displayed here too, providing a detailed picture of the period and the sacrificial ritual itself.

Shopping in Arequipa

There are numerous quality shops in Arequipa and the city is considered one of the best places in Peru to pick up alpaca clothing and other woollen items. Visit the boutiques close to the La Compañía church, behind the cathedral and on Calle Santa Catalina. **Alpaca 111** at Zela 212 and **Kuna** at Santa Catalina 210 are good bets. Look out for antiques on Calle Santa Catalina, and handicrafts in the **artisans market** close to Plazuela de San Francisco. For more on shopping in Peru, see *Chapter 4*, page 88.

Around Arequipa highlights
El Misti Volcano

There are three volcanoes situated close to Arequipa: Chachani, El Misti and Pichu-Pichu and all three hover around the 6,000m mark in height and are often snow-capped, although global warming has meant the snows on the summits last just a few months rather than all year round these days. Of these three, El Misti (5,822m), 19km away from Arequipa

and thought of as the city's guardian, is the most attractive. A picture-perfect, geometrically exact conical cone, as if drawn by a child imagining the ideal volcano, it is a staggering sight rising from the sierra. Popular with trekkers, the **two-day ascent** to the crater rim isn't technical but does require fitness, stamina and for you to be properly acclimatised to altitude. The volcano is best climbed between July and August.

Juanita, Ampato Ice Maiden

'Juanita' is the name given to the 13-year-old Inca girl sacrificed and subsequently found preserved in the ice on the summit of the volcanic Nevado Ampato, at 6,310m. Discovered by Johan Reinhard in 1995, she represents one of the most important archaeological finds in recent years. Other sacrifices had been found on summits before, but Juanita is the first female and far and away the best preserved. Because the body was still frozen at the time of discovery, none of her clothes or flesh had been unduly desiccated. Naturally mummified by the cold, her skin, organs, tissue, blood, hair and stomach contents were intact, affording scientists a rare but crystal clear look into the past. Killed during the mid to late 1400s, the body lay packed in ice for more than 550 years, and was only uncovered by hot ash settling on Ampato from an eruption on nearby Mount Sabancaya.

It is thought that the teenage girl was sacrificed on the summit in an elaborate ritual as a token to appease Ampato, who controlled the rain and

Scale El Misti for unparalleled panoramic views of the Arequipa area; pictured here, a crater-side view. (f/iS)

Laguna de Salinas

To the east of Arequipa, beneath the volcanoes of El Misti and Pichu-Pichu lies the large **Salinas (salt) Lake**. In the wet season, January to April, it hosts flocks of flamingos, including Andean, Chilean and puna flamingos, along with other water birds. During the warmest months, from May to December, it dries out completely and turns instead into a vast salt pan. Trek or mountain bike around the lake and look out for birds whilst on a day tour from Arequipa.

water and subsequently the quality of the harvest, and so ensure rainfall and healthy crops. Dressed in richly patterned fabrics, the girl is likely to have been an important, possibly royal figure. The Inca believed that mountaintops were the abode of their gods and that their priests could get closer to them by climbing the highest peaks. Led to the summit of Ampato by priests wearing colourful alpaca shawls, and caps made from red macaw feathers, Juanita was despatched with a blow to the temple, just above the right eye; sacrifice was at this time considered a great privilege and being chosen to appease the gods a great honour. She was then buried in a brightly coloured burial tapestry. All of the associated elements of the sacrifice have also been found next to the body along with a collection of grave goods including bowls, pins and figurines made of gold, silver and shell, allowing archaeologists to build up an accurate picture of the events leading up to the death. Many of these objects are now on display in the Museo Santuarios Andinos in Arequipa (see page 179). Latter ascents of Ampato found two more mummies, one a young girl, the other a young boy, though neither were as high on the mountain or as well preserved as Juanita.

Flamingoes flock to Reserva Nacional Aguada Blanca. (SS)

Aguada Reserva Nacional Aguada Blanca

The **Salinas and Aguada Blanca National Reserve**, constituting 300,000ha of high plateau, lies to the northeast of Arequipa, beyond El Misti. Standing at 4,300m, it is a good place to see timid alpaca and vicuña in the wild, with large herds roaming the high altiplano. Ascend to the highest point of the plateau and marvel at the views of the surrounding volcanic peaks. The road then descends onwards into the Cañón del Colca.

Valle del Colca

The **Colca Valley**, one of Peru's most striking and attractive regions, is a place of high drama and breathtaking beauty; the writer Mario Vargas Llosa, one of Arequipa's celebrated sons, described it as a 'Valley of Marvels'. At over 160km north of Arequipa, it is an essential detour to see traditional villages belonging to the Quechua-speaking Cabanas and Aymara-speaking Collagua groups, cleverly terraced hillsides, towering peaks including Coropuna (6,613m), Ampato (6,310m) and Sabancaya, along with a range of wildlife. To the north of the valley stands **Nevado Mismi**, a snow-capped peak considered by some to be the source of the Amazon River.

The main draw, however, is the 96km-long **Cañón del Colca (Colca Canyon)**, a precipitous gorge carved by the Colca River, which reaches

depths of around 3,400m, making it twice as deep as the Grand Canyon. Unknown until the 1970s, it came to fame when rafting expeditions explored its depths. Since then it has developed into a major destination for adventure enthusiasts, who come to hike, climb, mountain bike and white-water raft. Treks can be done year-round but are safer and easier from May to November, when it is driest. More recently, the area achieved fame when 'Juanita' was found buried on the summit of Ampato, one of the volcanic peaks in the region (see page 180).

Cruz del Cóndor

One of the most recognised places in Peru to see Andean condors is the Colca Canyon. A spectacularly sited **lookout point**, Cruz del Cóndor, known locally as Chaq'lla, overlooks the canyon, which is about 1,200m deep here. The viewpoint allows visitors to spot these enormous birds ascending silently on thermals from the canyon before sailing off effortlessly on their vast wings. Keep an eye out below and above and if you're lucky you'll lock gaze with one of these magnificent birds, the symbol of the Andes. The best time to spot the birds is June to September; arrive in the early morning, ideally between 07.00 and 09.00, when the cold overnight air heats up and the thermals are at their strongest. Look out too for vizcachas scurrying about amidst the rocks on the canyon rim. It can be cold first thing so bring warm clothes and, of course, binoculars.

Rafting

There is some superb, white-knuckle rafting in the Arequipa region for people looking to plunge through the narrow canyons. The best time to raft is April to November as during the rainy season – from December to March – the rivers are in full flow and considered too dangerous. The closest put-in point is on the Chilli River, about 8km from Arequipa. Trickier are the Majes River, with rapids rated Grade II and III, and the Colca River, a much more serious undertaking with far more turbulent water and larger rapids. Best of all though are the runs for more experienced river riders on the Colca and Cotahuasi rivers, which are best tackled between May and June and where rapids reach Grade IV-V. Extraordinary scenery, remote location and more or less constant adrenaline make these some of the most exciting rafting expeditions in Peru.

Colca Canyon

Why not take a two- or three-day tour to explore the wildlife and history of Colca Canyon? You will have the opportunity to see vicuñas, alpacas and llamas, as well as birds such as flamingos, ibises, condors, Andean geese and Andean eagles. In beautiful typical towns, like Yanque and Maca, you will discover colonial churches, locals in traditional dress, and hundreds of pre-Inca crop terraces. You can also enjoy dinner with typical folkloric shows at Colca Lodge.

Smaller towns along the Valle del Colca

Other than Arequipa, there are a number of smaller towns strung out along the rim of the Colca Canyon. Chivay, at the head of the Colca Valley and at 3,500m is a rather dry, dusty market town that nonetheless has brilliant views of the mountains, the 18th-century Ñuestra Señora de la Asunción church, and original Inca terraces. The Calera hot springs and thermal baths lie about a kilometre outside of town. Yanque, about 10km west from Chivay, has a Baroque 18th-century church, a small cultural museum and a number of hot springs, Baños Chacapi (☺ 15.00–19.00 daily), where you can soak. Walk out of town to discover an old stone bridge over the Colca River and some Inca tombs cut into a cliff face. At the far end of the valley, Cabanaconde, although small, provides access to some decent trekking routes in and around the Colca Canyon and is just a short distance from Cruz del Cóndor.

Toro Muerto petroglyphs
☺ 09.00–16.00 daily

Close to the town of Corire, about a three-hour drive from Arequipa, is Toro Muerto, a vast field of petroglyphs thought to be one of the largest in the world. Hundreds of carvings are scattered on volcanic boulders across an attractive area of desert several kilometres long. A little basic, the **stylised drawings** of people, animals and geometric shapes are attributed to the Huari culture and date from around 1,200 years ago. Remote, high and quite hard to reach – consequently little-visited – the arid site is atmospheric and unlike anything else you're likely to encounter in Peru. The scale and location are sufficiently impressive even before you take into account the primitive art. If you visit from Arequipa bring everything you'll need as there are no facilities here.

Condors can be seen rising on thermals from the depths of the Colca Canyon. (SS)

El Valle de los Volcanes

Just off the road north from Arequipa to the Cotahuasi Canyon, close to the village of Andagua and under the watchful gaze of the volcano Coropuna (6,613m), is the **Valley of the Volcanoes**. Some 64km long, straggled along a substantial fissure in the earth's crust, the valley is full of strange geological features, including 80 cinder cones up to 200m high and a host of lava flows that have issued from volcanoes over the years. Remote and off-the-beaten track but starkly beautiful and haunting, the valley is well worth the effort. Other features include a lake, the **Laguna de Chachas**, which is emptied by a stream that sinks below the lava and reappears more than 16km away; a 40m-high waterfall, **Izanquillay**; some pre-Columbian **ruins**; and a number of **funerary towers**, *chullpas*, at Soporo.

Cañón del Cotahuasi

The Colca Canyon may be better known, but it isn't the world's deepest canyon. That honour goes to the **Cotahuasi Canyon**, 200km northwest of Arequipa as the crow flies but more than 400km away by road. Stretches of the canyon, which has been carved by the Cotahuasi River, plunge more than 3,500m and it is around 150m deeper than its rival. Pretty to walk through and full of opportunities for trekking, the valley is best known for the high-quality white-water **rafting** that takes place here. The season runs from May to June and rapids reach Grade IV to V. To fully explore the canyon and its surrounding area, you'll need three to five days.

Puno and Lake Titicaca

Puno lies close to Peru's southern border, on the northwest shore of Lake Titicaca. Almost 400km south of Cusco, the city is also 300km northeast of Arequipa, making it fairly remote and the sort of place you have to make an effort to access. That said it's worth it, if not for the rather ramshackle town then for the surrounding countryside and for Lake Titicaca in particular.

The azure waters of Lake Titicaca, which looks more like an ocean than a lake, ripple across the altiplano – the waters are as deep as 270m in places. The lake's shoreline and islands, lapped by the cold waters, are lands of legend, ancient customs and colourful dress, with the locals continuing to hold firmly on to their pre-conquest traditions.

Established in the late 17th century to support a burgeoning silver-mining industry at Laicota, the town of Puno has evolved into a functional place without that much to immediately appeal to a visitor. Nonetheless, it has a certain vibrancy about it and the superb attractions on its doorstep more than compensate. It is perfectly placed for exploring the area and uncovering the nearby

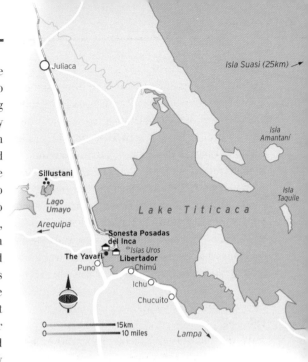

archaeological treasures along with the folkloric traditions that make the region famous. Set sail from here to explore the lake, stopping at the Uros Islands, made from totora reeds, and learn about the traditional

Festivals

Puno is renowned for its festivals and fiestas, and is widely considered the centre of Peruvian folklore. Amongst the most spectacular is the **Festival de la Virgen de la Candelaria** (Candlemass) during the first two weeks of February, when the city celebrates its patron saint with music, dancers in elaborate costumes, grotesque devil masks and animal outfits, and copious drinking. The most famous dance is La Diablada, which involves a struggle between elaborately costumed angels and frightening devils.

Carnival in late February and early March features native dancers and water fights and the obligatory consumption of yet more alcohol. The **Fiesta de San Juan de Dios** on 8 March is a little more muted and features processions of the saint on a litter through the streets. The island of Taquile celebrates the **Fiesta de San Diego** on 25 July, with wild dancing and a thunderous party that lasts several days, during which time traditional offerings are made to Pachamama. **Puno Week**, in early November, which marks the founding of the city and remembers the legend of Manco Cápac rising from the waters of the lake, is similarly impressive with processions, floats and dancing.

Practicalities

Puno, surrounded by mountains, can only be reached **overland**, as it doesn't have an airport. There are, however, daily **flights** to Juliaca (45km north of the city) from Lima and Arequipa. It's a straightforward and relatively quick transfer by road from here to Puno. Road access to the city is good, with improvements in particular to the route between Puno and Cusco, meaning that overland is now quicker and more comfortable than by train (the traditional way of travelling between the two cities). The highway between Puno and Arequipa has also made overland travel between these two cities far more practical and less time consuming. The **rail** route from Puno to Cusco, which operates three times a week, remains one of the most scenic in the country though, and something of an iconic journey despite the leisurely pace, breakdowns and frequent late arrivals. The **train station** is at Avenida La Torre 224.

Accommodation

If visiting Lake Titicaca's main islands, it's possible to arrange a homestay. The only private island, Suasi, boasts a smart ecolodge in a truly exclusive location; see below.

Upmarket

Casa Andina Private Collection (Suasi) Ⓦ www.casa-andina.com
Hotel Libertador (Lake Titicaca shore) Ⓦ www.libertador.com.pe
Sonesta Posada del Inca (Lake Titicaca shore) Ⓦ www.sonesta.com/laketiticaca
Titilaka (Lake Titicaca shore) Ⓦ www.titilaka.com

Moderate

Casa Andina Classic Puno Plaza (Puno) Ⓦ www.casa-andina.com
Casa Andina Classic Tikrani (Puno) Ⓦ www.casa-andina.com
Conde de Lemos Inn (Puno) Ⓦ www.condelemosinn.com

dress, customs and farming methods on the more substantial islands of Taquile and Amantaní from the islanders themselves.

Puno and around highlights
The city centre

To get an overview of the city and to see Lake Titicaca, climb to a

At 3,830m Puno is higher than Cusco, so will literally take your breath away upon arrival; take it easy when you first arrive and let your body acclimatise. The **altitude** also means that it can get very cold at night, particularly from June to August. The city is easy to navigate, although most people don't stay long enough to become well acquainted with it. You can get around the centre **on foot** and even walk down to the port, although a **taxi** is more usual and even essential if you're accessing several of the smarter hotels on the shore of the lake.

There are usually plenty of places to stay, except during the high season, June to September, and during the busiest festivals, when places book up well in advance. There's an **iPerú** information office at Jirón Lima 549 and **banks** and **ATMs** can also be found here. **Internet cafés** are widespread. For **souvenirs**, head to the artisans market beyond the railway line, between Jirón Melgar and Avenida Titicaca.

Hotel Colón Inn (Puno) ⓦ www.coloninn.com
Intiqa Hotel (Puno) ⓦ www.intiqahotel.com
La Hacienda (Puno) ⓦ www.lahaciendapuno.com

Budget

Casa Panq'arani (Puno) ⓦ www.casapanqarani.com
Hotel Los Uros (Puno) ⓦ www.losuros.com
Posada Don Giorgio (Puno) ⓦ www.posadadongiorgio.com

Eating out

The following eateries can be found in Puno:

IncAbar (international) Lima 348 ① 368 031
Los Balcones de Puno (international & Peruvian) Libertad 354 ① 365 300
Mojsa (international & Nuevo Andino) Lima 635 ① 363 182
Tulipans (café) Lima 394 ① 351 796
Ukukus (Peruvian) Libertad 216 ① 367 373

viewpoint in Huajsapata Park on a hill 400m to the west of the Plaza de Armas. There's a statue of Manco Cápac (the original Inca leader) here, too.

If you are exploring the centre, look out for the cathedral, **Catedral Basílica San Carlos Borromeo** (◷ 08.00–11.00 & 15.30–18.00 daily), on the Plaza de Armas, which has an elaborate exterior but is rather

Towns around Puno

There are a number of pleasant, historic towns in close proximity to Puno that are worth visiting to learn a little more about the area. **Lampa,** northwest of Puno is a small city, nicknamed 'La Ciudad Rosa' or the Pink City, because of its blush-coloured buildings. Once a thriving colonial centre, it's a perfectly preserved slice of what life in the area used to be like. The town has an attractive centre, with lots of low buildings with pretty balconies. There's also an interesting church, the Iglesia de Santiago de Apostol, dating from 1675, which contains colonial paintings, an elaborate pulpit and a copy of Michelangelo's Pietà.

South of Puno, 10km away, stands **Ichu,** a small lakeside community where an abandoned temple complex boasts some outstanding panoramic views of the landscape nearby. About 19km southeast of Puno, on the shore of Lake Titicaca, stands the small village of **Chucuito,** once the main town in the province. The village is home to the altiplano's oldest church, established in 1534. It's also well known for the rather bizarre Templo de la Fertilidad (Temple of Fertility; ⊘ 08.00-17.00), and the strange stone phalluses and other fertility symbols that are scattered throughout the site. The town is a pretty place, however, with some great countryside on the doorstep; from the main plaza walk out of town and climb Cerro Atoja for some superb views of the lake.

plain once you're inside. The small **Museo Municiapal Carlos Dryer** (Municipal Museum Carlos Dryer; ⊘ 09.30–19.00 Mon–Sat) at Conde de Lemos 289 has a collection of ceramics and textiles, local artefacts and several mummies that have undergone cranial deformation (see page 158). Nearby at Deústua 576 is the 17th-century **Casa del Corregidor** (⊘ 10.00–22.00 Tue–Fri), which is one of the city's oldest buildings and now houses an important cultural centre. There's also an eccentric **Coca Museum** (⊘ 09.00–13.00 & 15.00–20.00 daily) at Deza 301, which is full of information on the plant, the traditional use of it as a medicine and its place in Andean culture. There's also a display of traditional costumes that you might see during one of the many festivals held here.

The *Yavari*
⊘ 08.00-17.00 daily

The *Yavari,* an antique British **steamship** decorated black, white and red, is the oldest ship to have operated on the lake. It was one of a pair of iron gunboats ordered from a shipbuilder in Britain to patrol the waters. Built in 1862 in Birmingham, the iron boat was shipped around Cape Horn, in 2,760 parts. Having landed in South America at Arica (now in Chile), it was carried by mules across country to Puno over a period of six years. It was finally launched on Christmas Day 1870, using dried llama dung as fuel due to a lack of coal. It went on to operate on the lake as a cargo and passenger vessel for more than 100 years but is now retired and sits on the shore several kilometres from Puno behind the Sonesta Posada Hotel del Inca, where it has been converted into a small **museum**.

Sillustani towers
⊘ 08.00–17.00 daily

About 32km northeast of Puno is a wild, open peninsula almost entirely encircled by the pleasant, bird-rich **Lago Umayo**. Here, a series of about a dozen impressive granite funerary towers, *chullpas*, stand on desolate hilltops. These imposing cylindrical towers, which stand up to 12m tall, were in fact tombs belonging to the Colla people, who controlled the region prior to the arrival of the Incas; the Colla buried their leaders and celebrated members of their society in the base of the towers along with other family members, food, clothing and jewellery. The Incas conquered the Colla in the 15th century but maintained the practice.

The tombs are all empty but the spectacular structures that contained them remain. Smooth-sided, carefully sculpted and made without modern tools, the towers are engineering marvels. Two are unfinished, enabling you to see how the Colla constructed these remarkable buildings.

The funerary towers at Sillustani stand amidst the stark landscape.
(FR/PP)

To see some alternative, less well-visited *chullpas*, including a number of square structures, head instead to **Cutimbo** (☉ 08.00–17.00), which is south of Puno.

Lake Titicaca and its islands

Unlike anywhere else, Lake Titicaca, straddling the border between Peru and Bolivia, is truly a place of superlatives. The world's highest navigable lake, at 3,830m it is also the largest in South America and the largest above 2,000m anywhere in the world. A mythical, mysterious place, many people associate Lake Titicaca with folklore; the Incas believed that Viraocha, the creator god, drew the sun, moon and stars from the lake. The Inca also considered that their original leader, Manco Cápac, was directly descended from the sun and rose from the waters of Lake Titicaca with his sister Mama Ocllo, to go in search of a homeland for the future Inca civilisation. The lake is startlingly attractive, with intense deep-blue water stretching away from the shore, and enormous skies above.

The islands on the lake have been home to people for thousands of years. Each island, actual or manmade, has distinct traditions; explore them all to compare and contrast the ways of life here and to see traditional agrarian societies still functioning as they would have hundreds of years ago. Stay the night with a family and learn about the customs directly from the islanders themselves.

Islas Uros

One of Lake Titicaca's most surreal sites, the floating **Uros Islands** are just 5km east of Puno and are home to an Indian community of just a handful of families, who eke out an existence on manmade

The Uros people rely on reeds for their floating islands, traditional boats and crafts. (SS)

islands constructed from totora reeds; the islanders also use the reeds for boats, houses and handicrafts. The reeds are woven to form a giant mat, which slowly rots in the water and so has to be constantly replenished from the top. Walking on this giant raft is unsettling at first as it gives and sags under your step, but it is essentially safe and stable; the largest island even boasts a clinic, school and church. The Uros, who call themselves *kot-suña*, 'the people of the lake', took to the water, subsisting on fishing and hunting wild birds, to avoid the warlike Colla and later the Inca who occupied the area. They've maintained this lifestyle ever since, although now much of their income is derived by charging tourists for visits, rides in reed canoes and photographs. There are about 40 floating islands in total, with tourism restricted to about a dozen of these; on the back of continued exposure to visitors, one or two are little more than floating craft markets targeting tourists, where begging can be quite aggressive. A firm no, especially to children asking for hand outs, should help deter the practice.

Isla Taquile

Adrift in Lake Titicaca about 40km from Puno is **Taquile Island**, a small island that's home to 2,000 Quechua-speaking inhabitants. Just about a kilometre wide and 6km long, it's rugged and hilly, with several Inca terraces cut into the umber-coloured soil of the slopes, making it an attractive place to wander about. From the dock a series of 500 steps climb to the centre, which has no roads, streetlights or electricity after a certain time in the evening. The small country houses, farms and stone walls give the island a wonderfully rural feel. The island has been

Climb to the top of Isla Taquile for picturesque views of Lake Titicaca. (RC/S)

Lake Titicaca cruises

The legends about Lake Titicaca are as deep and old as the lake itself. Straddling the border between Peru and Bolivia, Lake Titicaca is said to be the birthplace of the Inca Empire. You can visit this beautiful, high-altitude lake by taking a catamaran cruise from Puno or Bolivia's Copacabana, stopping to explore the
Isla del Sol and the Isla de la Luna along the way. Spend the night on the 'Sun Island', where you will witness a spectacular sunset.

inhabited for thousands of years and the traditions that have grown up here are still strictly adhered to by the community. The men on the island wear distinctive floppy, knitted hats, coloured red if they are married or red and white if not; unlike elsewhere in Peru, the men knit their own headgear and are responsible for much of the weaving that's typically done on the mainland by women. The rest of their outfit is usually a coarse spun white shirt and calf-length black trousers, held up by a thick woven waistband. The women wear multi-coloured and multi-layered skirts with embroidered blouses. The overall effect of seeing a local couple walking together is striking. You can stay on the island overnight in a rustic homestay, where your hosts will probably cook for you, or there's always the option of trying one of the small restaurants on the island that are known for their quinoa soup and fresh fish dishes.

Isla Amantaní
To the north of Taquile Island lies the larger **Amantaní Island**, which is home to 4,000 people. The island is similarly historic, with traces of the Tiahuanaco culture found in the **temples of Pachamama** (Mother Earth) and **Pachatata** (Father Earth) that stand atop the hill in the centre of the island and date from 200BC to AD1000; the ruins are a great place to watch the sunset over the lake. Since the island is less frequently visited, it remains fairly rustic with no roads, vehicles or even dogs. It's possible to stay here and the locals have organised a rotational system of allocating visitors to homestays so that everyone benefits from tourism. The homestays are a great way to see daily life and take part in activities such as preparing food and meal times, and the villagers often throw impromptu music performances for their guests.

In conversation with...

Is Machu Picchu really Peru's one 'must-see' site?

Absolutely. Machu Picchu is not only the defining image of Peru but is South America's most iconic site and one of the New Seven Wonders of the World. Re-discovered in 1911, the Inca citadel often tops travellers' lists of once-in-a-lifetime experiences. As well as trekking the popular Inca Trail, it is also possible to travel to Machu Picchu by train from Ollantaytambo in the Sacred Valley. An overnight stay in Aguas Calientes is highly recommended.

Should visitors worry about their impact on Machu Picchu?

Everyone should be conscious of possible negative environmental impact. However, the Peruvian government does limit visitors through a permit system, and nearby Aguas Calientes can only be accessed by train or on foot, which automatically helps to restrict numbers. It's therefore very important to book well in advance.

What other sites should visitors be sure to include?

Lake Titicaca is another highlight. At 3,800m above sea level, its intensely blue waters are a stunning contrast to the snow-capped Andean peaks on the border between Peru and Bolivia. For a complete contrast to high altitudes and mountain scenery, visitors could spend some time in the Peruvian Amazon, home to an amazing diversity of flora and fauna. It is also really worth exploring the south of Peru, and visiting the historic city of Arequipa which is bursting with colonial charm and set against a backdrop of three volcanoes. It is also the gateway to the Colca Canyon. At twice the depth of the Grand Canyon this is the place to spot one of the region's other natural wonders: the majestic Andean condor.

Is altitude sickness a problem at key tourist sites?

Itineraries that take in destinations at high altitude, such as Machu Picchu and Lake Titicaca, are always planned meticulously to include plenty of time for rest and acclimatisation, so illness is rarely a problem for visitors. We do recommend drinking plenty of water at all times and sampling the local coca tea, which is said to help sickness and is also delicious.

What about the north of Peru?

Northern Peru is beautiful and much less visited than the south. Getting there is quite easy as there are regular flights to gateway cities such as Trujillo, and the region is a fantastic choice for visitors interested in history, culture and archaeological sites. The area is home to some of Peru's most spectacular

pre-Columbian ruins such as those at Chan Chan and the Temples of the Sun and Moon, or the pre-Inca ruins near Chiclayo. For visitors in search of adventure, the Chachapoyas region of the northern highlands offers a chance to get right off-the-beaten track, travelling by 4x4 through remote villages to discover ancient mountain-top sites.

What do you recommend of the local cuisine?

Peruvian cuisine is rapidly growing an international reputation and there are plenty of delicacies to try, so be adventurous! *Ceviche* is extremely popular and tastes amazing, while those who like local specialities may like to try alpaca steaks or even *cuy* (guinea pig). Don't leave Peru without sampling the classic *pisco sour* cocktail and refreshing local beers such as Cusqueña.

Rainbow Tours Latin America specialists have been providing expert advice and tailor-made tours to the region for over a decade. Rainbow's trips in Peru offer plenty of opportunities to visit the iconic sites or combine them with lesser-known destinations in order to soak up the rich culture and history of the region. We spoke with Amanda Sweeney of the company.

Ⓣ +44 (0)20 7666 1272 Ⓔ info@rainbowtours.co.uk
Ⓦ www.rainbowtours.co.uk

9 Cusco, Machu Picchu and around

The centre of the Inca Empire, Cusco has been a vital, vibrant city for more than 550 years. It is the main attraction for people in Peru, one of the undisputed highlights of South America, the archaeological capital of the continent, and a mecca for people drawn to see Machu Picchu or learn more about the Incas, who made the city the capital of their empire and who built many of their most spectacular sites in the surrounding area and nearby Sacred Valley. Much more than just a history lesson though, the city also has a contemporary feel, and all the development and evolution hasn't tarnished the traditional appeal of the place, which combines pre-Columbian and colonial history to dramatic effect. It's this juxtaposition that affords Cusco its unique charm.

Touring the region

Every tour operator will offer a day tour of the Sacred Valley, taking in the main highlights. To see everything and to get a better sense of what lies hidden in the region though, you'll need two to three days. Ideally you'll want to stay in the Sacred Valley, probably in or close to Ollantaytambo, to make the most of the area before returning to Cusco. Tour operators in Cusco will also organise treks on either the classic Inca Trail or one of the alternative routes to the ruins, and can also arrange train fares from Poroy, just outside the city, or Ollantaytambo in the Sacred Valley to Aguas Calientes, from where you can ascend to Machu Picchu. If you're trekking to the site you'll typically need four to seven days, depending on the route you take; if you travel on the train you'll want two to three in order to explore it properly.

If you choose to travel as part of an organised tour, five days should allow you to experience most of what Cusco has to offer, along with offering a chance to visit the Sacred Valley and take the train to Machu Picchu. Ten days would allow you to see a couple of the more unusual sites as well, before setting out on the Inca Trail to trek to Machu Picchu. Allow two weeks though to see everything that southern Peru offers by combining Lake Titicaca, Cusco and a trip into the Amazon.

Cusco and around

Cusco is a major destination in its own right and you can easily spend between three and five days just exploring the labyrinthine streets, taking in the first-class museums and exhibits, indulging in the café culture and restaurant scene, and visiting the outlying ruins and archaeological sites. The city is a perfect base from which to explore the Sacred Valley, and it's an ideal access point for the Amazon as flights and overland services leave here for Puerto Maldonado, the gateway to Tambopata and Manú. Cusco is also the departure point for Aguas Calientes and Machu Picchu, either on foot or by rail.

Although justifiably famous, Cusco wears its celebrity well and, despite the huge number of visitors, isn't overwhelmingly touristy. However, over the years the steady rise in visitor numbers has inevitably had an impact and the city is no longer the quiet introduction to the Andes it once was. Hordes of gringos, hawkers, restaurant touts and tour-operator reps ensure that you're rarely troubled by peace and quiet in the city centre, yet there are still corners you can escape to and places where you can avoid the sensory overload that comes with exploring the rest of the city.

History

The city has a long and interesting history. Founded by the Incas as the capital of their empire and heartbeat of their civilisation – the name means 'Navel of the Earth' – Cusco had an essential place in Inca mythology. Established during the 12th century, it remained a fairly small concern until the expansionist Inca Pachacutec began to grow the empire, at which time Cusco evolved into the capital of this territory. Pachacutec is also thought to have commissioned many of the great buildings within the city and to have ordered its distinctive shape. Constructed so as to resemble the sacred puma, the city reflected everything the Inca stood for and believed in.

Growth came to a halt with the arrival of the Spanish. The conquistadors recognised that to be successful in Peru they had to overthrow Cusco, and after a titanic struggle they duly took control of the Inca capital on 8 November 1533 and immediately sought to superimpose themselves on the city. As a show of dominance, they built churches on top of Inca temples and established colonial properties on palaces and places that previously had significance or importance to the Incas. This layered history is still visible; so good was the Inca engineering and architecture that the stonework and foundations remain strong to this

The great stones of Sacsayhuaman are a tribute to the longevity of Inca stonework – they still stand guard above Cusco today. (KD/S)

day, even after a succession of substantial earthquakes that damaged more recent colonial structures. The Spanish stripped Cusco of its wealth and monuments, and then relocated the capital to Lima, meaning that Cusco declined as a commercial centre. It wasn't until the arrival of Hiram Bingham in the early 1900s (see page 228) and the rediscovery of archaeological sites such as Machu Picchu that this highland town began to find favour again. With the broadcasting of the existence of the city's treasures to a worldwide audience, it enjoyed an immediate resurgence – a renaissance that continues today.

Cusco highlights
The city centre

Much of Cusco is an open-air museum, look out for streets such as Calle Loreto or Hatunrumiyoc, which are lined with magnificent Inca masonry and walls that fit together like intricate jigsaw puzzles. There

What's in a name

Nomenclature and the spelling of names in Cusco is even more haphazard than elsewhere in Peru; English and Spanish spellings of Quechua names vary due to the lack of a written guide to the language. Additionally, a movement to reclaim a lot of the colonial names for the indigenous language has also caused confusion and meant that in some cases, places now have two or three differently spelled versions of their name. For instance, Cusco is also spelled as Cuzco or even as Q'osqo in Quechua. The Coricancha temple can be the Koricancha or Qoricancha; Huanchac station can be Huanchaq or Wanchac; and the ruins at Sacsayhuamen can be shown as Sacsaywamen or Saqsayhuaman. And so on. Names are interchangeable, appear randomly on maps and signs, and generally cause confusion to the uninitiated. That said, most people will know where you mean, should you ask for directions.

is also a famous stone on Hatunrumiyoc that has 12 perfectly cut angles to ensure it sits alongside its neighbours seamlessly.

La Catedral
Plaza de Armas ⊙ 10.00–18.00 Mon–Sat, 14.00–18.00 Sun ⊗ *boleto religioso*
The monumental **cathedral**, which dominates the north side of the plaza stands on the site of an Inca palace belonging to Viracocha and is flanked by two churches, Jesus María and El Triunfo. Completed in 1669, it is a significant statement of religious superiority, designed to awe and impress the indigenous population. The imposing façade gives way to a cavernous interior that is packed with treasures, including hundreds of paintings from the Cusco School, intricate wood carvings, attractive cedar wood stalls and an enormous silver altar. One of the cathedral's most well-known sights is a painting of the Last Supper by indigenous artist Marcos Zapata that has been modified to suit an Andean audience; Christ is pictured eating guinea pig as the apostles drink *chicha*, fermented maize.

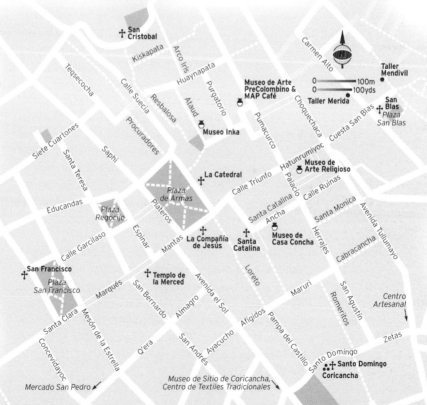

Practicalities

Most people travel to Cusco by plane; there are multiple **flights** from Lima as well as services from the other major cities in Peru. The **airport**, Aeropuerto Internacional Velasco Astete, is 5km southeast of the city. Most hotels operate pick-up services but if you aren't part of an organised tour or don't have a shuttle arranged, there are plenty of **taxis**. It is also possible to travel to Cusco **overland**. It takes around ten hours by bus or coach from Puno, 12 hours from Arequipa and more than 24 to travel from Lima. There's also a **rail** route, with services operating from Puno on the shores of Lake Titicaca. When you get to Cusco you might find that if you've arrived directly from the coast that you are easily out of breath, have a pounding headache and even feel a little nauseas; Cusco sits at just over 3,400m, meaning that your body will take a little time to adjust to the altitude. Take the first couple of days slowly, drink lots of water or coca tea, avoid excessive alcohol and don't overdo the sightseeing, especially since many of the attractions are at the top of steep cobbled streets.

Although the city has swelled and expanded rapidly in recent years, getting around Cusco is still easy as the centre is compact and the main sights all within **walking** distance. If you find yourself tiring or want to travel a little further, there are masses of registered taxis. There's also a **tourist tram**; the Tranvia trundles around a city circuit and takes about 1 1/2 hours to complete a loop. You can hop on or off at any point. The main Plaza de Armas, which today is only about half the size it used to be, is still the hub of activity, with most commercial and tourist-orientated businesses in close proximity. Tour operators, trekking agencies, shops, restaurants and bars can all be found here. Southeast from the centre, on Avenida El Sol, are the majority of **banks** and modern, bigger businesses. There are **ATMs** here too, and more can be found near the entrances of a couple of businesses and restaurants on the Plaza de Armas. **Internet cafés** are widespread, both on the Plaza de Armas and the surrounding streets. East of the centre is the **San Blas** district, which has always been Cusco's artistic quarter.

There's a **tourist information** office at the airport (⊘ 06.30–24.30 daily) but the main tourist office is located on Mantas 117-A (⊘ 07.00–19.00 Mon–Sat & 07.00–12.00 Sun), and you can buy the *boleto turístico* (see box, page 209) from here. There's also an **iPerú** office at Avenida El Sol 103 (⊘ 08.30–19.30). If you want an insider's view or advice, join the South American Explorers, who have a clubhouse at Atocsaycuchi 670 (⊛ www.saexplorers.org), although you won't need most of their services if you're on an organised tour.

Colonial architecture and Inca stonework survive side by side on the ancient streets of Cusco. (SS)

Accommodation

Exclusive
Casa Andina Private Collection Cusco Ⓦ www.casa-andina.com
Casa Catagena Ⓦ www.casacatagena.com
Fallen Angel Guest House Ⓦ www.fallenangelincusco.com
Hotel Monasterio Ⓦ www.monasterio.orient-express.com
La Casona Inkaterra Ⓦ www.inkaterra.com/en/cusco
Libertador Palacio del Inka Ⓦ www.libertador.com.pe
Marriott Ⓦ www.marriott.com
Palacio Nazarenas Ⓦ www.palacionazarenas.com

Upmarket
Hotel Arqueólogo Ⓦ www.hotelarqueologo.com
Novotel Cusco Ⓦ www.novotel.com
Picoaga Hotel Ⓦ www.picoagahotel.com
Sonesta Posadas del Inca Ⓦ www.sonesta.com

Moderate
Casa Andina Classic Cusco Koricancha Ⓦ www.casa-andina.com
Casa de Campo Ⓦ www.hotelcasadecampo.com
Casa San Blas Boutique Hotel Ⓦ www.casasanblas.com
El Balcon Ⓦ www.balconcusco.com
Hostal Corihuasi Ⓦ www.corihuasi.com
Hotel Rumi Punku Ⓦ www.rumipunku.com
Loreto Boutique Hotel Ⓦ www.loretoboutiquehotel.com

To the right of the main building is **El Triunfo**, the first Christian church in Cusco, which contains the famous **Señor de los Temblores** or Lord of the Earthquakes, a black-skinned Christ figure nailed to a cross who is considered the city's guardian after he was paraded round the plaza during a devastating earthquake in 1650 and the tremors subsided.

Iglesia de la Compañía de Jesús
Plaza de Armas ⊙ 11.00–12.00 & 15.00–16.00 Mon–Sat ⚿ *boleto religioso*
Overlooking the southern side of the plaza and competing with the cathedral for prominence and people's attention is the grand, Jesuit **Compañía Church**, which sits atop the Inca Huayna Capac's palace. Construction started during the late-16th century and caused

Los Apus Hotel Ⓦ www.losapushotel.com
Marqueses Ⓦ www.hotelmarqueses.com
Orquidea Real Hostal Ⓦ www.orquidea.net
Second Home Cusco Ⓦ www.secondhomecusco.com

Budget
Amaru Hostal Ⓦ www.cusco.net/amaru
Casa de la Gringa Ⓦ www.casadelagringa.com
Hostal Marani Ⓦ www.hostalmarani.com
Niños Hotel Ⓦ www.ninoshotel.com

Eating out

Bistrot 370 (centre; fusion) Triunfo 370 Ⓣ 224 908
Chicha (centre; Nuevo Andino) Regocijo 261 Ⓣ 240 520
Cicciolina (centre; Italian) Triunfo 393 Ⓣ 239 510
Don Esteban & Don Pancho (centre; café & bakery) Av El Sol 765A Ⓣ 252 526
El Buen Pastor (centre; café & bakery) Cuesta San Blas 579
Fallen Angel (centre; Peruvian), Plazoleta de las Nazarenas
Jack's Café (centre; international, café) Choquechaca 509 Ⓣ 254 606
Granja Heidi (San Blas; Peruvian, café) Cuesta San Blas 525 Ⓣ 238 383
Greens (centre; organic café) Santa Catalina Angosta 235 Ⓣ 243 399
Inka Grill (centre; Nuevo Andino) Portal de Panes 115 Ⓣ 262 992
Limo (centre; Peruvian) Portal de Carnes 236 Ⓣ 240 668
MAP Café (centre; international) Plaza de las Nazarenas 231
Pachapapa (centre; Peruvian) Plazoleta San Blas 120 Ⓣ 241 318

consternation, as it seemed to rival the cathedral. Badly damaged by the 1650 earthquake, it was finally finished in 1668 and duly did match its rival on the plaza, to the outrage of the pope. Often dark inside, its interior is in fact impressive, with a particularly beautiful gilded altar and a number of historically important and valuable art works that show a wealth of period detail.

Iglesia y Monasterio de Santa Catalina
Santa Catalina Angosta ⊘ 09.00–17.00 daily
Standing a couple of blocks west of the main Plaza de Armas is this small, interesting convent, dating from the first decade of the 17th century. **Santa Catalina Church and Monastery** was built on the site of the Acllawasi, where the Inca housed his chosen Virgins of the Sun,

and it was another attempt by the conquering religion to impose itself on what was there before. These days the convent contains a collection of colonial and religious art, including a number of fine examples from the Cusco School. Statues of Jesus covered in horrific wounds, designed to show the indigenous people that he suffered more than they did on a daily basis, are interesting if a little grisly.

Templo de la Merced
Calle Mantas ⊙ 08.30–12.00 & 14.00–17.00 Mon–Sat

Wrecked by the earthquake in 1650, **La Merced Church**, which stands to the southwest of the Plaza de Armas, is the third-most significant church in Cusco. It was originally built in the mid 1530s, and after being damaged was carefully restored and still boasts a beautiful façade and colonial cloister. Inside is a museum of religious art (which is a superb repository for Cusco School paintings) and a cage containing a priceless solid gold monstrance (a vessel used to hold the communion Host) which is encrusted with diamonds and precious stones. Below in the catacombs are the remains of two of the conquistador leaders, Diego de Almagro and Gonzalo Pizarro, brother of Francisco.

Iglesia y convento de San Francisco
Plaza de San Francisco ⊙ 09.00–16.00 Mon–Sat

The imposing and austere **San Francisco Church and Convent** stands on its eponymous square, southwest of the Plaza de Armas, and is best known for its collection of colonial artwork by celebrated artists including Zapata and Quispe Tito. There are also some attractive frescoes in the church, and macabre collections of bones and skulls in the crypts.

Cusco countryside walk

Des**t**inos
turísticos Group Perú

We suggest you spend an extra day in the Cusco area to explore the beautiful, tranquil countryside surrounding the city. The rolling hills and fertile river valleys with mountain views, Inca ruins and colonial villages are great for walking. We offer a range of half- and full-day guided walks (no camping) from easy to more demanding; you choose your level. Join us, the experts in the region, for a friendly excursion: have fun, get some exercise and learn a lot.

The tourist ticket

To see many of Cusco's primary sights and to explore some of the outlying archaeological sites, you'll need a tourist ticket or *boleto turístico*. This can be bought from the main tourist office at Calle Mantas 117-A, the office on Avenida El Sol and from Casa Garcilaso on the corner of Garcilaso and Heladeros. The ticket provides access to many of the most popular places of interest and is the only way of getting into some of the most important attractions. It costs S/130 (at the time of going to print) for adults and is valid for ten days from time of purchase, with one visit to each sight allowed during that time; guards at each sight will punch a hole in the ticket against the relevant site when you arrive. You probably won't check off everything on the ticket in the time you have available, but you will certainly want to see most of the sights in Cusco and access the nearby ruins and attractions of the Sacred Valley. Sights on the ticket include: Museo de Arte Contemporáneo de la Municipalidad de Cusco, Museo Historico Regional, Museo de Sitio Coricancha, Museo de Arte Popular, Centro Qosqo de Arte Nativo, Monumento al Inka Pachacuteq, Sacsayhuaman, Q'enko, Puca Pucara, Tambo Machay, Pikillacta, Tipón, Pisac, Chinchero and Ollantaytambo.

There is also a **religious tourist ticket**, *boleto religioso*, which is valid for entry to a number of Cusco's main religious sites and costs S/50.

Coricancha and Santo Domingo
Plazoleta Santo Domingo ⊘ 08.30–18.30 Mon–Sat, 14.00–17.00 Sun

This unlikely pair of buildings most clearly illustrates the conquistador desire to subjugate the indigenous Inca culture. The **Inca Temple of the Sun**, Coricancha, dating from the mid 15th century, was the most impressive and significant temple not just in Cusco but in the Inca Empire. Constructed from exceptionally fine stonework, it has a smooth, curving outer wall that stands 6m high. At the temple's height it would have been home to 4,000 priests and attendants dedicated to worshipping the sun. On the solstice the sun's rays fall on a particular niche in a feat of clever engineering and astronomical observation. Mummies of preserved Inca rulers were also kept here in special niches. Decked in gold and decorated with precious metals and stones, the temple contained life-size gold figures, fields of golden corn, a solid gold altar and a giant golden sun. The site was stripped by the Spanish, who stole the panels of gold and the precious stones. Francisco Pizarro's brother, Juan, was given the site but he died shortly after during a battle at Sacsayhuaman.

Shopping in Cusco

There is an exceptional range of shops in Cusco; the city is considered one of the best places to buy **handicrafts** and you'll be spoiled for choice when choosing hand-woven textiles, ponchos, blankets, woodcarvings, picture frames, ceramics, reproductions of Cusco School religious paintings and silver jewellery.

The streets around the plaza are good places to start looking, especially on Plateros and Triunfo. Alternatively, head up to San Blas and browse the artisan shops and market stalls there: **Taller Olave** at Plaza San Blas 651, **Taller Mendivil** on Cuesta San Bas and **Taller Merida** at Carmen Alto 133 are among the best workshops. If it's alpaca goods and clothing you want, try **Alpaca III** at Ruinas 472, **Alpaca's Best** on Plaza Nazarenas, **Kuna** on Plaza Regocijo or at Portal de Panes 127, and **World Alpaca** at Portal de Carnes 232. Another shop of note is the **Centro de Textiles Tradicionales del Cusco** (☺ 07.30–20.30 Mon–Sat) at Avenida El Sol 603, which is a non-profit, fairtrade outfit supporting weavers and communities specialising in textiles. Prices are a little higher than elsewhere but the quality is better and more of your money is going to the people who actually do the work. There are also high-quality textiles and weavings for sale in the courtyard of the Museo Inka. You can see more examples of handicrafts for sale in the courtyard of the Museo de Arte Precolombino on Plaza Nazarenas. The **Centro Artesanal Cusco** (☺ 09.00–22.00) at the southern end of Avenida El Sol is the largest indoor craft market in Cusco, with a vast array of stalls and items for sale.

For **antiques**, head to San Blas and explore the shops there. Whilst in the district look out too for **art galleries** and **ceramic workshops** where you can watch people at work and also buy the goods they produce.

For a different type of experience, go to the **Mercado San Pedro** near the San Pedro Railway Station, where you'll see fresh food, mounds of meat, household items and all sorts of other produce for sale. There are also food stalls and fresh juice stands here. Essentially for locals, who come here to shop and gossip, it's a great place to get a glimpse of daily life. Be aware, however, that pickpockets have been known to operate amidst the hustle and bustle of the crowded market.

Juan Pizarro bequeathed the temple to the Dominicans, who constructed an uninspiring Baroque church on top of the exquisitely crafted Inca masonry. However, the engineering of the **Santo Domingo Church** and convent wasn't as sophisticated as that of the Incas and during repeated earthquakes the church collapsed and had to be rebuilt, whilst the Inca foundations endured. These expertly shaped blocks remain the epitome of Inca stonework and are probably the finest intact Inca masonry in Cusco.

The Coricancha and Santo Domingo (SS)

Museo de Sitio de Coricancha

Av El Sol ⊘ 9.30-17.30 Mon-Sat, 08.00-13.00 Sun ⊜ boleto turístico

Housed in a subterranean set of three rooms across from the Coricancha itself, the small **Coricancha Museum** is actually much less interesting than the main site. There's a collection of ceramics, textiles and crafted metal objects from both pre- and Inca eras but they pale in comparison to the buildings above and the stories associated with them.

Museo de Arte Precolombino

Casa Cabrera, Plaza de las Nazarenas ⓦ http://map.perucultural.org.pe ⊘ 10.00-22.00 daily

Within an old convent that was first converted into a conquistador's colonial mansion and then into the sophisticated **Pre-Columbian Art Museum** are some exceptionally beautiful and well-presented artefacts. Almost 500 pieces of pre-Columbian art are presented here, dating from 1250 to 1532 and showcasing the skills and achievements of the Nazca, Moche, Huari, Chimú and Inca cultures. Carvings, ceramics, pottery, jewellery and stunning silver and gold metalwork are carefully curated and clearly lit. Carefully chosen, the museum gives you a good impression of the variety of skills possessed by these cultures without being overwhelming. There's also an excellent restaurant, the **MAP Café**, in a transparent box in the courtyard.

Museo de Casa Concha

Santa Catalina Ancha ⊘ 09.00-17.00 Mon-Sat

The **Casa Concha Museum** was opened to house the artefacts returned to Peru by Yale University after they were removed by Bingham from Machu Picchu (see page 228). The museum is in a renovated colonial mansion that was constructed on top of an Inca palace; there are fine fireplaces, ceilings and other architectural details to see that are worth the visit in their own right. The museum has a number of interesting original photographs, a selection of ceramics, stone and metal objects, fragments of bone and a virtually complete skeleton of a male aged around 25 years old, used to debunk Bingham's theory that Machu

Entertainment in Cusco

Cusco has some of the best nightlife and entertainment in Peru, centred on the Plaza de Armas, with a raft of pubs and watering holes, both traditional and modern, catering for locals and visitors alike, along with sophisticated bars and raucous *discotecas*, which open late and get going later. If these are all a little too rowdy, then retreat to San Blas where there's a selection of laidback alternatives.

Cross Keys (centre; pub) Triunfo 350
Fallen Angel (centre; bar) Plazoleta de las Nazarenas
KmO (San Blas; bar) Tandapata 100
Los Perros (centre; bar) Tecsecocha 436
Mama Africa (centre; club) Portal de Panes 190
Siete Angelitos (San Blas; bar) Siete Angelitos 638
Ukuku's (centre; bar & club), Plateros 31

Picchu was populated largely by chosen women. As pieces are returned and studied so the collection will grow. There's also a large site model and an interesting virtual tour of Machu Picchu that puts the place in context and explains elements of the site and Inca daily life. It's well worth a visit, especially if you're going to visit the ruins later.

Museo Inka
Cnr Atud and Tucumán ⊘ 09.00–18.00 Mon–Sat
To get an overview of Peruvian history through the various pre-Columbian cultures and especially the Inca era, visit the superb **Inca Museum**. It is housed in the grand **Admiral's Palace**, an impressive colonial mansion that once belonged to Admiral Francisco Aldrete Maldonado and which is worth a visit in its own right; the main staircase climbing to a balconied first floor is guarded by mythical creatures and is especially impressive.

Along with the world's largest display of *queros*, Inca drinking vessels, there are good displays of ceramics, textiles, mummies and jewellery. The architectural models of archaeological sites help put the cultures and places into context whilst also exploring the impact of the Spanish conquest and the legacy of civilisations such as the Incas. In the mansion's courtyard you'll find a collective of women weaving and making traditional textiles that are wonderfully intricate and available to buy.

Museo de Arte Religioso
Cnr Hatunrumiyoc and Palacio ⊘ 08.00-12.30 & 15.00-18.00 Mon-Fri ⊗ *boleto turístico*

A former Inca Palace that was then taken over by the Archbishop of Cusco, the building has now been converted into the **Museum of Religious Art** and houses colonial religious paintings. The house is architecturally interesting, boasting Moorish-style balconies and doorways, carved wooden ceilings and pretty stained-glass windows. The paintings themselves are impressively detailed and offer a valuable insight into the past.

Iglesia de San Blas
Cuesta San Blas ⊘ 10.00-18.00 Mon-Sat, 14.00-18.00 Sun ⊗ *boleto religioso*

This rather small, simple looking adobe church is reputed to be the oldest in Cusco. Don't let the deceptively simple façade put you off popping inside to see the Baroque gold-leaf altar and the stunning carved cedar-wood pulpit. The pulpit has been crafted from a single tree trunk with elaborate detailing and is thought to be an example of some of the most impressive colonial woodwork in the Americas. Legend has it that upon his death, the skull of the man responsible for the work was placed at the feet of St Paul, towards the top of the pulpit, as tribute for the magnificent carving.

Around Cusco highlights
Sacsayhuaman
⊘ daily ⊗ *boleto turístico*

Above Cusco stand the extraordinary, **enormous ruins** of Sacsayhuaman. Built as a **fortress-temple**, the site dates from the mid 15th century but took many years to finish. Huge blocks of stone were moved to the site from a good distance away and worked into precise shapes, cut to fit angles and corners to such a degree that they slot together impossibly tightly. Stones over 8.5m high and unimaginably heavy – the largest is thought to weigh more than 350 tonnes – have been hauled into place and then carefully built around. The main walls remain today, which were built in a zigzag formation about 400m long to ensure an attacker always exposed a flank during an assault. They are said to resemble the teeth of a puma; Cusco was thought to have been built in the shape of a puma, with Sacsayhuaman forming the head of the animal.

Behind the three-tiered walls are the remains of three circular towers up to 22m in diameter, used for storing food and water. There are great views over Cusco from here. Before the walls is a broad plaza, known as the **Esplanade**, and from its far side rises a small mound, **Rodadero**,

The massive, tiered walls of Sacsayhuaman, set above Cusco (Y/D)

known as the Inca's seat or throne, with more carefully cut steps, seats and altars. Behind this are some more structures, including tunnels cut into the hillside, and a series of smoothed rock slopes that are used as slides by children.

This site was also famously the scene of one of the bloodiest battles between the Incas and the conquistadors, when the rebel Inca, Manco Capac, staged a rebellion and attempted to re-take Cusco from the Spanish in 1536, two years after the initial conquest. Having captured Sacsayhuaman, he laid siege to Cusco. A desperate break out by the conquistadors to avoid defeat saw the siege turn into a brutal, bloody fight, where Spanish cavalry proved decisive. Stories about the battle finish with accounts of thousands of corpses being left as carrion for the condors.

You can visit the ruins as part of an organised tour; drive to the site or tackle the steep half hour walk from the Plaza de Armas. The ruins cover a huge area and take time to explore properly. Impressive at any time, they are perhaps at their most spectacular during the festival of Inti Raymi, when a huge re-enactment of an Inca ceremony is held at the site.

Q'enko, Puca Pucara and Tambo Machay ruins

☺ daily ⌗ *boleto turístico*

Beyond Sacsayhuaman there are **a series of ruins** that can be visited as part of an organised tour; combine them with a trip to Sacsayhuaman itself for a fuller day exploring. Closest to Sacsayhuaman and just under a kilometre due east of the site is **Q'enko** (☺ 07.00–18.00 daily). This giant limestone boulder is covered in channels as well as carvings of a condor, llama and snakes, and conceals a carved altar in its cave-like core. North of Q'enko, about 1½ hours' walk away and just off the Cusco to Pisac road stands **Puca Pucara** (☺ 07.00–18.00 daily). This site, whose name means 'Red Fort', is thought to have been a hunting lodge or possibly a guard post on the approach road to Cusco and is the simplest of the three sites. There are pleasant views of the countryside from here.

A short distance further north and about 300m from the Cusco to Pisac road, stands **Tambo Machay** (☺ 07.00–18.00 daily), which is sometimes referred to as Los Baños del Inca or the Inca Baths. A spring issues from a hillside close by and the water is channelled through a sophisticated series of aqueducts to a number of ceremonial pools and terraces. Rather than bathing though, the site was probably used for the ritual worship of water, with the high-quality stonework and carefully cut shapes suggesting that it was primarily used by priests and Inca nobility.

Sights east of Cusco

Travelling east from Cusco there are a number of sites worth seeing as part of a half-day trip. **Tipón** (☺ 07.00–18.00 daily ⌗ *boleto turístico*) lies about 32km away from Cusco and is a substantial archaeological site made up of some large terraces. The clever irrigation network here hints at the site being an experimental farm much like Moray in the Sacred Valley. **Pikillacta** and **Rumicolca** (☺ 07.00–18.00 daily ⌗ *boleto turístico*) are a little further east still; Pikillacta means 'Place of the Fleas' and is the only major non-Inca site in the area. Dating from 1100, the large ceremonial centre and its defensive wall here are attributed to the Huari culture, who had their centre at Ayacucho. Rumicolca, less than 1.5km east is an imposing gate arch built by the Inca on Huari foundations; the latter stonework is substantially more sophisticated. Finally **Raqchi**, almost 130km southeast of Cusco, is the remains of the Temple of Viracocha, once one of the most important shrines of the Inca Empire. Sadly, the Spanish conquistadors destroyed the 22 mighty columns that supported the shrine roof and the site is still in a state of disrepair.

Inti Raymi celebrations (GT/PP)

Festivals

Cusco is home to some of the most exciting, energetic festivals and fiestas in Peru's calendar of events. Visit at the appropriate time to see the city at its traditional, vibrant best but beware that accommodation books up far in advance. Cusco is a great place to spend **Semana Santa** (Easter week) in late March or early April, as there are dramatic processions throughout the city, building towards a parade on Easter Monday led by El Señor de los Temblores, the 'Lord of the Earthquakes', the giant crucifix kept in the cathedral (see page 203). Early May sees the highlands in general celebrate the **Fiesta de las Cruces** (the Festival of the Crosses), where local communities decorate large wooden crosses that are then displayed on hilltops. **Corpus Christi** in early June sees effigies of celebrated saints carried through the city and then displayed in the cathedral for a week. The biggest event, however, is **Inti Raymi**, the celebration of the winter solstice, which takes place on 24 June but seems to go on for days before and after; Cusco's carnival is often the start point for the celebrations. Folk dances, parades with participants dressed in elaborate Inca costume and huge processions culminate in a giant pageant that takes place on the flat central plaza of Sacsayhuaman, above the city. A careful re-enactment of an ancient festival, it is hugely significant and an essential expression of folk culture. The year culminates on 24 December with the **Santuranticuy Festival**, where artisans gather in the Plaza de Armas to display and sell traditional carved figures, ceramics and *retablos* (carefully crafted wooden boxes containing intricately decorated scenes and figures).

El Valle Sagrado

The Sacred Valley, through which the Urubamba River flows, is just to the north of Cusco. It's a fascinating, historic stretch that was a key area for the Incas and which is still home to a number of important villages and towns where typical traditions are maintained. There are also a host of essential sights, from Sunday markets to unique archaeological ruins that tell the story of the Incas in the area. Along with history and culture, the valley is home to all sorts of activities and sports, making it a destination in its own right rather than just an add-on to a stay in Cusco.

Pisac

Pisac, sometimes spelled Pisaq, can be found at the eastern end of the Sacred Valley, 32km northeast of Cusco. A traditional place, the colonial town built on an Inca settlement boasts some impressive Inca ruins and a fully functioning **Sunday market** that's essentially for the locals although it's now a little touristy. The outdoor market is lively and a great place to pick up handicrafts, with artisans offering all manner of goods for sale in and around the central square. Clothes, ponchos, weavings, musical instruments and carvings are all here, and there's also a food and produce market on the main square. Look out for locals dressed in traditional clothing. During the week the town hosts mildly more muted markets on Tuesdays and Thursdays, although such are the visitor numbers that the place is never quiet. Busy at the best of times, Pisac becomes even more so from 16 to 18 July when the town hosts a tumultuous party for the Virgen del Carmen Festival, which includes dancing, drinking and parades with people dressed in outlandish costumes.

The Inca ruins

☺ 08.00–17.30 daily *boleto turístico*

On a hillside above the town of Pisac is a substantial Inca **fortress-cum-ceremonial centre** that has excellent views of the valley and surrounding countryside. You can either drive to the site, or climb up from Pisac; the two-hour walk is quite long and arduous but rewarding, arriving at the triangular plateau where the main ceremonial centre stands.

On an upper level stands the **Templo del Sol (Temple of the Sun)**, which was used as an astronomical observatory. Within it stands one of only a few surviving *intihuatanas*, the so-called 'hitching post of the

Practicalities

The Sacred Valley, about 16km north of Cusco, is best explored on an organised tour, which can be arranged in Cusco; a full circuit is over 160km long, so logistically a tour makes sense. Typically a tour will combine a number of the sites in the valley in the course of a day. Better though are the tours that take two to three days to see everything and stop overnight in places such as Urubamba and Ollantaytambo as well. There's so much to see, it makes no sense to rush through. Day trips from Cusco are busiest on Sundays, to coincide with the markets in Chinchero and Pisac and tend to follow a similar route. Although these markets are must-see stops, try to arrange to travel in a different direction and arrive at different times. Alternatively, stay over

Accommodation

Upmarket

Aranwa Sacred Valley (Urubamba) Ⓦ www.aranwahotels.com
Casa Andina Private Collection (Urubamba) www.casa-andina.com
Hostal Sauce (Ollantaytambo) Ⓦ www.hostalsauce.com.pe
Libertador Valle Sagrado Lodge (Urubamba) www.vallesagradolodge.com
Pakaritampu (Ollantaytambo) Ⓦ www.pakaritampu.com
Rio Sagrado Hotel (Urubamba) Ⓦ www.riosagradohotel.com
Sol y Luna Lodge (Urubamba) Ⓦ www.hotelsolyluna.com
Sonesta Posada del Inca Sacred Valley (Urubamba) Ⓦ www.sonesta.com

Moderate

El Albergue (Ollantaytambo) Ⓦ www.elalbergue.com
Hostal Sauce (Ollantaytambo) Ⓦ www.hostalsauce.com.pe
Hotel San Agustín Monasterio de la Recoleta (Urubamba)
Ⓦ www.hotelessanagustin.com.pe
K'uychi Rumi (Urubamba) Ⓦ www.urubamba.com
Pisac Inn (Pisac) Ⓦ www.pisacinn.com

sun'; another is at Machu Picchu. The exact use of these aesthetically pleasing stone sculptures is unknown but it is thought Inca priests used them during astronomical and religious ceremonies to determine the seasons. Adjacent to this is the more basic **Templo de la Luna (Temple of the Moon)**. A series of water channels lead to a ritual bathing station close by. Climb to the top and admire the defensive

somewhere and be on site well before the first bus makes its way out of Cusco. In **Pisac**, there's an **ATM** on the main square but you're better off coming with cash from Cusco. A handful of places to stay make stopping over possible and there are a number of cafés and restaurants as well. **Urubamba** has some good places to stay and eat, and there are ATMs on the main road and **internet cafés** dotted throughout the town. There's virtually nowhere to stay in **Chinchero**, meaning that most people visit only as part of a tour, moving on to somewhere better at the end of the day. **Ollantaytambo** stands on the **rail** line between Cusco and Aguas Calientes, halfway between the two, and there are also good **road** connections to Cusco (96km southeast) and Urubamba (24km east). There are no banks in Ollantaytambo but there are a couple of ATMs on the Plaza de Armas. There are several internet cafés here, too.

Budget

Hotel Pisaq (Pisac) Ⓦ www.hotelpisaq.com
KB Tambo Hostal (Ollantaytambo) Ⓦ www.kbperu.com
Las Chullpas (Urubamba) Ⓦ www.chullpas.uhupi.com
Las Orquideas (Ollantaytambo) Ⓦ www.hotellasorquideas.com/pe
Paz y Luz (Pisac) www.pazyluzperu.com

Eating out

Café Mayu (Ollantaytambo; café) Train station Ⓣ 204 014
El Maizal (Urubamba; Nuevo Andino) Main Rd Ⓣ 201 454
Hearts Café (Ollantaytambo; café) Plaza de Armas Ⓣ 204 078
Puka Rumi (Ollantaytambo; fusion) Ventiderio Ⓣ 204 091
Restaurante Cuchara de Palo (Pisac; Nuevo Andino) Plaza Constitución Ⓣ 203 062
Tres Kerros (Urubamba; Nuevo Andino) Cnr Highway & Señor de Torrechayoc Ⓣ 201 701
Tunupa (Urubamba; Nuevo Andino) Main Rd Ⓣ 963 0206
Ulrike's Café (Pisac; international) Plaza de Armas Ⓣ 203 195

ramparts and sweeping agricultural terraces that step down the steep slopes to the south and east of the site in broad curves. Behind the site in the Kitamayo Gorge is a cliff pocked with Inca tombs, although they have all been plundered and are now empty. To wander throughout the site and really get a feel for all its features you'll need three to four hours.

Urubamba

Sitting centrally in the Sacred Valley, Urubamba is around 80km from Cusco and can be reached via Pisac or Chinchero. It's the biggest and busiest town in the valley, although it is less appealing than many of the smaller places and has less to offer the casual visitor in terms of historical sights. The attractive Plaza de Armas is home, however, to a twin-towered **colonial church**, and there are a couple of exceptional sights close to town although neither is all that accessible, as the main roads don't go anywhere nearby. Organised tours from Cusco should ferry you to each sight though.

Salineras de Maras
⊘ 09.00–17.00 daily

The Salineras de Maras, also known as Salinas, is an ancient set of **terraces and pools** where salt is extracted from subterranean spring water. Thousands of shallow pools hold the water, which evaporates to leave salt crystals.

Shallow pools spill down the slopes of Sal

These are then gathered by hand, in backbreaking conditions, just as they have been since Inca times. The pools step down a narrow valley and make quite a surreal sight. The scale of the place is dizzying and it's only when you spot a small figure standing ankle deep in saltwater that you realise how substantial the enterprise is.

Giant, concentric terraces at Moray (AB/PP)

Moray
⊘ 09.00–17.00 daily

Moray, south of Salineras, is an **Inca farm and laboratory** that comprises a number of giant concentric ringed terraces, set deep into natural hollows in the earth; the largest has 15 steps. As you descend the terraces, the climate changes, and this allowed the Incas to experiment with farming techniques and crop types. Today, the terraces

eras de Maras. (GH/S)

have been repaired and are still used to demonstrate what happened here as a sort of living museum; visit after the rainy season to see them coloured green.

Chinchero

⌖ *boleto turístico* to enter the main plaza & ruins

The gloriously located **village** of Chinchero, 27km northwest of Cusco on a high plateau, is held to be the mythical birthplace of the rainbow and is renowned for its **Sunday market**. Considered more authentic even than the market in Pisac, most of Chinchero's main sellers set out blankets as stalls in the principal square in front of a smart **17th-century church** (⊘ 09.00–17.00 Mon–Sat, 09.00–18.00 Sun) filled with pretty, faded floral frescoes and religious designs. The market is a particularly good place to pick up woollen items, textiles and ceramics. Views from the square are sumptuous, with the peaks of Salcantay and the summits of the Vilcabamba and Urubamba mountains clear to see; sunsets from up here are particularly spectacular. Beyond the village are a series of **Inca terraces** and some carefully sculpted Inca stones, steps and channels.

Ollantaytambo

At the far end of the Sacred Valley is Ollantaytambo, a great place to spend time and the final stop before Aguas Calientes and Machu Picchu. The **town**, known locally as Ollanta, has a superb setting on the floor of a steep-sided gorge, surrounded by peaks. The historic **town square**, a fine example of Inca planning, is attractive and vibrant, while narrow cobblestone streets lead off to reveal irrigation channels, quiet courtyards and residential blocks that have housed people since the 13th century. A small museum, **Museo Catcco** (⊙ 08.00–17.30 daily), houses a wealth of information about the area and the town.

The Inca ruins

⊙ 07.00–17.30 daily *boleto turistico*

The enormous Inca ruins that sit above a series of terraces behind the town of Ollantaytambo were built by the Inca Pachacutec as a **fortress-temple**, and were used both for protection and for astronomical observation. Ollantaytambo was one of the few places where the Incas defeated the Spanish conquistadors; the rebel Manco Inca retreated here after defeat at Sacsayhuaman and successfully defended the position in a pitched battle in 1536. He was later forced to flee though when the conquistadors returned with reinforcements.

Between the town and the bottom of the ruins are the **Baños de la Ñusta**, or Princess Baths, where ceremonial washing would have taken place. Rows of substantial terraces climb a hillside beyond this to a flattened ridge, where some of the Inca's most impressive stonework

Adventure sports

The Sacred Valley is developing into one of the prime adventure sports destinations in Peru, with world-class activities easily accessible and catering to all skill and thrill levels. **Trekking** is the number one activity, with countless opportunities for getting into the hills. **Mountain biking** has taken off and there are routes that range from easy to rigorous, with one- to five-day rides through the Sacred Valley and the surrounding area. **Horseriding** is also available and the ranches close to Urubamba are the best places to arrange trips. **White-water rafting** is well established, with river runs offering everything from Grade II to Grade V rapids. The Urubamba River offers a good introduction, whilst the Apurimac River is more challenging. Alternatively, you can go **hot-air ballooning** or **paragliding** and enjoy superb aerial views of the valley.

stands. Steps ascend between the terraces in a steep staircase. At the top, an elegant doorway leads to the main site and adjacent to this is the **Temple of Ten Niches**. Beyond are six enormous granite blocks, carefully carved to fit together, which make up the **Temple of the Sun**. There are great views across the valley from this point, to the quarry where the stone was cut and to the Inca granaries high on an opposite hillside. A path climbs the hill behind the temple to some residential areas, a defensive wall and yet more terraces.

Aguas Calientes and around

In some respects, Aguas Calientes is literally the end of the line. The trains from Cusco and the Sacred Valley come to a stop here and there's nowhere really to travel to beyond. For many years the town, officially known as Machu Picchu Pueblo but hardly ever referred to as such, existed solely as a staging point for people trying to access Machu Picchu or recover after trekking to the ruins; the town's economy is still based almost exclusively around tourists. It was a pretty grubby gringo haunt with a frontier feel. More recently, however, the place has undergone a makeover and whilst the cheap pizza joints and bunkhouses are still here, there's a much more cosmopolitan air and a far wider range of accommodation and restaurants than there used to be. One thing hasn't changed though, and that's the stunning setting, alongside the Urubamba River and in the lee of the most magnificent ruins in the Americas, which are just a short bus ride away or a slightly longer trek uphill.

Aguas Calientes – also known as Machu Picchu Pueblo – is the base for visitors exploring the celebrated Inca site. (CH/S)

Aguas Calientes and around highlights

The town centre

Aguas Calientes has little for the casual visitor in terms of historic or cultural attractions. The **Museo de Sitio Manuel Chávez Ballón** (Manuel Chávez Ballón Site Museum; ⊙ 09.00–17.00 Wed–Sun), which can be found at the foot of the climb to Machu Picchu – by the bridge that crosses the Urubamba River – has some good information on Machu Picchu and its excavations and discoveries. Visit before you climb to the ruins to build anticipation, or after a tour of the site to help put some of the things you've seen in context. The detail on Inca building methods is especially enlightening. There's a small botanical garden here, too.

Baños Termales

⊙ 05.00–20.30 daily

To the north of the town are a series of **hot springs**, which have lent their name to the town. Around a ten-minute walk up Pachacutec, they are frequently crowded and a little dirty and sulphurous but there's nowhere else to soak your aching limbs after you've hiked so lots of people still flock here. The springs are widely used by the locals as well. Along with a couple of hot pools, there's one filled with ice-cold mountain water that frequently catches people out. Perhaps save pampering yourself until you're back in Cusco.

Putucusi

⊙ dawn to dusk daily

Just to the southwest of town stands Putucusi, a **sacred mountain** with sumptuous views of Machu Picchu which is immediately opposite on the far side of the Urubamba River. There's a path to the top that's a scramble up vertical ladders in places and it takes almost 1½ hours. The effort is worth it though for the alternative view of the celebrated ruins across the valley, which lie straggled along a ridge, with terraces stepping steeply down the cliff face. The descent is quicker but watch where you put your feet as the trail is uneven and some of the short climbs are treacherous if wet.

Fixed ladders make the ascent of Putucusi a rather demanding challenge. (L)

Practicalities

To get to Aguas Calientes you have to catch the **train** most usually from Ollantaytambo in the sacred valley, go overland by **road** to Santa Teresa and then sneak in the back door, or trek the **Inca Trail** and descend from Machu Picchu.

The train service between Ollantaytambo and Aguas operates regularly in each direction. There are three grades of train travelling from Poroy, just outside Cusco – Expedition, Vistadome and Hiram Bingham – which increase in comfort and price exponentially. The Expedition and Vistadome services are comparable, whilst the Hiram Bingham service from Poroy is the most luxurious and elegant, invoking the spirit of the 1920s' Pullman services; you'll be incredibly conspicuous in your lavish carriage of polished wood, gleaming glass and glittering cutlery though. Most tour operators will structure a trip using these services. A small number offer an arduous overland route that goes via Santa Maria and Santa Teresa instead, but the trip is time consuming and tricky, so isn't widely embraced. Trains from Aguas Calientes leave from the train station to the east of town, while local trains to Hidroelectrica, on the way to Santa Teresa, operate from the older station on Avenida Imperio de los Incas.

Accommodation

Accommodation in the town is very varied with something for every budget. At the top end are some of Peru's better and most expensive properties, including one adjacent to Machu Picchu itself. There are also a couple of mid-range options and a number of budget hostels. To ensure you stay in the place you'd like, make sure to plan your trip well in advance, especially during the peak season of May–September.

Upmarket
Inkaterra Machu Picchu Hotel Ⓦ www.inkaterra.com
Machu Picchu Sanctuary Lodge Ⓦ www.machupicchu.orient-express.com
Sumaq Machu Picchu Hotel Ⓦ www.sumaqhotelperu.com

Moderate
Gringo Bills Ⓦ www.gringobills.com
El Mapi Ⓦ www.elmapihotel.com

Train tickets can sell out well in advance, especially during the peak months May to September; your tour operator should book them several days ahead of time. If arranging travel is down to you, book online at Ⓦ www.perurail.com, who run virtually all the train services, print your e-ticket and change it at the station for an embarkation ticket before checking in. Make sure you leave enough time before departure to do this. The only competition comes from Inca Rail (Ⓦ www.incarail.com), although they have a vastly reduced timetable.

In Aguas, the **bus** for Machu Picchu leaves from a pick-up point close to where the train tracks cross a small stream; there's a ticket office nearby that opens at 05.15 daily if your tour operator hasn't arranged the fare.

Aguas Calientes essentially comprises two streets, Avenida Imperio de los Incas, which has train tracks running down its length and Avenida Pachacutec, which hosts the majority of the hotels and restaurants.

There's an **iPerú** office (☉ 09.00-13.00 & 14.00-20.00 daily) in the INC building on Pachacutec. The **Machu Picchu ticket office** (☉ 05.00-22.00 daily) is in the same building; if you're travelling with a tour group or trekking, then your agent ought to have arranged a ticket in advance. It's not possible to buy an entrance ticket for Machu Picchu at the ruins, so they must be sourced in Aguas Calientes or in Cusco in advance. There are **ATMs** on Avenida Imperio de los Incas and Avenida Pachacutec and you can change money all over town, although the rates tend to be in the *casas de cambios*' favour; bring plenty of cash to avoid losing out on the exchange. **Internet cafés** are widespread and easy to find.

Hostal Mayurina Ⓦ www.hostalmayurina.com
Rupa Wasi Ⓦ www.rupawasi.net
Wiracocha Inn Ⓦ www.wiracochainn.com

Budget
Hostal Machu Picchu Ⓦ www.hostalmachupicchu.com
Hostal Presidente Ⓦ www.hostalpresidente.com
La Cabaña Hostal Ⓦ www.lacabanamachupicchu.com

Eating out

Café Inkaterra (Nuevo Andino) Machu Picchu Pueblo Hotel ☏ 211 122
Indio Feliz (international fusion) Lloque Yupanqui 4 ☏ 211 090
Inka Wasi (Peruvian and international) Av Pachacutec
Pueblo Viejo (Peruvian) Av Pachacutec 108
Toto's House (Peruvian, pizza) Av Imperio de los Incas
Tree House (Nuevo Andino) Huanacaure ☏ 211 101

Machu Picchu

Northwest of Cusco, 120km away amidst a series of ridges and valleys cloaked in dense vegetation and often shrouded in cloud, stands Machu Picchu. Exceptionally well known, this is the most revered archaeological site in the Americas. Despite its image being widespread, however, nothing equates to the first impression you have of it; it truly has to be seen to be believed. The history of the site, its stunning location and the mystery surrounding its purpose combine to make a visit here something remarkable.

History

American archaeologist and historian Hiram Bingham began to explore the region in 1911, lured by reports of hidden cities and potential treasure. A week into his explorations Bingham unearthed Llactapata, at what is now the start of the Inca Trail. On meeting a local Indian *campesino*, Melchor Artega, Bingham learned of some fine ruins

Machu Picchu, seen from Huayna Picchu, lies straddled along a ridge in a stunning setting. (MS-A/W/C)

nearby. Artega duly led Bingham up the steep slope of the valley to a massively overgrown site where Bingham stumbled upon 'the ruined walls of buildings built with some of the finest stonework of the Incas.'

By clearing thickets and vegetation he got a sense of the scale of the site and the quality of the architecture contained therein. Bingham recognised the importance of the find but mistakenly thought it to be Vilcabamba, the last city of the rebel Incas who valiantly held out against the conquistadors. This error endured for 50 years, until US explorer Gene Savoy found the actual Vilcabamba at Espiritu Pampa, further into the jungle. Bingham had previously come across part of these ruins but discounted them as being insubstantial. In the meantime, Bingham cleared Machu Picchu and over a period of three years discovered ceramics, stone artefacts and bones, which were spirited back to Yale University in the USA; some 45,000 pieces were removed and after much wrangling several hundred museum-quality artefacts are being returned to be displayed in Peru.

A railway to the site was started in 1913, and reached Aguas Calientes in 1928. A road from here to the ruins was finally finished in 1948 and

Practicalities

Machu Picchu opens at 06.00 and stays open until 18.00. You must have a ticket to enter the site and tickets can't be bought at the ruins themselves. To add to the rules and regulations governing the Inca Trail, the Peruvian government has restricted the number of people able to access Machu Picchu every day to just 2,500.

Machu Picchu remained hidden from the outside world for so long due to its remote location; the ridge it stands upon is fairly inaccessible, even though thousands of people now descend upon it. The nearest town is Aguas Calientes (see page 223), at the foot of the mountain on which the site stands. The ideal way to visit the site is on foot along the **Inca Trail** (see page 232) treating the trek as a pilgrimage, with each section a swelling towards an enormous crescendo as you arrive at the ruins; Machu Picchu is the final act of an outstanding performance and it's best enjoyed as part of a whole, as it was intended. The classic four-day Inca Trail is the most common route, although it is possible to tackle a shorter two-day version of the trail and also to bypass the regulations and red tape by trekking to the site via the 'back door' on the Salkantay Trek (page 233). Alternatively, from Aguas Calientes you can ascend to the ruins by **shuttle bus** along a narrow zigzag track. The 20-minute drive is quite scenic as you pass through lush cloudforest, with vertiginous views falling away on one side. The first bus departs Aguas Calientes at about 05.20,

inaugurated by Bingham. The Peruvian government declared the area a Historical Sanctuary in 1981, and UNESCO afforded it World Heritage status in 1983. Since then it has been nominated one of the seven modern wonders of the world. All these accolades and the corresponding fame and interest from visitors have also seen it gain less popular plaudits, including a warning from the World Monuments Fund; the site has endured 500 years and survived the Spanish conquistadors and various natural disasters, but it was never built to withstand quite so many visitors and it is these excessive numbers and a lack of structured conservation that have put it at risk.

The mystery as to what Machu Picchu was continues to rumble on; unknown by the Spanish, it wasn't found by the conquistadors, suggesting it had been abandoned prior to their arrival and had fallen from the Incas own consciousness. The architectural style suggests it was commissioned by Pachacutec, the man responsible for much of the expansion of the Inca Empire, dating it to the early or mid 1400s. Wild suggestions are often bandied about regarding the site, and it's

with the final shuttle returning from the ruins at 17.30. It's a long walk down, taking around an hour, if you miss this.

However you travel to the ruins, their continued popularity means that you must plan well in advance. It's possible to take a small daypack into the site but larger luggage must be left at the entrance in a secure luggage store. Almost a million people a year visit Machu Picchu – the site is busiest from June to September – and as many as 5,000 a day were descending on the site before restrictions were put in place to reduce this number. The solstice days of 21 June and 21 December are probably the worst in terms of numbers, as people flock to see the sun's rays fall on certain features in a deliberate and carefully curated way. Typically, Monday is the busiest day of the week and Sunday the quietest, although this is relative as there are still hordes of people. Mornings before 11.00 and afternoons after 15.30 are again fractionally quieter than the middle of the day.

Most trips to Machu Picchu give you about a half-day at the ruins, which allows you to cover the main sites and get a feel for the history of the place. Ideally though, you should spend a whole day and even stay overnight in Aguas Calientes in order to return for a second visit, to see some of the less heavily visited sections and soak up more of the atmosphere and history. You do not need a guide to visit the ruins; however, if you are on an organised tour then you will have someone talk you round the site and its features, so will get more from the experience.

sometimes easier to identify what we know is not true in relation to these: we know that there was no settlement on the site prior to Machu Picchu, the site was built to a plan, it was never a temple filled with virgins, the Spanish never found it, and aliens weren't involved in its construction. Theories that do stand up, however, maintain that the site was a ceremonial and administrative centre for a large population, supporting up to 1,000 inhabitants. The location would have been chosen for its aesthetic appeal and dramatic surrounds, as well as its proximity to the jungle and sacred summits such as Salkantay. The position close to the Vilcanota River was also auspicious. Seen in this light, the Inca Trail ceases to be just a road to the ruins and becomes a pilgrimage route to a celebrated ceremonial centre. The abandonment of the site may have been down to the death of Pachacutec and the decision to build another centre for the next Inca elsewhere as was the custom. Alternatively, Machu Picchu may have run out of water. Listen to the ideas circulating and see what works for you. The one you choose may even be true.

The Inca Trail and alternative treks to Machu Picchu

One of the best known walks in the world, the classic Inca Trail is justifiably famous. The four-day mountainous jungle hike is, however, just one of a vast network of Inca trails. These routes connect archaeological sites and places of interest all across the region and the classic Inca Trail to Machu Picchu is simply the best known of them all. Passing through outstanding scenery, dramatic landscapes and encountering a series of ruins that increase in quality and drama as you get closer to the finish, it's a spellbinding way to approach Machu Picchu.

Typically starting at Km82, 82km from Cusco on the railway line to Aguas Calientes, the route climbs a series of passes, reaching a maximum elevation of 4,200m, meaning that you must be acclimatised before setting off. A licensed guide and team of porters is mandatory, so you must trek with a tour operator; there are a huge number based in Cusco and you should take time to select one appropriate for your trip. Nights are spent camping in designated sites. Prices vary according to group size, service and standard of kit and food. This is very much a case of you get what you pay for, and the cheapest options are not the best, as operators have a series of fixed costs, so to turn a profit on a cut-price trek they're cutting corners somewhere or exploiting their porters and crew, both of which are big no-nos. The trek is fairly demanding but any reasonably fit person should be able to complete it.

You can extend the classic Inca Trail by starting in Mollepata, ascending over the shoulder of Mount Salkantay and joining the celebrated route midway through what would be the first day. This extended route takes five to six days and is tougher, as the high pass is around 5,000m.

way run by Mountain Lodges of Peru. Another alternative -day **Lares Trek**, which sees you walk through a series of valleys, stopping at traditional villages, before again arriving alientes in order to take the bus up to Machu Picchu.

Picchu highlights

of the site

discovery and initial excavation, Machu Picchu has entranced d in equal measure. The 'Lost City of the Incas' is steeped in legend, and this extends to the features of the site and their purpose. A masterpiece of architectural and landscape art, erraces, plazas, temples, water channels and staircases seem m from the rock, echoing the surrounding mountains and r celebrating features in the landscape. The natural beauty of staggering.

he entrance, there's a staircase that climbs to a good above the ruins. Stop at the restored **Caretaker's Hut** and arved **Funerary Rock** to look out over the site and put all of nts into context. It's the classic postcard overview, with rows s falling away towards the main plaza. To the left is a defined al zone and to the right are urban living areas and agricultural Cleverly engineered terraces can be seen on all sides. From escend into the site past a series of burial grounds to reach ssive trapezoidal archway that acts as the **main gateway** to A **quarry** where stones for the various structures were cut yond this. Descend a steep set of stairs alongside a series of ourses to the Torreón, or **Temple of the Sun**, a circular tower

on (Sun Temple) at the heart of Machu Picchu was an ceremonial and astronomical centre of the site. (HC/S)

along the
is the fou
unspoiled
at Aguas (

Machu
Features
Since its r
and baffle
myth and
potential
the steep
to be hev
framing o
the site is

Inside
viewpoint
the low, c
its elemer
of terrace
ceremoni
sections.
the Hut, c
an impre
the site.
stands be
16 water

The Torre
important

Inca Trail regulations

There are a host of regulations and rules regarc
adhered to. To ensure you don't fall foul of the
in advance as possible, and up to five or six mc
if you're visiting during the busiest months of
the trail is closed during February, the wette:
repair work.

• Independent trekking on the Inca Trail is bann
by a licensed, accredited guide.
• Tour operators running Inca Trail treks must ha
body that controls access to Machu Picchu. The
basis and is meant to ensure a minimum standai
• The number of trekkers is restricted to 500
This number includes all guides, porters and ass
reality around 200 tourists a day can start the t
• You must pay an entrance fee to trek on the Inc
the trek; all guides and porters must have a perr
• The maximum group size is 16 people. For gr
must be two guides.
• There is a minimum working wage for porters
operators must pay and a maximum weight they a

Should you be short of stamina or time, ther
the **Camino Real de los Incas**, which skips
of the ruins but does allow you to walk the
Machu Picchu on foot. It starts at Km104 ar
Huinay Huayna, where it joins the classic Ir
it is still steep to start and requires a degre
is spent walking to Machu Picchu, although
arrival as it'll most likely be too late, so yo
Aguas Calientes overnight, returning to expl
day of the trek.

The five-day **Salkantay Trek** is increasingly
a number of tour operators as an alternative
Picchu. It starts in Mollepata, skirts Mount Sal
to Santa Teresa, from where you can acce
thereby the shuttle bus service to Machu Picc
where you don't have to camp as there are a s

What are your favourite treks in the Andes?

I first trekked to the Inca citadel of Choquequirao 15 years ago, and it is still one of the most amazing hikes we offer. You can now connect right through to Machu Picchu in eight days. If you have less time, you still can't beat five days on the classic Inca Trail, or – for something less busy – Lares, Ausangate, even hotel-based day hikes around Cusco and the Sacred Valley are all brilliant. For a total adventure, trek to Espiritu Pampa – the very last city of the Incas.

What are your favourite river journeys in Peru?

After 23 years, I still love three or four days of rafting world-class rapids through the 3,000m-deep canyon of the Río Apurimac, the true source of the Amazon, or for true wilderness, wildlife and white water, you've got to raft the Río Tambopata. Even a day by raft, inflatable canoe, or – new for 2013 – stand-up paddle-boarding on the Río Urubamba, is a lot of fun.

Where are your favourite bike rides around Cusco?

For the best day out, cycle via the circular ruins of Moray and descend through the incredible saltpans of Maras, or try any of the amazing trails that crisscross Cusco and the whole Sacred Valley – we live in single-track heaven!

Amazonas Explorer is the only Peruvian member of Ⓦ www.onepercentfortheplanet.org and has helped plant over 165,000 native trees in the Lares Valley. They organise trips throughout Southern Peru with 'getting off-the-beaten track' their specialty. We spoke with Paul Cripps, owner/operator of the company.

Ⓣ +51 (0)84 25 2846 Ⓔ enquiries@amazonas-explorer.com
Ⓦ www.amazonas-explorer.com

that seems to grow organically from the rock, with perfect masonry and a window aligned just so, ensuring that on the winter solstice the sun falls though it onto an altar. You aren't allowed to actually enter the temple but can admire the precision with which it was built from close up; Bingham considered the back wall of the temple the most elegant in all the Americas. Beneath the temple is a cave that appears to have been moulded from the rock, such is the smoothness and elegance of the stonework. Bingham named this the **Tomb of the Princess**, even though there was no evidence found to support this name.

On the southern side of the site is the main ceremonial area. First to be reached is the **Temple of the Three Windows**, which lines one side of the **Scared Plaza**, and which looks out on to exhilarating views of the Andes and Urubamba Gorge. Further on is the **Principal Temple**, made of some exceptional stonework, with niches all along one wall. Behind this is the **Sacristy**, a small cell that is celebrated for the finesse of its stonework, with a particular rock cut to have 32 distinct angles, ensuring it fits the space perfectly. Climb a staircase from here to the *intihuatana*, known as the 'hitching post of the sun'. A gorgeously carved, aesthetically pleasing bit of sculpture, the rock's shape echoes the outline of Huayna Picchu; it was thought to have been used during astronomical and agricultural ceremonies to judge seasons and solar events. Having survived the Spanish, who ritually smashed these structures anywhere they found them, the *intihuatana* was instead badly damaged by a camera crew filming a beer commercial as they dropped a crane on it and chipped the top.

Descend from the most significant ceremonial part of the site and cross the plaza to a clearing backed by a **Sacred Rock**, the shape of which mirrors the mountains beyond it. To the left of here is the access

Alternative Inca Trail treks

www.SouthAmerica.travel

There are several Inca trails that offer great alternatives to the classic one to Machu Picchu. The five-day Salkantay trek through Apurimac Valley passes villages, lakes and snow-capped peaks. The challenging four-day Choquequirao Trek includes a hike to an abandoned Inca city. The Lares Valley trek is a popular option,

beginning at hot springs and ending in Ollantaytambo. The seven-day luxury lodge-to-lodge trek includes accommodation in mountain lodges each night.

Implausibly positioned terraces and ruins atop Huayna Picchu (SW)

Huayna Picchu

Rearing up at the back of the site like a rhino horn is the mountain Huayna Picchu, which peaks at 2,700m, 350m above Machu Picchu. There's a trail that scrambles and hauls itself to the summit of this impregnable looking rock, where there are some Inca terraces and small ruins, along with aerial views of Machu Picchu and its surrounds. The government have started to charge admission to Huayna Picchu; to climb to the Inca eyrie on the summit you must now purchase a combined Machu Picchu-Huayna Picchu entrance ticket. The ticket must be bought well in advance, either online from ⓦ www.machupicchu. gob.pe or from the official ticket office in Cusco or Aguas Calientes.

Just 400 people a day can climb the peak; 200 set off between 07.00 and 08.00 and return by 10.00, and a second wave of 200 then go from 10.00 to 11.00, and are required to be down by 13.00.

to the climb up **Huayna Picchu** (see above), which although it looks daunting is not as formidable as it first seems. A path dips down below Huayna Picchu and descends into the cloudforest to the **Temple of the Moon**, a cavern full of niches and other features of unknown use that have been likened to thrones and altars.

On the opposite side of the site to the ceremonial centre are a series of living quarters and storage rooms, as well as an industrial sector. Within this area is the **Temple of the Condor**, a giant carving of the sacred bird that uses natural rock formations and shaped stones to create a dramatic impression of the bird in flight.

If you have enough time, head west from the main site to see the **Inca Bridge**, a retractable defence on a sheer cliff with plunging drops below and steepling rock faces above. Additionally, walk away from the site and up towards the **Sun Gate** or Intipunku, where people completing the Inca Trail get their first glimpse of Machu Picchu. Turn and look back over the site to see it laid out like an architectural model, and marvel once more at the audacity and engineering genius required to build something so extraordinary in such a remarkable location.

Beyond Machu Picchu

Unusual decorated terraces depicting creatures such as llamas can be found at Choquequirao. (H)

Aside from the classic Inca Trail and other treks to Machu Picchu, there are a number of other treks in the Cusco area that explore different sections of the landscape and which access different ruins.

The most celebrated after Machu Picchu is **Choquequirao**, sometimes described as its sister site. Built in a similar, if not even more dramatic location, Choquequirao is still being excavated and only about a third of the site has been uncovered, which adds to its mystique. Although the stonework is less refined than that at Machu Picchu, there are plazas, ceremonial centres and some unique terraces decorated with patterns of llamas to discover. The site can be reached on a four-day trek from Cachora, which sees you walk in to the site for two days, via the vertiginous Apurimac Gorge, and then retrace your steps to return home. Just before the turning to Cachora, there's a giant sculpted monolith, **Saywite**, which is covered in carvings and symbols.

For the ultimate outing in this area combine a trek to Choquequirao with a wilderness route to Machu Picchu, this will take about eight days to complete. Or for an even more dramatic wilderness trek, follow the retreating Inca along the **Vilcabamba Trek**, as they fled into the jungle pursued by the Spanish, to reach Vilcabamba Vieja, also known as **Espiritu Pampa**, the Last City of the Incas. Barely uncovered at all, it's the perfect place to get in touch with your inner Indiana Jones. The trek takes four to five days but the remote trailheads mean you need at least a week to complete the route and return to Cusco.

In conversation with ...
Walking Perú

What tours do you recommend in Cusco?

Cusco has an incredible richness in its culture and natural environment. If you have an adventurous spirit, we encourage you to experience this richness by taking the Inca Trail to Machu Picchu, which leads you through diverse natural areas, breath-taking views, changing climates and ecosystems, and fascinating ruins to Macchu Picchu, rightfully named a world wonder for its stunning beauty and enigmatic history.

What makes your treks on the Inca Trail to Machu Picchu special?

In contrast to the other companies, we personalise your experience by providing a choice between three levels of service: Basic, Plus, and Imperial, though in each we are proud of the high quality of our service. Not only do we provide all tents and equipment, but also make your journey as comfortable as possible by using an 'all-included' system: even the Basic tour includes all food, transport and even a thermal sleeping bag and blanket!

Basic, Plus, and Imperial? What is included in each?

Firstly, they are all high-quality experiences, and even in the Basic we guarantee your satisfaction. What differentiates each category for the Inca Trail is the train service and the quality of equipment used. The Imperial package includes more spacious tents with inflatable mattresses and lamps, buffet-style meals and even glass cups! We include this distinction for every tour we offer, which we think really makes our company special. In addition to these levels of service, we also specialise in tour packages to fit the unique interests and schedules of private groups.

Walking Perú is based in Cusco and specialises in personalised tour packages designed to meet each group's preferences. In addition to traditional tours like the world wonder of Machu Picchu, they offer a variety of treks, including Inca Trail, the snow-capped Salkantay, and Choquequirao. Well-trained staff ensure that you have the best experience possible. We spoke to manager Lizett Flores Linares.

☎ +51 (0)973 58 2815
✉ info@walkingperu.com ⊕ www.walkingperu.com

10 The Amazon

The Peruvian Amazon inevitably captures the imagination and conjures up impressions of deepest, darkest Peru. Up to 60% of the country, an area approximately six times the size of England, is covered in rainforest and much of it still primary. Few people live here so there's more room for birds and wildlife. The territory isn't uniform, however, and different sections offer different possibilities to the visitor. There are two main regions: in the north of the country, visits are centred on Iquitos, the Amazon River itself and the waterlogged reserves such as Pacaya Samiria that surrounds it in the south, Puerto Maldonado provides a more accessible and easier-going gateway to the Madre de Dios River and Tambopata-Candamo National Reserve, whilst the more remote and more exclusive Manú National Park perhaps provides the ultimate Amazon experience. Regardless of where you head though, everyone who ventures into the tangled, humid forest comes out affected by the experience of exploring one of the great wilderness areas on earth.

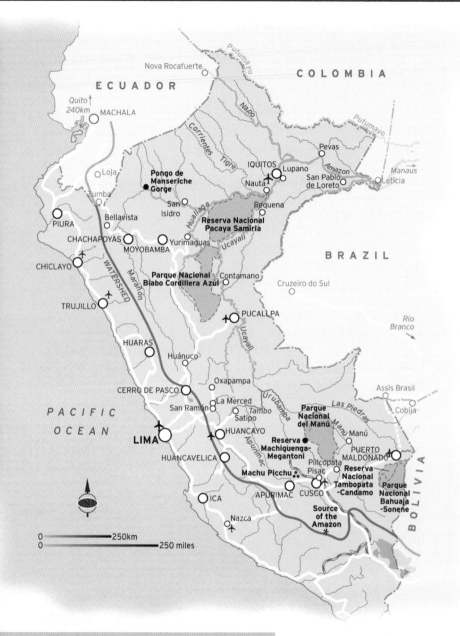

Iquitos and around

Despite its size and status as the largest city in the Peruvian Amazon and the third largest in the entire jungle, Iquitos, capital of the vast Loreto department, remains relatively unknown. To those that have heard of it, it is a loud, raucous frontier town with a unique, sultry charm and a way of getting under your skin. Hot and humid, the waterlogged air gives Iquitos a steamy feel. The city is remote, isolated amidst the jungle at the confluence of the Itaya and Nanay rivers, without road access of any kind. At 3,700km from the sea, it's still only 115m above sea level, meaning that the mighty Amazon flows slowly and sluggishly east, having already travelled 2, 840km to reach the city.

History

Iquitos, known originally as Santa Maria de Iquitos, was founded by the Jesuits during the early 1750s as a mission station and trading post. In 1864, port facilities were built. Up to this time and immediately after, Iquitos stayed small and isolated. The rubber boom of the late 1800s changed all that and transformed the city's fortunes, swelling its status almost overnight. Rubber barons got rich and the city enjoyed an almost glamorous period, with the appearance of ostentatious houses decorated in European style. Bust followed boom but export industries, recent oil discoveries and the increase in ecotourism have ensured the city continues to prosper. Today, the influx of workers and visitors means the city has a surprisingly cosmopolitan air for what's ostensibly a jungle town. Rubber is still exported and other areas of business include the export of mahogany and Spanish cedar, jute and fish.

Iquitos highlights
The city centre

The city retains some relics of its rubber boom heyday, although the mansions are now faded testaments to what the grand port of old would have looked like; on older buildings look for fine tile work and ironwork

Otorongo Lodge

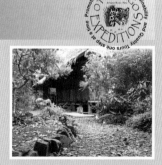

Located 100km downstream from Iquitos, Otorongo Lodge is surrounded by one of the hottest biodiversity zones in the region. Below the confluence of the Napo and Amazon rivers, more than 15 different ecosystems are found around the lodge: terra firme, lowland igapo forest, beaches, lakes, rivers, palm swamps, and more. Dodge hummingbirds and tanagers, and admire butterflies and flowers as you walk the lodge's exotic gardens. Let the wildlife come to you.

Practicalities

It's possible to spend weeks, months or even a lifetime exploring the Amazon and it's also possible to parachute in for just a brief foray using airports and jungle lodges. The main criteria affecting where you travel and how long you stay to explore will inevitably be budget, time and the extent of the jungle experience you're after. Work out how much you have to spend, how easy you need access to the jungle to be and how deep into the rainforest you want to travel in order to target your trip and choose the right tour.

Iquitos is the gateway to the northern Amazon Basin and standing on the Amazon River, it's an excellent introduction to life in the jungle. This is also the part of the jungle to visit if you want to undertake an **Amazon River cruise**, see page 252. Iquitos is the world's largest city inaccessible by road; realistically, to reach the city you have to catch one of the **daily flights** from Lima to the outlying **airport**, 8km southwest of the centre. It is also possible to **sail** and dock at the world's most inland river port. To reach the port, 3km north of the centre, ships must sail 3,700km from the mouth of the Amazon, making this stretch of waterway the longest navigable river. On an organised tour you ought to be provided with transport to the city and to get around, usually in a minibus or chartered local bus. If you're on your own jump on a *motocarro*, a

Accommodation

The jungle lodges around Iquitos act as excellent bases for exploring the rainforest, discovering indigenous communities and watching wildlife.

Upmarket
Amazon Yarapa River Lodge (130km from Iquitos) Ⓦ www.yarapa.com
El Dorado (Iquitos) Ⓦ www.hoteldoradoiquitos.com
Hotel El Dorado Plaza (Iquitos) Ⓦ www.groupo-dorado.com
Hotel Victoria Regia (Iquitos) Ⓦ www.victoriaregiahotel.com
Pacaya-Samiria Amazon Lodge (190km from Iquitos)
Ⓦ www.pacayasamiria.com.pe

Moderate
Acosta (Iquitos) Ⓦ www.hotelacosta.com
Amazonas Sinchicuy Lodge (30km from Iquitos)
Ⓦ www.paseosamazonicas.com

Motocarros provide noisy, cheap transport around Iquitos. (DK/S)

three-wheeled motorised rickshaw, but agree a price before you set off.

An important commercial centre, Iquitos has decent accommodation options, restaurants and tourist facilities; look for **banks** and **internet cafés** on Próspero and Putumayo. There are **iPerú** tourist offices at the airport, and in town at Loreto 201 (⊘ 08.00–20.00 Mon–Sat). The office responsible for the **Pacaya Samiria National Reserve** is at Pevas 339 (⊘ 08.00–16.00 Mon–Fri). Travel beyond the city isn't easy though and on an organised tour your operator ought to make arrangements; some lodges manage their own boats for instance. Otherwise, the riverboats that run up and down the Amazon are the only option.

Explorama Lodge (Iquitos) Ⓦ www.explorama.com
Hotel Europa (Iquitos) Ⓔ hoteleuropasac@yahoo.es
La Casa Fitzcarraldo (Iquitos) Ⓦ www.lacasafitzcarraldo.com
Marañón Hotel (Iquitos) Ⓦ www.hmaranon.k25.net
Muyuna Amazon Lodge (140km from Iquitos) Ⓦ www.muyuna.com
Otorongo Lodge (100km from Iquitos) Ⓦ www.otorongoexpeditions.com. See page 243.
Rio Grande Hotel Aguirre (Iquitos) Ⓦ www.riograndehotel.com
Tahuayo Lodge (140km from Iquitos) Ⓦ www.perujungle.com

Budget

Hostal Ambassador (Iquitos) Ⓦ www.peruamazonecotours.com
Hostal La Pascana (Iquitos) Ⓔ pascana@tsi.com.pe
Hotel la Casona (Iquitos) Ⓦ www.hotellacasonaiquitos.com
Hotel Real Malécon (Iquitos) Ⓣ 65 231 011

imported at considerable cost and effort from Europe. The finest example of this can be found at **La Casa de Fierro** (the Iron House), on a corner of the Plaza de Armas, a two-storey structure with silver-grey iron panels that was designed by Gustave Eiffel and imported by a rubber baron after the Paris Exposition of 1889. Elsewhere, wooden huts stand on stilts, or float tethered to poles to accommodate the fact that the river rises up 6m when in full flow.

To get an idea of what living in Iquitos is like, stroll along the **waterfront boulevard** *malecón*, overlooking the Itaya River, which provides a window on to local life. Families congregate, kids play, street vendors hawk handicrafts and entertainers ply their trade. Further insights are available at the unusual **Belén Market** in the southeast corner town, where anything and everything is on sale, from toys to trinkets, fresh produce and unidentified animal parts for

Eating out

The following eateries are all found within Iquitos itself.

Al Frio y Al Fuego (Peruvian) floating restaurant ① 224 862
Antica Pizzeria (international) Napo 159 ① 241 988
Fitzcarraldo (international) Malecón Maldonado ① 243 434
El Cauchero (international/fusion) Raimondi 449 ① 231 699
El Nuevo Mesón (Peruvian) Malecón Maldonado ① 231 837
La Gran Maloca (Peruvian) Lores 170 ① 233 126

Explore Ciudad Flotante on the edge of Iquitos by *peke-peke* canoe. (SG)

the pot. Crowded, noisy, and an assault on several senses, the market is visceral but the best introduction to the city there is. Close to the market is the **Ciudad Flotante** (Floating City), consisting of hundreds of squalid shacks, hovels and huts afloat on the river; it's estimated that some 7,000 people live here. You can explore the shantytown in a *peke-peke* motorised canoe by day but keep out at night as muggers operate here.

Standing on the waterfront boulevard is the **Museo Amazónico** (Amazonian Museum; Tarapacá 386 ⊘ 08.00–13.00 & 15.00–19.00 Mon–Fri, 09.00–13.00 Sat), in a building that dates from 1863. The main attraction is the 50 plaster statues of Indians cast by Lima artist Felipe Lettersten, although there's also pottery, portrait pictures, photos of

Ayahuasca <small>(WC)</small>

Whilst you are in Iquitos you may encounter *ayahuasca* and *ayahuasca* tourism. *Ayahuasca*, from the liana *Banisteriopsis caapi*, is a powerful hallucinogen used to bring on an ecstatic experience. Indigenous shaman and their communities traditionally ingest it as part of their rituals and as a way of connecting with their ancestral world. The drug is also reputed to have powerful medicinal properties. These days the experience has been rolled out to everyone, and it's possible to sign up to an *ayahuasca* session with a shaman. Should you wish to try the drug, be careful about taking too much, investigate the reputation of the person who will be leading the session, and make sure you're happy with the setting before you start.

Iquitos, and military memorabilia. In the **Plaza 28 de Julio** to the south of the centre stands a miniature locomotive that was once used to haul raw rubber to the river, from where it was floated to market. It stands testament to the boom that built the town in the first place.

To whet your appetite for what's living in the Amazon, visit the **Santa Fe Aquarium** on Calle Abtao and see a wide variety of Amazon River fish. Alternatively, travel out of town on the Nauta Road to the **Acobia Manatee Rescue Centre** at IIAP, the Peruvian Amazon Research Institute, where you can see these unusual creatures up close; a great opportunity since they're very hard to find in the wild. The **Pilpintuwasi Butterfly Farm** (⊘ 19.00–16.00 Tue–Sun) has a range of the region's butterflies on display but is also an animal orphanage, where a number of rescued animals, including caiman, capybaras, coatis, turtles and monkeys, now live. Don't visit the zoo in Quistococha Park, however, as the animals are kept in excessively small enclosures.

Around Iquitos highlights
Reserva Nacional Pacaya Samiria
Ⓦ www.pacaya-samiria.com

Around 185km southwest of Iquitos on the Rio Ucayli, lies Pacaya Samiria, the only officially protected part of Peruvian lowland forest. Covering 20,000km², it's the world's largest **flooded forest**. Given the remoteness and red tape required to access the reserve, much of it is off-limits and it is only accessible on a tour.

River trips depart from Iquitos and Nauta, which is about a 2½-hour drive from the main city on a reasonable road. Boats then cruise along the river, past dense jungle where giant kapok trees poke through the canopy. Wildlife is prolific, with more than 100 species of mammal, 130 species of reptile and amphibian, and more than 450 species of bird. Egrets roost on the riverbank while macaws, parrots, tanagers and kingfishers provide splashes of colour against the vegetation; pink dolphins frolic in the water and use sonar to navigate through the flooded forest. Giant otters, manatees and four species of caiman can also be seen, especially during low water season (from September to March) when they are easier to spot. If you travel during the high water season (April to August) you can explore smaller tributaries, increasing your chance of spotting primates and other mammals.

Parque Nacional Biabo Cordillera Azul

To the south of Pacaya Samiria and usually accessed from Pucallpa, 800km upstream from Iquitos, is an attractive area of cloudforest. **Biabo Cordillera Azul National Park** is vast but receives very little publicity, meaning that it is genuinely off-the-beaten track. It does, however, contain some of Peru's most bio diverse habitats. Although tourism to the park itself is prohibited, it is possible to visit the surrounding area on a tour, which will give you a feel for the exceptional landscapes of this beautiful area.

Visiting the Amazon sensitively

For all its size and sprawling scale, the Amazon is a very delicate environment and there are a number of guidelines that you ought to adhere to when visiting, to ensure that you minimise your impact. They are:

• Always travel with a tour operator that sets and adheres to a stringent code of conduct when it comes to minimising environmental impact.
• Travel in small groups and use a guide.
• Put something back into the local economy by using tour operators that employ local people.
• Never harass wildlife – it's not worth disturbing a creature's routine for that perfect picture. Instead, take in the spectacle from a distance.
• Leave no trace after travelling through the forest or staying overnight. Pack up all of your rubbish – it wasn't there before you visited, so it shouldn't be there once you've left.

Pongo de Manseriche

In a remote and largely inaccessible part of the rainforest, well to the west of Iquitos, is the spectacular Pongo de Manseriche, a narrow **gorge** 5km long and just 30m wide at its slimmest point. Through the gorge rushes the Marañón River as it cascades from the mountains to the lowlands. In places, the cliffs stand 600m above the swirling waters. A handful of tour operators offer **rafting** trips through the Pongo, and this is one of the most adventurous expeditions to undertake in the Amazon. There are no lodges in the vicinity and it takes around a week of travel to get there, but it is genuinely spectacular.

Puerto Maldonado and around

The Amazon in the south of Peru is best accessed from Puerto Maldonado, a boisterous, ramshackle settlement at the point where the Madre de Dios and Tambopata rivers converge. Once a rubber boom town, logging and gold mining have replaced this as the town's primary reason for being; continued expansion and new roads mean it'll only get bigger and easier to access, which hopefully won't threaten the remarkable reserves on its doorstep. Smaller and much more relaxed than Iquitos in the north, Puerto Maldonado is a compact town that quickly gives way to the jungle. Most people barely see the town though, as they are ferried into the rainforest soon after arrival and on to one of the lodges along the Madre de Dios River or deeper in the Tambopata-Candamo National Reserve or Manú National Park.

The Amazon

RAINBOW TOURS

To experience the true wonder of the Amazon rainforest, stay in one of the luxury reserves run by the local indigenous communities. Experience the jungle at night, immersing yourself in the rich cacophony of sound; pan for gold along the Madre de Dios River; take a boat trip on Lake Sandoval; and go piranha fishing with your guide. There are also luxury cruises on small river boats from Iquitos, one of the main gateways in the north, if you have more time.

Rafting through the Pongo de Manseriche allows you to get up close to the Amazon's many delights and mysteries. (CC/MP/FLPA)

Cruise along the Amazon for a chance to see the daily life of the river unfold. (SS)

Amazon River cruises

Around Iquitos, cruises generally take place on the Amazonas River although it's also possible to drift along the Itaya and Nanay rivers. Beyond the outpost of Nauta, boats explore the Marañón and Ucayli rivers as well, which lead into the Pacaya Samiria Reserve. Cruises tend to be all-inclusive of food, transfers and guide and last three days, although it's possible to be on the water for just one if time is tight. In general, the longer you have and the further you sail, the more you'll see; aim to get well away from Iquitos and onto the secondary waterways to increase your chances of seeing wildlife. To get the best out of Pacaya Samiria you should dedicate at least five days to the reserve.

Your cruise itinerary may allow you to pause in Nauta, in which case visit **Grippa's Art Gallery**, where one of Peru's most accomplished painters of wildlife and jungle people has a workshop and gallery. Grippa is internationally successful and displays in the US, but will show people around his studio and describe his work, which is of course available to buy.

Cruiseships include *Amazon I* (Ⓦ www.dawnontheamazon.com), which sails deep into the reserve; MV *Amazon Journey* (Ⓦ www.amazoncruise.net), which has twice weekly sailings of three- or six-days; the three ships, *Ayapua* (with Green Tracks Ⓦ www.amazontours.net), *Delfin I* and *Delfin II*, (Ⓦ www.delfinamazoncruises.net) which tend to operate four-, five- or seven-day cruises; and MV *Amatista*, MV *Turmalina* and MV *Turquesa* (Ⓦ www.ietravel.com), which sail for up to nine days. Perhaps the most luxurious cruises though are aboard the MV *Aqua* (Ⓦ www.aquaexpeditions.com).

Puerto Maldonado highlights
The town centre

Puerto Maldonado is a little scruffy but all the more authentic because of it. To put the place in context and to gaze out over the jungle, climb the **Obelisco** (☉ 10.00–17.00 daily) at the junction of Fitzcarald and Madre de Dios, a viewing tower 30m high that affords you great views. To get a small sense of what sailing on the river is like, take the **Madre de Dios ferry**, from the dock off Avenida 26 de Deciembre, and weave amongst river craft bustling along the waterway, which is about 500m wide at this point.

Around Puerto Maldonado highlights
Parque Nacional del Manú

Manú National Park, in a beautiful, unspoiled corner of Peru, is the country's largest protected area and covers a vast 9,300km² of rainforest. UNESCO recognise it as a World Heritage Site and World Biosphere Reserve and it is considered to be the most species-rich protected area on earth, with an ever-expanding inventory of plants, animals and birds found here. Less accessible than the rainforest in the north of the country, it is correspondingly more exclusive, and therefore more expensive to visit.

Beginning in the foothills of the Andes at elevations as high as 4,200m and then descending and stretching east, the conservation area includes lowland tropical forest and montane forest. These habitats are home to an exceptional biodiversity; 200 mammal species have been recorded here, along with around 1,000 bird species and over 15,000 plant species so far. Giant otter, black caiman, jaguar, ocelot and various primates are often spotted, whilst birdwatchers will marvel at

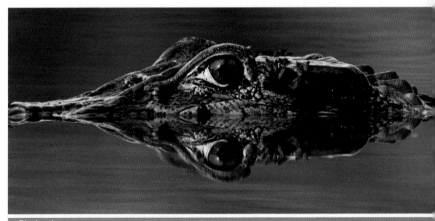

Black caiman (FL/FLPA)

Practicalities

It's possible to **fly** from Lima via Cusco to Puerto Maldonado; there are daily scheduled flights and the hop from Cusco takes from as little as half an hour to 45 minutes. There are two **airports** in the region, in Puerto Maldonado and at Boca Manú, adjacent to the Manú National Park (the latter

Puerto Maldonado (m/s)

is only used by charter planes connected with tour groups). Alternatively, it's

Accommodation

As well as the accommodation options in town there are also a number of lodges on the banks of the Madre de Dios River which are between 5km and 32km east from the town, and from where you can explore the jungle.

Upmarket

Amazonia Lodge (Manú National Park) Ⓦ www.amazonialodge.com
Cayman Lodge Amazonie (Tambopata-Candamo National Reserve)
Ⓦ www.cayman-lodge-amazonie.com
Cock of the Rock Lodge (Manú National Park)
Ⓦ www.tropicalnaturetravel.com
Heath River Wildlife Center (Bahuaja-Sonene National Park)
Ⓦ www.incanatura.com or Ⓦ www.tropicnaturetravel.com
Inkaterra Reserva Amazonica (Puerto Maldonado) Ⓦ www.inkaterra.com
Manú Lodge (Manú National Park) Ⓦ www.manuperu.com
Manú Wildlife Centre (Manú National Park) Ⓦ www.manuexpeditions.com
Pantiacolla Lodge (Manú National Park) Ⓦ www.pantiacolla.com
Posada Amazonas (Tambopata-Candamo National Reserve)
Ⓦ www.perunature.com

Moderate

Anaconda Lodge (Puerto Maldonado) Ⓦ www.anacondajunglelodge.com
Casa Machiguenga (Manú National Park) Ⓦ www.manuexpeditions.com
Corto Maltes (Puerto Maldonado) Ⓦ www.cortomaltes-amazonia.com
EcoAmazonia Lodge (Puerto Maldonado) Ⓦ www.ecoamazonia.com.pe
Estancia Bello Horizonte (Puerto Maldonado)

a rather gruelling 480km **drive** from Cusco (two days), although the road is constantly being improved and is even sealed in places. After crossing the high-altitude grasslands and cresting a pass in the Andes, the road descends into the Amazon Basin. Small river ports on the Madre de Dios and Tambopata rivers then serve the surrounding jungle lodges. Travel tends to continue from Puerto Maldonado by **boat**, depending on your final destination.

Hotels are solid if unspectacular but there is a range of good value restaurants to try. There's a **bank** on the Plaza de Armas and several **internet cafés** downtown; try Avenida 2 de Mayo. There's a **tourist office** at the airport, whilst the **national park office**, SERNAP, at Avenida 28 de Julio is a good place to pick up information.

Ⓦ www.estanciabellohorizonte.com
Explorer's Inn (Tambopata-Candamo National Reserve)
Ⓦ www.explorersinn.com
Hostal Cabaña Quinta (Puerto Maldonado) Ⓔ cabanaquinta_reservas@hotmail.com
Hotel Don Carlos (Puerto Maldonado) Ⓔ reservasmaldonado@hoteldoncarlos.com
Libertador Tampobata Lodge (Tambopata-Candamo National Reserve)
Ⓦ www.tambopatalodge.com
Tambopata Research Centre (Tambopata-Candamo National Reserve)
Ⓦ www.perunature.com
Wasai Lodge (Tambopata-Candamo National Reserve) Ⓦ www.wasai.com
Wasai Maldonado (Puerto Maldonado) Ⓦ www.wasai.com

Budget
Amarumayo (Puerto Maldonado) Ⓔ residenciamarumayo@hotmail.com
Tambopata Hostel (Puerto Maldonado) Ⓦ www.tambopatahostel.com

Eating out

The following establishments are all based in Puerto Maldonado itself.

Burgos's (Peruvian) Bilinghurst 480
El Califa (Peruvian) Piura 266
Gustitos del Cura (ice cream/juice bar) Loreto 258
La Casa Nostra (café) Velarde 515
Tsaica (bar) Loreto 335

Giant river otters are often seen fishing and feeding in the Amazon. (B/JML & FR/FLPA)

the macaws and parrots lured to clay licks throughout the reserve by the minerals in the soil. The park is divided into three zones: by far the biggest, the **National Park Zone** is strictly preserved in its original state and is off-limits to unauthorised visitors; the **Reserve Zone** is set aside for scientists, researchers and controlled ecotourism, and access is by permit only and is strictly controlled with all visitors having to be accompanied by a guide; the **Cultural Zone** is where most casual tourism occurs. Viewing platforms and observation towers allow you to see animals such as tapir at close quarters, whilst boat trips on oxbow lakes often find giant river otters, caimans and other creatures. Ideal times to visit are during the dry season, June to November.

Reserva Nacional Tambopata-Candamo

South of Puerto Maldonado is the **Tambopata-Candamo National Reserve**, which can be reached by boat or car. More accessible and less restrictive than Manú, the reserve comprises mainly lowland forest although three ecosystems actually converge here. The reserve is home to many species, including more than 100 species of mammal, around 600 species of bird and more than 1,200 types of butterfly. It is especially famous, however, for its clay licks or *colpas*, and the numbers of macaws and parakeets that congregate at them; best known is the **Colpa de Guacamayos**, one of the largest natural clay licks in Peru, where the copper-coloured cliffs attract thousands of birds every day. Although

Birdwatching in Manú National Park

It is said that Manú has the highest concentration of bird life on earth. Around 1,000 species have been recorded, some 10% of all the species of bird in the world. No other protected area contains as many birds and on a two-week trip to Manú you might expect to see up to 500 species, a staggering number. Altitude within the park ranges from more than 4,000m above sea level to just 350m, meaning there's an enormous diversity of landscapes and habitats. Descending from the higher elevations, look out for tinamous and finches, tanagers, toucans and nightjars. In the humid subtropical forest you might see Andean cock-of-the-rock, quetzals, flycatchers and wrens. The tropical forest at lower elevations hides skimmers, terns, lapwings, spoonbills, egrets and herons. Stake out a clay lick during the early morning and enjoy a multi-coloured mêlée of macaws and parrots as they flock to the riverbank for their daily dose of mineral-rich soil; watching them wheeling over the clay licks is one of the great wildlife experiences of the world.

(SS)

you can stay for as little as two days and just one night, you should try to stay much longer as a lot of the time will be taken up by travelling.

Parque Nacional Bahuaja-Sonene

Bahuaja-Sonene National Park is a rarely visited enclave between the Tambopata and Rio Heath rivers by the Bolivian border. It has some superlative wildlife; 600 bird species have been recorded here along with more than 170 species of mammal and 100 different reptiles. There's not much in the way of infrastructure, however, and accommodation is very limited.

Santuario Nacional Machiguenga Megantoni

To the west of Manú National Park is **Machiguenga Megantoni Reserve**, established to protect a swathe of upland forest and the ten zones of vegetation found within it. It is especially well known for orchids and is also home to a number of endangered species of mammal, including jaguar, puma and tapir. Indigenous groups including the Machiguenga and Yine Yami live within the Urubamba River watershed, too. Tour operators currently don't run trips here but this is bound to change and those operating within Manú will doubtless incorporate this section of rainforest into their itineraries in due course.

Indigenous communities continue to live traditionally along the river in the Santuario Nacional Machiguenga Megantoni. (FL/FLPA)

In conversation with ...
Otorongo Expeditions

What sets OtoEx apart from other local operators?

We provide personalised itineraries for every client. Each has their own personal bilingual naturalist guide to help form their ideal itinerary. We provide a broad knowledge of the Amazon, its ecosystems and inhabitants. We are also very active with local communities and the sustainable management of their communal lands. We do not take shortcuts on customer service; we strive to be the best.

What could you recommend to someone seeking an environmentally and socially responsible tour company?

Do not pick the cheapest! Workers and locals always get the bad end of the deal with cheap services. Our local staff and the communities we work with are very content. They realise the importance of tourism in their area. Every year our environmental consciousness spreads through the population with positive first-hand experiences.

What do clients enjoy most about OtoEx Jungle Lodge?

It is designed in a rustic fashion similar to local houses with palm-thatch roof. Although we are in the middle of the jungle, people always seem to be comfortable in their mosquito-netted room with private bath and toilet. It is easy to relax and see wildlife right from the patio. You can catch exotic fish, watch birds, learn

medicinal plants, smell exotic flowers in the rock gardens or take a siesta in a hammock. Exquisite meals from superb Peruvian chefs will make your taste buds dance. And our stellar staff will stop at nothing to accommodate.

Owned and operated by American/Peruvian naturalists, Otorongo specialises in personalised itineraries for all types of adventures in the Peruvian Amazon. Tailor-make your trip: choose from camping in the rainforest to jungle lodging or cruising on the Amazon. They work extensively with local communities to promote environmental sustainability in tourism. We spoke to owner/operator Anthony Giardenelli.

① +51 (0)65 22 4192 ⓜ +51 (0)965 30 7868
ⓔ otorongoexpeditions@gmail.com ⓦ www.otoex.com

Canoeing at sunset on the Amazon River Basin (DD/A)

Appendix 1

Language

The lingua franca of Peru is **Spanish**. It is widely spoken in all urban areas and places heavily associated with tourism, although there are still more rural parts of Peru where it isn't spoken, with indigenous people instead using Quechua or another local tongue. The Spanish spoken, Latin American Spanish, is a variation of the European language, Castilian Spanish, which was exported to the continent by the conquistadors. Pronunciation is subtly different and some of the vocabulary varies, not unlike the variation between British English and US English, but by and large you'll be able to make yourself understood if you can speak traditional Spanish.

Educated Peruvians and those who deal regularly with tourists generally also speak English and since you're likely to be on an organised tour, your guide will certainly have a good grasp of the language and should to all intents and purposes be fluent.

Visitors who learn a little Spanish will find the effort appreciated. Those that pick up a phrase or two of **Quechua** in order to be able to talk to villagers, porters or other people will also win plenty of friends, even if they mangle the complex, guttural language in their attempts to pronounce it.

Pronunciation

Pronunciation of Latin American Spanish isn't that difficult, as most of the sounds are similar to those in the English language. Peruvian Spanish is one of the easier variations to master, with fewer colloquialisms and less slang, and fairly clear enunciation. Pit falls include 'll', pronounced 'y'; 'hu', pronounced 'w'; 'q', pronounced 'k'; and 'ce' or 'ci', pronounced 's'.

Greetings and goodbye

All conversations should start with a greeting, of which the most common, at least when dealing with tourists, is *hola*, meaning 'hello'. Others you'll come across include *¿cómo está usted?* ('how are you?'), *¿que tal?* ('what's up?') and variations of *buenos días, buenas tardes* and *buenas noches*, meaning 'good day', 'afternoon' and 'evening' respectively. If you're being formal, address people as *señor* ('Mr') or *señora* ('Madam'). When it comes to saying goodbye, close the conversation with *adiós*, ('goodbye') or *hasta lluego* ('see you later').

Numbers

0	*zero*	11	*once*	30	*treinta*
1	*uno/una*	12	*doce*	40	*cuarenta*
2	*dos*	13	*trece*	50	*cincuenta*
3	*tres*	14	*catorce*	60	*sesenta*
4	*cuatro*	15	*quince*	70	*setenta*
5	*cinco*	16	*dieciséis*	80	*ochenta*
6	*seis*	17	*diecisiete*	90	*noventa*
7	*siete*	18	*dieciocho*	100	*cien*
8	*ocho*	19	*diecinueve*	200	*doscientos*
9	*nueve*	20	*veinte*	1,000	*mil*
10	*diez*	21	*veinte-y-uno*		

Time

What time is it?	*¿Que hora es?*	afternoon	*tarde*
What time is ...?	*¿Que hora ...?*	evening	*noches*
when	*cuando*	soon	*pronto*
morning	*mañana*	later	*más tarde*

Days of the week

Monday	*lunes*	Friday	*viernes*
Tuesday	*martes*	Saturday	*sábado*
Wednesday	*miércoles*	Sunday	*domingo*
Thursday	*jueves*		

Months

January	*enero*	July	*julio*
February	*ebrero*	August	*agosto*
March	*marzo*	September	*septiembre*
April	*abril*	October	*octubre*
May	*mayo*	November	*noviembre*
June	*junio*	December	*diciembre*

Shopping

money	*dinero*	That's expensive	*¡Esta caro!*
Do you sell ...?	*¿Me vende...?*	That's too much	*¡Esta demasiado!*
I want	*quiero*		

I don't want	*no quiero*	How much?	*¿Cuánto es?*
I would like	*quisiera* or		or *¿cuánto*
	me gustería		*cuesta?*

Foodstuffs

the meal	*la comida*	I don't eat ...	*no como ...*
breakfast	*desayuno*	chicken	*pollo*
lunch	*almuerzo*	fish	*pescado*
dinner	*cena*	meat	*carne*
That was delicious!	*¡Estaba buenísimo!*	beer	*cerveza*
Bring the bill please	*La cuenta, por favor*		

Other useful words and phrases

Excuse me	*Disculpe*	towel	*la ropa*
	or *perdóneme*	soap	*el jabón*
You're welcome	*De nada*	telephone	*el téléfono*
very good	*muy bien*	currency	*la casa de*
thank you	*gracias*	exchange	*cambio*
many thanks	*muchas gracias*	bank	*el banco*
please	*por favor*	ATM	*un cajero*
yes	*sí*		*automatico*
no	*no*	airport	*el aeropuerto*
What is your name?	*¿Cómo se llama?*	bus station	*stacion del*
My name is ...	*Mi nombre es ...*		*autobus*
I don't understand	*no comprendo*	street	*la calle*
	/no entiendo	house	*la casa*
Do you speak ...	*habla ...*	market	*el mercado*
... English?	*.... inglés?*	museum	*el museo*
Help!	*¡Socorro!*	tourist office	*la officina de*
I am lost	*estoy perdido*		*turismo*
To the left	*a la inquired*	guide	*el guía*
To the right	*a la derecha*	luggage	*equipaje*
Where is?	*¿dónde está?*	What is	*¿Que es su ...?*
restaurant	*el restaurante*	your ...?	
bathroom	*el baío*	phone	*número de*
hotel	*el hotel*	number	*teléfono*
bedroom	*la habitación*	address	*dirección*

Appendix 2

Selected reading

History

Hiram Bingham's account of his explorations and discoveries, *Lost City of the Incas* (republished by Phoenix, 2003) should be the starting point for any visitor to Peru interested in its history and archaeology. Slightly self-serving and designed to inflate the cult of Bingham, it nonetheless has a wealth of information and detail on some of the most remarkable discoveries in the Americas and is a rollicking good read. Bingham's book, *Inca Land* (Forgotten Books, 2012), is also worth a read. For a look at the man himself, try Chris Heaney's biography *Cradle of Gold: The Story of Hiram Bingham, a Real-Life Indiana Jones, and his Search for Machu Picchu* (Palgrave Macmillan, reprint 2011).

To understand the conquest and put the Inca civilisation in context, pick up a copy of John Hemming's seminal *The Conquest of the Incas* (Pan, 2004), the definitive history of the subject. For a fascinating, more contemporary account and for descriptions of finding new Inca sites, look out for Hugh Thomson's book *The White Rock: An Exploration of the Inca Heartland* (Phoenix, 2002). His second book, *Cochineal Red: Travels Through Ancient Peru* (Phoenix, 2007), has a broader focus and also looks at other pre-Columbian cultures and their place in Peru's history. Kim MacQuarrie's *The Last Days of the Incas* (Simon & Schuster, reprint 2008) is worth a follow up read for its rip-roaring style. If you've more time, look out for *The Discovery and Conquest of Peru* (Duke University Press, 1999) by Pedro de Cieza de León or *Conquest of Peru* (New York, originally published 1847, reprinted 2002) by William Prescott. *The Incas: Empire of Blood and Gold* (Thames and Hudson, 1994) by Carmen Bernand is a handy, pocket-sized introduction to the Incas and their civilisation, whilst *The Machu Picchu Guidebook: A Self-Guided Tour* (Johnson Books, revised 2011) by Ruth Wright and Alfredo Zegarra is a good commentary on the site and its key features.

Travel literature

The most widely read account of travels in Peru is *Inca Kola* by Matthew Parris (Orion, 1993), which is full of wonderful descriptions but is now a little dated. *Three Letters from the Andes* by Patrick Leigh Fermor (Hodder, 2005) is a slim but beautifully observed account of a trip by the master travel writer. *Eight Feet in the Andes: Travels with a Mule in Unknown Peru* (John Murray, 2003) is Dervla Murphy's account of a journey during the early 1980s. If you're heading to the Cordillera Blanca or Huayhuash at all, then read Joe Simpson's stunning account of a mountaineering disaster, *Touching the Void* (Vintage Classics, 2008), which captures the harsh beauty of the mountains and tells a harrowing tale of survival against the odds. Chilean poet Pablo Neruda was moved to write *The Heights of Machu Picchu* after a visit; it's an epic poem often compared to TS Eliot's *The Waste Land*.

Fiction

Peru's leading novelist, Mario Vargas Llosa, writes extensively about Peru; start with *Conversation in the Cathedral*, *The Green House*, *The Time of the Hero* or *Aunt Julia and the Scriptwriter* (all Faber & Faber) to gain an insight into everyday life as well as the political and historical events that have helped to shape Peru. His novel, *Death in the Andes* (Picador, 2007) deals with the Shining Path terrorists during the 1980s and looks at the impact they had on rural communities and the country in general. *The Dancer Upstairs* (Anchor, 2002) by Nicholas Shakespeare looks at a similar era but tells the story of the capture of the Shining Path leader Abimael Guzman. Travel writer Colin Thubron used his personal experiences of trekking in Peru to inform his novel *To the Last City* (Vintage, 2003), about a journey to Espiritu Pampa, which is full of colour and sound and captures the experience well. Henry Shukman also penned a colourful account of a quest for a mythical city, *The Lost City* (Vintage, reprint 2009), which is full of intrigue and adventure. Daniel Alarcon, a rising star of the Peruvian literary scene and Santiago Roncagliolo are also worth looking out for; try *Lost Radio City* (Harper Perennial, 2008) and *Red April* (Atlantic Books, 2011) respectively.

Photographic books

Photographer Edward Ranney and historian John Hemming collaborated to produce a set of stunning black-and-white photographs and detailed text on *Monuments of the Incas* (Thames & Hudson, revised 2010). *Machu Picchu: Unveiling the Mystery of the Incas* (Yale University Press, 2008) edited by archaeologist Richard Burger has some great photographs of the ruins and a detailed overview of the features and the site's significance. The photographer Max Milligan lived in Peru for many years and his book *Realm of the Inca* (Idlewild, 2003) is a set of stunning photographs culled from his time there; they capture the Cusco region, ruins and lives of the people who live there. *Peru's Amazonian Eden: Manu* (Jordi Blassi, 1992), featuring photographs by André Bärtschi, wonderfully captures the diversity of the Peruvian rainforest and gives a great impression of what you might see if you visit the jungle.

Field guides

Start with the Bradt's *Peruvian Wildlife* (2007) by Gerard Cheshire, Huw Lloyd and Barry Walker, which covers fauna found in the high Andes. Alternatively, look for *The Travellers Wildlife Guide to Peru* (Interlink Books, 2004) by Les Beletsky, a substantial tome that describes 500 of the most common mammals, birds, amphibians, reptiles and insects. Birdwatchers should carry the *A Field Guide to the Birds of Peru* (San Diego NHM, 2001) by James Clements and Noam Shany, or the *Field Guide to the Birds of Machu Picchu* (Profonanpe, 2002) by Barry Walker.

Online

Ⓦ **www.andeantravelweb.com/peru** The most comprehensive advice site on travel in Peru and in particular on the Cusco region.

Ⓦ **www.saexplorers.org** Site of the South American Explorers, full of advice and information for members of the club.

Ⓦ **www.peru.info** Official site of iPerú, the government tourism agency.

Ⓦ **www.peru.travel** Official government site with useful data for travellers, travel FAQ, weather, accommodation, travel agents, restaurants and other tourist services.

Ⓦ **www.peru.com** Comprehensive information about Peru, including history, geography, statistics and useful sections on each department.

Ⓦ **www.perulinks.com** Peru links directory, with around 800 Peru-related sites, including some 200 travel sites.

Ⓦ **www.theperuguide.com** A broad travel overview site.

Ⓦ **www.peruviantimes.com** Contains all the latest news and information coming out of Peru.

Ⓦ **www.livinginperu.com** An expat guide to the country and a good source of information on what's on when.

Ⓦ **www.cusco.info** Comprehensive site for travel to Cusco, with package tours and hotel and travel information.

Index

Index

First published February 2013
Bradt Travel Guides Ltd
IDC House, The Vale, Chalfont St Peter, Bucks SL9 9RZ, England
www.bradtguides.com
Published in the USA by The Globe Pequot Press Inc,
PO Box 480, Guilford, Connecticut 06437-0480

Project Manager: Anna Moores; Picture research: Kelly Randell

ISBN: 978 1 84162 440 2

British Library Cataloguing in Publication Data
A catalogue record for this book is available from the British Library

Photographs Adam Kumiszcza (AK); Adrienlenoir (A); Alamy: Danita Delimont (DD/A), Emmanuel Lattes (EL/A), Jeff Greenburg (JG/A), John Warburton-Lee Photography (JW-LP/A); ChildofMidnight (C); Corbis: George Steinmetz (GS/C); Ines Menacho (IM/C), Ivan Kashinsky (IK/C), Marcos Ferro (MF/C), Paolo Aguilar (PA/C); Communist Party of Peru (CPP); Daniel Barker (DB); Dardanelo (D); Dreamstime: Cascoly (Ca/D), Chrishowey (Ch/D), Chicco7 (Chi/D), Hotshotsworldwide (H/D), Jarnogz (J/D), Jumiati (Ju/D), Kpics (K/D), Lizzgiordano (L/D), Michael Zysman (MZ/D), Noamfein (N/D), Rickymats (Ri/D), Rjlerich (Rj/D), Sohadiszno (S/D); Edubucher (E); Felipe Guaman Poma de Ayala (FGPA); FLPA: Biosphoto/JM Labat & F Rouquette (B/JML & FR/FLPA); Carr Clifton/Minden Pictures (CC/MP/FLPA), Cyril Ruoso/Minden Pictures (CR/MP/FLPA), David Tipling (DT/FLPA), Frans Lanting (FL/FLPA), Gerard Lacz (GL/FLPA), Imagebroker/FB-Fischer/Imagebroker (I/FB-F/I/FLPA), Ingo Arndt/Minden Pictures (IA/MP/FLPA), JM Labat & F Rouquette/Biosphoto (JML and FR/B/FLPA), Kevin Schafer/Minden Pictures (KS/MP/FLPA), Luciano Candisani/Minden Pictures (LC/MP/FLPA), Markus Friedrich/Imagebroker (MF/I/FLPA), Pete Oxford/Minden Pictures (PO/MP/FLPA), Tui De Roy/Minden Pictures (TDR/MP/FLPA); Getty: William Albert Allard (WAA/G); Harleyca (H); Heinz Plenge (HP); iStock: fixelpics (f/iS); Lmuellerleile (L); Martin St-Amant/Wikipedia/CC-BY-SA-3.0 (MS-A/W/C); Museo Larco (ML); PromPeru: Alex Bryce (AB/PP); Beatrice Velarde (BV/PP), Denise Tejada (DT/PP), Enrique Castro-Mendívil (EC-M/PP), Flor Ruiz (FR/PP), Gihan Tubbeh (GT/PP), Heinz Plenge Pardo (HPP/PP), Luis Garnero (LG/PP), Miguel Carrillo (MC/PP), Renzo Giraldo (RG/PP); Sascha Grabow (SG); Sascha Wenninger (SW); Shutterstock: Alexander Ryabintsev (AR/S), Antonella865 (A/D), Chris Howey (CH/S), colacat (c/S); Dennis Ku (DK/S), e2dan (e/S), Gail Johnson (GJ/S), gary yim (gy/S), Giles Harvey (GH/S), Hailin Chen (HC/S), Ildi Papp (IP/S), Jarno Gonzales Zarraonandia (JGZ/S), jaroslava V (jV/S), Kobby Dagan (KD/S), Maksym Gorpenyuk (MG/S), meunierd (m/S), Mrpeak (M/S), P. Zonzel (PZ/S), Rafal Cichawal (RC/S), RIRF Stock (RS/S), Thomas Barrat (TB/S), Tomaz Kunst (TK/S), Yeolka (Y/D); SuperStock (SS); Thomas Somerscales (TS); Wikipedia Commons (WC)

Front cover (Top, left to right) Peruvian children (Chi/D); Traditional reed boat on Lake Titicaca (SS); An inquistive alpaca (Ju/D) (Bottom) Machu Picchu (MF/I/FLPA)
Back cover Red and green macaws (SS); Wooden idol, Chan Chan (HPP/PP)
Title page (left to right) Detail from Chavín de Huántar (SS); El Misti Volcano and surrounds (SS); Colourful Andean cock-of-the-rock (H/D)
Page iv Blue-footed booby (TDR/MP/FLPA)

Part & chapter openers Page 1: Uros Indian girl, Lake Titicaca (SS); Page 2: Bora tribesmen in the Amazon (SS); Page 3: Chan Chan (HPP/PP); Page 24: Curl-crested aracari (DT/FLPA); Page 25: Vicuñas (N/D); Page 49: Birdwatching at dawn in the Tambopata Reserve, Amazon (SS); Page 77: Andean condor soaring above birdwatchers in Colca Canyon (TDR/MP/FLPA); Page 95: An iconic shot of the famous Machu Picchu site (JGZ/S); Page 96: View of the Miraflores coastline, Lima (TB/S); Page 97: Plaza de Armas, Lima (SS); Page 120: Hiker at sunset, Cordillera Blanca (SS); Page 121: Beach at Trujillo (SS); Page 150: Nazca pottery in Museo Antonini (BV/PP); Page 151: Inca terns along the Paracas coastline (GL/FLPA); Page 170: Alpacas in front of El Misti (c/S); Page 171: Harvest festival in Puno (M/D); Page 198: *Mestiza cuzqueña* dancer, Cusco (SS); Page 199: Central Cusco (AR/S); Page 240: (Top) Olive oropendola (DT/FLPA) (Bottom) Brown-throated, three-toed sloth (IA/MP/FLPA); Page 241: Iquitos (SS)

Maps David McCutcheon FBCart.S. Includes map data © OpenStreetMap contributors (Under Open Database Licence)

Typeset from the author's disc by Chris Lane, Artinfusion
Production managed by Jellyfish Print Solutions; printed in India